CW01627898

SCOTTISH GAELIC TEXTS

NEW SERIES

VOLUME ONE

ALASDAIR MAC MHAIGHSTIR ALASDAIR

SELECTED POEMS

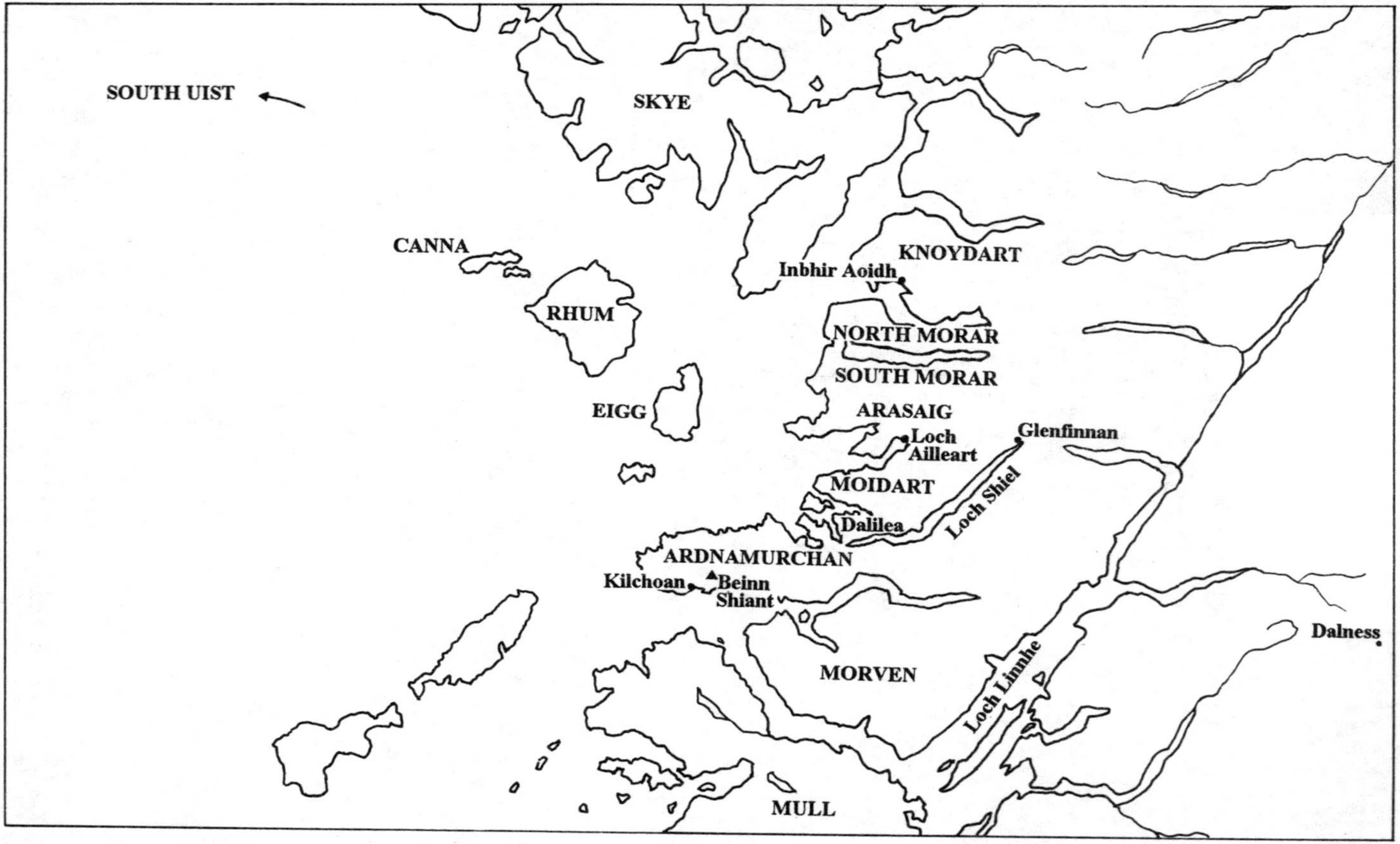
SOUTH UIST
SKYE
CANNA
RHUM
EIGG
KNOYDART
Inbhir Aoidh
NORTH MORAR
SOUTH MORAR
ARASAIG
Loch
Ailleart
Glenfinnan
MOIDART
Loch Shiel
Dalilea
ARDNAMURCHAN
Kilchoan
Beinn
Shiant
MORVEN
Loch Linnhe
Dalness
MULL

ALASDAIR
MAC MHAIGHSTIR ALASDAIR

Selected Poems

edited by

Professor Emeritus
Derick S Thomson
MA, BA, DLitt (Wales & Aberdeen),
FRSE, FBA

Published by Scottish Academic Press
for the

SCOTTISH GAELIC TEXTS SOCIETY

Published in 1996
by Scottish Academic Press Ltd.
56 Hanover Street, Edinburgh EH2 2DX
on behalf of The Scottish Gaelic Texts Society

ISBN 0 7073 0748 1

ACKNOWLEDGEMENTS

The Society gratefully acknowledges grants from the following towards the costs of publication of this volume:

The Glasgow Highland Society
Highland Regional Council
The Sir John MacDonald Study Fund
Strathclyde Regional Council Education Department
The University of Aberdeen
The University of Edinburgh
The University of Glasgow

CONTENTS

PREFACE

Over a long career of teaching and writing I have been repeatedly intrigued by the life and poetry of Alasdair Mac Mhaighstir Alasdair. Both the life and the poetry raise problems of interpretation, some of which will never be solved, but this book is presented as an attempt to clarify some aspects of the puzzle, and to give a more rounded account of the poetic achievement.

The fourteen poems were selected to illustrate both the range and the highlights of the poet's surviving work, and also to include poems from widely different parts of his career. The introduction has brief discussions of other examples of his work, and sets out to relate his work to his life insofar as this can be done with the fairly meagre biographical evidence.

This edition is intended to be useful to a varied reading public: the general reader interested in Scottish eighteenth-century literature and history, the Gaelic literary public generally, and the pupils and students who are making a serious study of Gaelic literature. In large part the Notes and Glossary are intended to smooth the path in such studies, without offering the trap-door of complete translation.

The work of earlier editors and writers is acknowledged at many points in the book. Here it is appropriate to refer to the help of the custodians of various manuscript collections that have been used. I would wish to refer specifically to the staff of the Special Collections Department at the University of Glasgow Library, particularly Mr David Weston, and to Mr Ian Maciver, of the Department of Manuscripts at the National Library of Scotland. I am also indebted to the staffs of Edinburgh University Library and of the RHASS Library at Ingliston, Edinburgh.

Finally I offer thanks to the Scottish Gaelic Texts Society's Secretary Mr James Gleasure and its Publisher Dr Douglas Grant for their work behind the scenes, and to the Society itself for providing windows over the last sixty years for serious Gaelic scholarship.

Derick S. Thomson January, 1996

INTRODUCTION

1. *Biographical*

Considering his posthumous fame, it is strange that relatively little hard detail can be identified regarding Alasdair Mac Mhaighstir Alasdair's life. Considerable periods are almost totally bare of evidence of a documentary nature, and one has frequently to have recourse to folk tradition and to the evidence of the poems. Some traditional accounts come from fifty to seventy years after his death, and are coloured by editorial preference or prejudice. The main documentary evidence dates between 1727 and 1751, spanning the Presbyterial notices associated with his teaching and catechising career which ended in 1744-45 and his interviews and correspondence with Robert Forbes between December 1747 and April 1751.

In the following account an attempt is made to construct a fuller biography, using all the different kinds of evidence (documentary, traditional, inferential), and assessing the validity of that evidence, in some cases more stringently than in earlier biographical accounts. It is hoped that there will be fewer instinctive prejudices in this account, and care will be taken to distinguish firmer evidence from conjecture.

The Reverend authors, A. MacDonald of Killearnan and A. MacDonald of Kiltarlity, have assembled a large amount of detail about MacDonald families in their three-volume opus *The Clan Donald.* This helps considerably to place the poet in his family and clan background, and to explain some aspects of his life and work. This clan and family network was extensive and influential, and an understanding of it throws light on the poet's career, movements, personality and choice of subjects for his poems. But in many cases there is a crucial shortage of precise dating, and we are obliged to make some conjectures as to where exactly Mac Mhaighstir Alasdair fits into the general framework.

There is no certainty as to the date of the poet's birth. His father, Alexander MacDonald, known as Maighstir Alasdair, graduated M.A. at the University of Glasgow on 16th July, 1674, and went on to study Divinity thereafter. The MacDonald editors of the 1924 edition of the poems claim that he was still a student of Divinity in 1681, and after that became an Episcopal clergyman at Islandfinnan/Eilean Fhìonain in Moidart. Hew Scott, in *Fasti* IV, 106, suggests 'about 1687' as the date of admission. In several papers in the Clanranald charter chest, in Maighstir Alasdair's hand, and with dates before and after 1688, he designates himself 'Minister of Islandfinnan'. Students at the University of Glasgow matriculated at that time at ages ranging from twelve to the late teens, so that, working back from his graduation in 1674, we can conjecture that Maighstir Alasdair may have been born in the mid-1650s. He died in 1724, probably about the age of seventy.

Maighstir Alasdair was the fourth son of Angus Og MacDonald of Milton in South Uist. His grandparents were Ranald MacDonald, 1st of Benbecula, and Margaret MacDonald of Dun Naomhaig (Islay), and that Ranald was a son of Alan MacDonald, Chief of Clanranald. Maighstir Alasdair's eldest brother, Ranald, succeeded his father at Milton, and Flora MacDonald of the '45 was his daughter. A younger brother, Angus, in 1710 married Mary, daughter of Lachlan MacDonald of Laig in Eigg, and this tack was to be taken up much later by the poet's son Ranald. Maighstir Alasdair had a sister who married John MacDonald of Glenaladale, and the poet was to have close connections with that family.

Alasdair Mac Mhaighstir Alasdair was his father's second son. His elder brother was Angus (Aonghas Beag), and he had two younger brothers, Lachlan and James, and several sisters. We do not know the year of birth of any of the family. At least a pointer to the dates of birth of his two younger brothers may be provided by the references in Bishop Forbes' *The Lyon in Mourning* to the poet's two brothers James and Lauchlan visiting the Prince (p.327), and to two nephews of the poet, Lieutenant John MacDonald and Lieutenant Rory MacDonald his brother (p.328). According to the *Clan Donald* account (Vol. 3, 284) John and Roderick were the second and third sons of Lachlan, the elder of the poet's two younger brothers. In 1746, then, we see two sons of the poet's younger brother holding the rank of Lieutenant. This would seem to suggest a birth year for that brother hardly later than 1700, and possibly a few years earlier.

Keith Norman MacDonald (p.25) reports the tradition that Maighstir Alasdair's four sons lived to a good old age. Angus is thought to have died soon after 1760, and this could suggest a birth year about 1690 or soon afterwards, with a birth year for Alasdair Mac Mhaighstir Alasdair in the mid-1690s or slightly earlier. Such a date would fit in with the suggestion that the poet took part in the 1715 Rising. This possibility is supported by the detailed references to Sheriffmuir in 'Diomoladh Chabair Fèidh', and also by his references in the Lockhart Papers.

Lockhart includes a very detailed 'Journal and Memoirs of P----- C------ Expedition into Scotland 7c. 1745-6. By a Highland officer in his Army' (*Lockhart Papers*, Vol. 11, 479-510), and it is clear from internal evidence that this Highland officer is Mac Mhaighstir Alasdair. This is confirmed particularly by the passage on p.482

where the writer of the Journal says "After we had all eaten plentifully [in the house of Angus McDonald of Borradel in Arisaig] and drunk chearfully, H.R.H. drunk the grace drink in English which most of us understood; when it came to my turn I presumed to distinguish myself by saying audibly in Erse (or highland language) *Deochs laint- an Reogh*; H.R.H. understanding that I had drunk the King's health made me speak the words again in Erse and said he could drink the King's health likewise in that language, repeating my words; and the company mentioning my skill in the highland language, H.R.H. said I should be his master for that language, and so was made to ask the healths of the P. and D." He reports a later incident, at the battle of Prestonpans, when he passed near by the Prince, and "he with a smile said to me in Erse, "Gres-ort, Gres-ort", that is, Make haste, make haste" (*Ibid.*, 491).

There are two passing references to the 1715 Rising in this Journal. As the writer and three other MacDonald gentlemen board the Prince's ship on 20th July 1745 "we were most chearfully welcom'd by the Duke of Athole to whom some of us had been known in the year 1715" (p.480). Again, referring to the army's encampment near Dumblane, he says "It was in this neighbourhood that many of our fathers and severalls of us now with the P. fought for the same cause just thirty years ago at the battle of Sherriffmuir" (p.486). The tone of this second reference seems to suggest that he included himself in the group who had fought in 1715.

An earlier birth date also leaves space for attendance at Glasgow University, before the '15 Rising, and perhaps a period of service to a Clanranald official between the '15 and the mid-1720s. The MacDonald editors of the 1924 edition (p.xxvi) report "It is said further that his chief, Allan, who fell at Sheriffmuir, desired him to study law with a view to his succeeding Farquhar McCulloch, the notary who did the legal business of the estate. The fact that there remain in the Clanranald charter chest a few legal documents in the handwriting of Alastair would seem to lend colour to this suggestion". If we can accept this tradition, it suggests that the poet may have been at University before the '15. John Reid (p.79) reports the tradition that the poet went to live on Canna, as ground officer to Clanranald, adding "The date of this residence seems to have been 1725, or perhaps some years before". Caution must be expressed as to Reid's views, but in general this suggestion seems feasible. A document in the Clanranald papers written and witnessed by 'Alex^{r}. MackDonald second son to the Deceast Mr Alex^{r}. mackDonald Min^{r}. of Islandfinan', and dated 28 February 1727, is reproduced in the 1924 edition (facing p.viii). This was witnessed at Nuntown in Benbecula. There is therefore some persuasive evidence that the poet was employed on legal or semi-legal tasks, and had presumably some training (probably in the form of apprenticeship) before the mid-1720s.

The poet's father, Maighstir Alasdair, as we saw, had taken up residence at Islandfinnan and/or Dalilea, almost certainly in the 1680s, and probably before the middle of that decade, and had himself performed scribal tasks for Clanranald. His allegiance was to the Episcopal Church, and it was a strong and obstinate allegiance. He was deposed in 1697 for nonjurancy, i.e. the stance of clergy who refused to take the oath of allegiance to William and Mary in 1689, but he continued to minister as an Episcopalian in Ardnamurchan and Moidart until his death in 1724. He was seemingly acquainted with the traditional style of writing Gaelic, including the old script, and may have passed these skills on, in part, to his son, along with a grounding in classical studies. Maighstir Alasdair's wife was a MacLachlan from Morven. A strain of rugged independence is clearly to be seen in this MacDonald family generally, whether it shows in the reported excesses of the minister's grandfather, in his own doggedness, or in his son's enormous political enthusiasm and his virulent opposition to individuals.

Father Charles MacDonald, in his book *Moidart or among the Clanranalds*, was able to draw on relatively recent memories of this family, and has vivid stories about the physical strength and fearlessness of Maighstir Alasdair, his eldest son Aonghas Beag, and his great-grandson, the son of Ranald son of Alasdair the poet. Fr. Charles also relates the firm tradition that the minister and his family lived for a time on the islet of Camustroloman, in Loch Shiel, close to Eilean Fhìonain: it is thought that they moved there when there was an outbreak of fever or smallpox.

From what we know of Maighstir Alasdair's career it seems most likely that the poet was born at Dalilea or in that vicinity, and brought up there, despite the reference in the Eigg version of 'Smeòrach Chlann Raghnaill' to *Caisteal bhuiribh*, Borve Castle in Benbecula. Angus MacLeod (*Sàr Orain*, 23) comments "later versions have *dhuibh* for *bhuiribh*, and the reference might be to Castletirrim, the mainland seat of Clanranald, which he mentions in the next stanza of the poem."

The farm of Dalilea had been given in life-rent as early as 1630 to a so-called "parson" (according to Charles MacDonald, *Moidart* – – – 121-2) who seems not to have actually lived in Moidart, and it passed to a Donald Gorm, possibly the "parson's" nephew, and ultimately to Maighstir Alasdair. The farm stayed in the minister's family until late in the eighteenth century. Fr. Charles also relates (p.158) the tradition that the poet planted a number of trees near the house of Dalilea, including an oak-tree which survived into the present century.

The poet's life was intertwined with the Clanranald and MacDonald clans, and with their territories. The Clanranald lands were located both in the islands (especially South Uist and Benbecula, but also Canna and Eigg) and on the western mainland, and the poet seems to have spent the greater part of his life in these territories or within close reach of them. His father's people came from the Outer Isles and continued to hold tacks of land in Benbecula and South Uist. Two of the poet's brothers followed this pattern. We have specific accounts of his presence in Uist and Benbecula in 1727 and in 1746, but no doubt he had visited these islands throughout his life. He may have spent two separate periods in Canna, and on the Mainland he lived in Moidart, Knoydart, Morar and Arisaig. During his teaching career he lived in Ardnamurchan latterly, but still within easy reach of earlier haunts. His wife was a MacDonald, from the Dalness family, which was a branch of the Glencoe MacDonalds. The eulogy of the poet in the Eigg Collection was composed by John MacDonald, IV of Arnabidh (Aird na Bìth in the Glengarry lands), described at one point as the poet's *dalta*, probably a courtesy reference implying discipleship rather than specific fostering. This MacDonald had also been a Captain in the '45 Rising. These MacDonald allegiances come over very clearly in the '45 poetry, but there can be little doubt that they coloured his whole career and life, though he seems to have fallen out with his patrons from time to time.

There seems no reason to doubt the strong tradition that he married Jane MacDonald of Dalness, though there is no documentary evidence for this. The 'Oran d'a Chèile' evidently refers to the location of her home, and the reference to the *Reumhair* from whom he got her is surely to her father, whether the appellation here means 'Reiver' or 'Rhymer'. The MacDonalds of Dalness were known as *Clann Reumhair/Reubhair*, and certainly some of them were poets. Jane's brother was apparently the original author of 'Cuachag nan Craobh', later reworked by William Ross, and her mother also came from a poetic family, the MacLachlans of Coire Uanan in Lochaber, from whom the poet Ewen MacLachlan came. At one time it was assumed that it was the poet's involvement with Jane which had terminated his University career. This is not feasible, as it appears that the poet's eldest child, Ranald, was born about 1728 (as he is said to be about eighty in 1808 – see Black, p.15), and his wife was delivered of a child while the family was on the run after Culloden in 1746. In a letter from Robert Forbes, dated 10th July, 1749, he says that Ranald had told him that the poet and his family "had got safe to Glenco" (*Lyon in Mourning*, Vol. 2, 336). There is also a reference to *Sìne* in 'Moladh Mòraig'. There is a brief passage in the 'Oran d'a Chèile' which shows deep emotion, but surprisingly little reference to his wife either in the surviving poetry or in tradition. It is likely that she pre-deceased him, as he appears to have been living on his own at the end.

Probably the most frustrating period of the poet's life, for a biographer, was the decade from 1715 to 1725. There seems a strong possibility that he took part in the '15, and his poem 'Diomoladh Chabair Fèidh' has very specific references to the behaviour of the Mackenzies in the '15 campaign. I have argued elsewhere (TGSI, Vol. LVI, 187-90) that this poem probably dates to the year 1725. What he had been doing in the years from 1715 to 1725 can only be conjectured, but this period is likely to contain whatever training he did for legal or quasi-legal duties.

It is tempting to surmise that he may have done some training of this kind in Edinburgh, sometime between 1715 and 1725. Contacts and influences from that location surface at various times in his life and work. We know that he visited Edinburgh in 1738, in 1745 and in the years from 1747 to 1751. More intriguingly, his perfunctory borrowing from Allan Ramsay in 'Oran an t-Samhraidh', the influence of Thomson's *Seasons* (1726-38), and the influence of Gavin Douglas's Prologues and possibly his 'Palice of Honour', may well have come about through some acquaintance with Edinburgh literary circles. Douglas's *Aeneados* was edited by Thomas Ruddiman and published in 1710, and Douglas's reputation was clearly boosted thereafter, as is instanced by Allan Ramsay's adoption of his name c. 1713-14 as his Easy Club pseudonym. It would not be surprising to discover that the 'Entreaty to the Muses' (*Guidhe no Urnaigh an Ughdair don Cheòlraidh*) was written in Edinburgh in that post-'15 decade.

There is another probable reference to Allan Ramsay in the first section of 'Mìomholadh Mòraig'. This is supposed to be spoken by Alasdair's wife Jane, and she says that if he does not stop his nonsense she will contact Alan Bard and other poets who care for her in Edinburgh:

Tàmh do d' sgeig dhìom tràth
Neo ruigim Ailean Bàrd
'S gach filidh ga bheil càs
An Dun Eideann dìom.

'Ailean Bàrd' is probably a playful way of referring to Allan Ramsay, and the reference to other poets in Edinburgh may even suggest that he had introduced Jane to some of his friends there.

Yet another pointer to Edinburgh influences may be the considerable number of instances where he names an English/ Scots air as the melody/metrical model for songs in the 1751 collection. There are ten such named. Four of these feature in William Thomson's *Orpheus Caledonius* which appeared in editions dated 1725 and 1733; 'Tweedside', given as the 'air' for a song on p.43 of the 1751 collection, was an art-song by Robert Crawford, dating from the early part of the eighteenth century, and 'Good night, and God be with you', the 'air' for a song on p.134 of 1751, was included in Henry Playford's *Collection of Original Scotch Tunes – – – for the Violin* (1700). William Thomson and Allan Ramsay had the reputation of re-cycling each other's publications to some extent, and the relationship between Scots and Gaelic airs is itself a highly complex matter.

The period for which most documentary evidence exists is that from 1729 to 1745, and is connected with his work as teacher and catechist. The evidence is in Presbyterial records of the time. Much of this was assembled in William Mackay's 'Presbyterial Notices of Mac Mhaighstir Alasdair, and some of his contemporaries in Ardnamurchan and Morven', in TGSI, Vol. XI, 171-84 (1885), and this evidence is set in a wider context in Ronald Black's important monograph *Mac Mhaighstir Alasdair: The Ardnamurchan Years*. The Royal Bounty Committee of the General Assembly of the Church of Scotland had begun in 1728 to fund certain appointments to the joint duties of teacher and catechist. It seems likely that Mac Mhaighstir Alasdair, recently married and with a newly-born or soon-to-be-born son, and probably estranged from his former Clanranald employer in Canna, was attracted to this type of appointment. In any case, he took up duties as teacher at Islandfinnan and catechist in the parish (usually referred to as Ardnamurchan). His annual stipend was £16. He probably lived at Dalilea, now farmed by his brother Angus. (He had looked forward, in the 'Oran d'a Chèile nuadh-phòsda', to bringing Sìne home to Moidart.) But in December 1730 he wrote from Kilmory, on the northern coast of Ardnamurchan (some fifteen miles from Dalilea) to Sir Alexander Murray his local landlord, urging that Kilmory should be the site of the parish school (the letter, in the National Library of Scotland Adv. MS 29.1.1 (iii), ff.258r-259v, is quoted by Black, *op. cit.*, 20). After various negotiations a school was set up at Kilmory, with a small additional salary input from the SSPCK, and the poet began teaching there in November 1732, with a salary of £18. In the following month he appears as Commissioner from the parish of Ardnamurchan, asking the Presbytery of Mull "to moderate a call for a minister to them". In May 1733 he appeared before the Presbytery again "to prosecute a call to Mr Daniel Maclachlan, a probationer". Maclachlan became minister of Ardnamurchan in September 1734, although he had previously stood trial accused of drunkenness, swearing and singing of indecent songs. After two months as minister he was given leave of absence to go to Edinburgh, but he never returned, being finally 'excommunicated'. There are other tales of roistering clergymen at this period and in close neighbourhoods, and we may suspect that the poet fitted easily into such company at times. We should remember too that his mother was a MacLachlan from Morven. Perhaps as an indirect result of the Maclachlan case the poet's school was visited by a committee from the Presbytery, and his salary was reduced in late 1735, but partly restored a year later.

These early schools were often switched from one locality to another, to extend the opportunities of education within the limited budget available, and his school was moved back to Islandfinnan in late 1736. By 1737 his salary had risen to £18 again. In 1738 his school was moved to Kilchoan on the south coast of Ardnamurchan, and in 1739 to Corryvullin, where he stayed until the end of his teaching career in 1745. (The detailed references to these moves and salary changes are given in William Mackay's article referred to above, and in Black *op. cit.*, the latter quoting also from Scottish Record Office sources).

Late in his Corryvullin incumbency, Mac Mhaighstir Alasdair became involved in another clerical scandal, when Francis MacDonald, Presbyterian preacher at Strontian, and formerly a Roman Catholic priest in Moidart, was accused of incest with his sister. The 'information' on this charge was said to be written by John Stewart, drover in Knock, Mull, and Alexander MacDonald, schoolmaster at Ardnamurchan. The case fizzled out, as Francis MacDonald moved to Skye (see TGSI, Vol. XI, 178-80).

The part Mac Mhaighstir Alasdair took with prominent Roman Catholics in this case, against an ex-priest, suggests a strong sympathy with the Catholic Church while he was still acting as catechist and teacher for the rival establishment, whereas in the 1741 Vocabulary he had placed 'Popish Emissaries' among the evils from which the Highlands then suffered. It is likely, however, that his religious beliefs and allegiances had been fluid for some time, perhaps since his youth. His public identification with Presbyterianism, in 1729, came five years after his Episcopalian father's death. His elder brother Angus, reputedly under his wife's influence in this, had converted to Catholicism. But many of the

Clanranald hierarchy were Catholic, and some of the Chiefs had probably been Protestant in name only. When he came to make a public switch to Catholicism, apparently just before the start of the '45 campaign, it seems likely that he was throwing in his lot with his clan and political allies rather than expressing a religious conversion. His motives were thought by the Mull Bard and others to be connected with personal advancement and court sycophancy, but it is at least as probable that they were determined by his burning enthusiasm for the Jacobite cause.

The important topic of his involvement with the 1741 Vocabulary falls within his teaching career, but will be discussed later, in relation to his views on language and his involvement with Edinburgh.

Hopes of another Jacobite rising were surfacing in 1744, and Mac Mhaighstir Alasdair was absent from his teaching duties for part of that summer, while early in 1745 he appeared before the Royal Bounty Committee in Edinburgh, where his conduct of his school was apparently in question. In June 1745 the Presbytery of Mull reported that he was wandering through the country, "composing Galick songs, stuffed with obscene Language", and this was recorded in the SSPCK minutes on 4th June 1745 (see J. L. Campbell, 'The Expurgating of Mac Mhaighstir Alasdair', SGS, Vol. XII, Pt.1, 59-60). Some of these pre-campaign poems survive. Two of them were said by John Mackenzie (*Eachdraidh a' Phrionnsa* (1844ed.), 254*n*) to have been sent to Aeneas MacDonald, brother of the Laird of Kinlochmoidart, and a banker in Paris, and to have been translated by him and shown to Prince Charlie (see D. S. Thomson (1991), p.6). Aeneas's brother Ranald was married to Marcella, daughter of Angus of Dalilea and the poet's niece. One of these two poems is the 'Oran nam Fineachan Gaidhealach', in which many clans are appealed to, and urged to join the coming Rising, including the unlikely clan, the Campbells.

Our knowledge of the poet's involvement in the '45 comes mainly from the poems themselves, but also importantly from his extended conversations with and reports to the Rev. Robert Forbes, later Bishop Forbes, on various occasions from December 28th, 1747 to April 22nd, 1751. Forbes was born in 1708, graduated at Marischal College, Aberdeen, in 1726, came to Edinburgh in 1735, and soon afterwards started his long incumbency as an Episcopalian clergyman in Leith. He was an ardent Jacobite, but was imprisoned in 1745 on his way to joining the Rising. His relationship with the poet seems to have been a warm and respectful one. He refers to him repeatedly as 'Captain Alexander MacDonald', 'Captain MacDonald' and 'the Captain', describing him at one point (Forbes, *The Lyon in Mourning*, Vol.

1,354) as "a very smart, acute man, remarkably well skilled in the Erse, for he can both read and write the Irish language in the original character – – –". The poet on December 28th, 1747 brought Forbes "a journal of several sheets in his own handwriting, and in the handwriting of young Clanranald, and in the handwriting of MacDonald of Glenaladale, the Journal having been drawn up in the presence, and by the mutual assistance of all the three". This account is largely concerned with post-Culloden events, though later Forbes gets the poet to comment on some entries in Aeneas Macdonald's Journal which relate to the Prince's landing, and Mac Mhaighstir Alasdair tells of his meeting with the Prince before he knew who he was (*Lyon in Mourning*, Vol. 1,352), and also of his and his family's experiences on the run after Culloden (*Ibid.*, 354).

Some different details emerge in the account given in the 'Journal and Memoirs of P----- C------ Expedition into Scotland etc. 1745-6', printed in the *Lockhart Papers*, Vol. II in 1817. This tells how the poet was sent to Ardnamurchan to recruit, "and soon returned with 50 cliver fellows". The Prince gave him command of them, and told him that he was "the first officer he had made in Scotland; which compliment encouraged my vanity not a little – – –" (p.483). There follows a fairly detailed account of the campaign, from the raising of the standard at Glenfinnan to the beginning of the battle of Culloden. The various places passed through, stopping places, smaller and larger military incidents, all the way to Derby and on the return journey are detailed, with additional detail about battles such as Prestonpans and Falkirk, the entry to Edinburgh and later to Glasgow, the skirmish at Clifton near Penrith etc. It seems quite clear from this account that Mac Mhaighstir Alasdair was involved throughout, and also at Culloden, although he does not describe that battle, saying that there are sufficient accounts of it in existence already. That last remark suggests an addition, perhaps a year or two after 1746, but the Journal is probably based on notes taken during the campaign, and written up into a continuous narrative later.

In the main, the accounts in *The Lyon in Mourning* and in the *Lockhart Papers* cover different aspects of the campaign and its aftermath, but there are one or two instances of common ground, especially the accounts of the poet's first meeting with the Prince. These are similar, but the *Lockhart Papers* one is much more detailed. The editor of *The Lyon in Mourning*, Henry Paton, is wrong in suggesting (Vol. II, 321, footnote) that the 'Account of the Young Pretender's Escape' in the *Lockhart Papers* (II, 537-62) seems to have been taken from Mac Mhaighstir Alasdair's Journal (if by that he means the version Forbes used), for the author of the later Lockhart account has additional references e.g. to his brother Rorie and his nephew Lieut. Alexander MacDonald (p.544). It is important, in assessing Mac Mhaighstir Alasdair's involvement in the '45, to take account of both the *Lyon* and the *Lockhart* journals.

The poems provide detail of a different sort, not concerned much with personal matters, but rather with political exhortation, reporting of battles, hopes for future success, praise of the Prince and hatred and satire directed at the Hanoverians. I have discussed elsewhere (TGSI, Vol. 56, 185-213, and separate booklet with the same title) Alasdair Mac Mhaighstir Alasdair's political poetry, and will briefly summarise the conclusions reached there. There are probably some other poems, besides the two reputedly sent to Paris, which are pre-campaign ones, the drinking-poem 'Ho-rò mo bhobag an dràm' being one, with its references to James and not to Charles, whereas 'Oran rìoghail a' bhotail' is a campaign one, dating between July 1745 and March 1746. Only one or two other poems can be closely connected with the actual campaign. The 'Moladh air pìob-mhòir MhicCruimein', apparently referring to the piper Dòmhnall Bàn MacCruimein who was killed at the Rout of Moy on 24th February 1746, is probably one such, and the popular 'O hì ri rì, tha e tighinn' may be another. The 'Oran a rinneadh a' bhliadhna 1746' has some pre-Culloden elements in it, but a significant part was composed after that battle, and comments on the Hanoverian ravaging of some West Highland districts thereafter. But even in these stressful conditions the poem has a fairly cool historical perspective and philosophical argument, though it is interspersed with vituperation and satire. It gives us a classic window on the poet's heart and mind, showing us a landscape of historical knowledge, genealogical interest, reflections on justice, and vitriolic abuse of the Hanoverians. An important aspect of his technique was the ability to express such a range in vivid and colourful language, calculated to appeal to 'ordinary folk'.

There is evidence in some of the poems that though they were begun during the campaign they were added to later, before the 1751 publication. And there are several poems that can be dated to the post-campaign years. The fragmentary 'Brosnachadh gu èirigh le Teàrlach an dèidh 1745' (An Incitement to rising with Charles after 1745), known only from MS 63 in the National Library, is one such, dating from not later than September 1746. Other poems of this period are reactions to the Disarming Act of 1746 and the Disclothing Act of 1747 (e.g. 'Am Breacan Uallach'). And another group of poems seem to refer backwards to Prince Charlie's departure for France, and forwards to hopes of his return (e.g. 'Oran luadhaidh no fùcaidh', 'Oran do Raghnall Og Mac Mhic Ailein', the poem beginning *'S eutrom, uallach, mear* – 1924 ed., p.126, deriving from MS 63 – and 'Oran Mhorair Mhic Sìomoin', dating from 1747). Some of the satirical anti-Campbell poems, including the Bana-bhàrd an Obain ones, have post-campaign references in them, and it is important to remember that Campbells were involved in the post-Culloden ravaging of Moidart. He seems to have gone through a period of intense bitterness in the two years after Culloden in particular, but to have made a recovery from this state of mind: this recovery seems to show in 'An Airce' (The Ark), an anti-Campbell poem which tolerates some fun as well as satire. Hopes of a further rising probably persisted into the early 1750s, and may well have been an important part of the motivation for the 1751 publication of his poems.

The 1751 volume includes three translations of short poems by the seventeenth-century Duke of Montrose. These may have been made about the time of the centenaries of Charles I's execution (30th January, 1649) and of Montrose's (21st July, 1650). They are placed near the end of the 1751 volume, which follows, but only sporadically, a chronological sequence.

As we have seen, when he visited Forbes in Leith (December 28th and 29th, 1747, January 9th, 1748, and April 22nd, 1751) we get no impression from Forbes of that post-campaign bitterness. The Act of Indemnity, passed in June, 1747, would have relieved some of the pressure on him, and he may have lived with his own or his wife's relatives for some time. Dr J. L. Campbell (*Canna*, 106) refers to a note in Bundle 117 of the Dunvegan Papers which proves that Alexander MacDonald, the "Famous Composer of Morack" was installed on Canna by 10th April, 1750. He may have been there somewhat earlier, for Forbes writes to him on 10th July, 1749, "You told me you intended to take up your abode in Egg or Canna". Forbes asked him on that occasion to supply full details of the pillaging of Eigg and Canna (after Culloden presumably), and on April 22nd, 1751 the poet brought Forbes his answer to that request. There is a tradition that he composed the *Birlinn*, or part of it, on Canna. His stay there seems to have ended sometime in 1751.

Keith Norman MacDonald (*MacDonald Bards from Medieval Times*, 26), probably building slightly on John Mackenzie's account in *Sàr Obair* (p.103) reports the tradition that "He had been invited to Edinburgh by some Jacobite friends there to take charge of the education of their children, and it is supposed that he was in Edinburgh in 1751, the year in which his first volume of original Gaelic poetry, the first ever published, took place – – – –

His mission to Edinburgh having proved unsuccessful he returned to the Highlands and settled at 'Eignaig' in Moidart".

After 1751 there seems to be little or no documentary evidence of the poet's movements, and we have to rely on reported tradition and such evidence as can be extracted from the poetry, to give some picture of his movements and activities. The sequence suggested by these is as follows. Firstly there is a stay in Eigneig, probably leasing a farm on the Glenuig estate of the Clanranald chief. From the poem 'Imrich Alasdair ás Eigneig', and related tradition, we can deduce that he quarrelled badly with the local priest, Fr. William Harrison (who apparently did not have Jacobite sympathies), and perhaps also with Clanranald, and moved to Inbhir Aoidh on the southern shore of Knoydart. From there he moved to Morar, which he describes lovingly in the poem 'Fàilte na Mòrthir', and then he moved to Arisaig, living (according to the Rev. Charles Macdonald, *Moidart* – – – p.156) first at Strath-Arisaig, then "at a place between Camus-an-Talamhainn and Rhu", and finally at Sanntaig, where he died, being buried in the Arisaig churchyard.

In none of these traditions of his final twenty years or so is there any specific reference to his wife, and none of his poems, apart from the 'Oran d'a Chèile' and the Morag poems, mention her either. We do not know when she died, but he seems to have been isolated from his family at the time of his death, for the Rev. Charles Macdonald (*Ibid.*, 156-7) reports the story of how two young men were sent to watch at his bedside as he approached death, and how he helped them with his final breaths to make some verses. It is a marvellous symbol of the poet's life. He is said to have composed satiric verses in his father's household as a young boy, and the gift of verse stayed with him to his final moments.

His son Ranald is said to have operated the inn at Strath Arisaig until his move to Eigg, where he took over the lease of the farm of Laig not later than 1770. Mac Mhaighstir Alasdair's uncle, Angus, had married Mary, daughter of Lachlan MacDonald of Laig in 1710, but he died in 1716. Ranald's move may well have taken place before the poet's death. The earliest MS source of the poem 'Fàilte na Mòrthir' is in the MacDiarmid MS, and comes near the beginning of that MS (pp.6-11), which suggests it was copied close to 1770. The editor ascribes the poem to 'Mr. Alastair Mac-Dhomhnuil', and this suggests that the poet was still alive as far as MacDiarmid was aware. It is usually assumed that he died in 1770 or soon afterwards.

There were various satirical exchanges between Mac Mhaighstir Alasdair and other poets, especially his dialogues with the Aireach Muileach and with the Campbell 'Bana-bhàrd (female poet) an

Obain', but apparently only one eulogy of him by a fellow-poet. This was included in his son Ranald's *Eigg Collection* of 1776, and is worth looking at in some detail. The poem is entitled 'Oran le fear Arnabidh, do Alister Mac Domhnuill', and appears on pp.322-4 of the Collection. It is rather badly spelled, and some phrases are obscure. Ardnabi is now a ruined village, west of Ardochy which is just south of Loch Garry. The authors of *Clan Donald* identify Fear Arnabidh as John MacDonald of Ardnabie who was a Captain in the Glengarry regiment in 1745 (Vol. III, 346). Dr J. L. Campbell (SGS XII, 73), referring to Mac Mhaighstir Alasdair's comment in his 1751 Preface that the poems were written 'for the amusement of a private gentleman', speculates that this gentleman may have been Fear Ardnabie. John Reid, in his *Bibliotheca Scoto-Celtica* (p.79) had speculated in 1832 that the private gentleman was connected with the poet's stay in Canna c. 1725. It is scarcely possible to make a secure judgement, but on the whole a Clanranald connection seems the more likely, as some of the poems are likely to pre-date the '45 by many years. The poet's legal mentor (possibly an Edinburgh lawyer of MacDonald stock?) is another possibility.

Returning to the eulogy, it seems clearly in praise of a poet who is still alive, and it refers very specifically to a number of Mac Mhaighstir Alasdair's subjects and individual poems, ending with drinking a health to the poet. His 'collection' of the virtues of piping (*Co chnuaisach buaidh gach piobarichd*) is referred to, his being Morag's sweetheart for a time and his dispraise of her (*Ga be chualla a duais 's neo ebhin e*), his involvement with the nine (Muses) and his pre-eminence even over Homer (*Gun tuig u bar air h omar,/Ga ba ceol fhear mòr sa greigas e*), his popularity among poets, his learning and knowledge. In a later stanza he says that when the Messenger (i.e. Death) inevitably comes, many will be sad, including the Muses (*Na miusas bigh gu gallach,/Nuair ni Alistar air faigalse*). Then he brings Nature into the circle of mourning, with references to streams and rivers, the birds, plants and flowers, the salmon etc., with a specific reference to Allt an t-Siùcair (*'S fear feanais ault an t shuicar air*). The closing stanza sends regards/a farewell from the poet's foster-brother, and this may suggest that the poem was composed close to 1700.

Some episodes in the poet's life have still to be discussed, in relation particularly to his work on the 1741 Vocabulary, but this section on his biography generally may be concluded with reference to some of the traditions reported about him after his death. John Mackenzie in the 1830s and 1840s undoubtedly had a closer access to such traditions than some later commentators and one contemporary one (Reid). Some of these surface in his edition of 1834-39, his *Sàr Obair* of 1841, and his *Eachdraidh a' Phrionnsa* of 1844. Some caution must be exercised with his accounts of these traditions and his interpretations of them.

Mackenzie has a couple of good stories about the poet and his encounters with a local clergyman and with his brother Angus. They ring true, though it would have been better to have them in their original Gaelic form. In one instance, Mackenzie quotes his source, a Duncan McKenzie, from Kilchoan, who lived to the age of ninety-four, and in 1828 told John Mackenzie of when he was a pupil in the poet's school, and when examiners came to see how it was being run, he was called up and asked to read the scriptures, which he did competently in spite of having come to school only in the preceding term. Duncan Mackenzie was presumably aged ten or more at the time, and he recalls that the following summer he was taken from school to tend cattle. John Mackenzie comments briefly on some of the poems, saying that the descriptive ones were composed from 1725 to 1745, and that 'Oran an t-Samhraidh' was composed "at Glenscribisdale, situated on the south side of Loch-Suainart, in the parish of Morven. He came there on a visit the last day of April; and rising early next morning, and viewing the picturesque scenes around, was powerfully impressed with the varied beauties of nature, displayed in such ample profusion". The detail of date and location sound wholly authentic. In the Memoir prefixed to the 1839 edition Mackenzie says: "After the defeat at Culloden, the bard was obliged to skulk and hide himself for a year or two, in the wilds of Moidart and Arasaig. It was during the time of his concealment that he composed the greater part of those fiery and enthusiastic Jacobite songs – – – –". In that Memoir also he gives his account of the Morag poems: "Morag was a common country girl, and, according to tradition, the poet's wife became jealous of her rival. The bard had talked of the marriage ties with the greatest contempt, and regretted that he was fettered with the bonds of wedlock. This raised a storm, and the bard sacrificed the mistress to appease the wife, and composed his Mi-mholadh – – – –". This interpretation needs to be treated with caution, as it is not the only possible one. Mackenzie also comments on the tally of unpublished poems: "We have good authority for saying that a tenth of these poems and songs have not been given to the world. His son Ronald had them all in manuscript; but having published a collection of Gaelic poetry, and not meeting with much encouragement for a second volume, he allowed his MS. to be destroyed. Dr. McEachen, a friend and connection, had the mortification of seeing leaves of them used for various purposes through the house". The reference to "a tenth" reads oddly, and MacKenzie's intention may have been to suggest that a lot of poems were unpublished. But his story, and the reference to Dr. McEachen, makes one wonder if he was referring to what is now MS 63/Adv. MS 72.2.13 in the National Library of Scotland, with its many missing pages, and with its note in the margin of p.133: 'Mary McDonald Eachen'. Mary, a daughter of Aonghas Beag, the poet's brother, was married to Charles MacEachen of Drimindarach (according to *Clan Donald*, III, 285), and Dr. McEachen may have been a son of hers.

In 1832 John Reid published his *Bibliotheca Scoto-Celtica*, and on pp.78-82 he gives an account of Mac Mhaighstir Alasdair which may well mingle fact with fiction. Of the poet's early education he says: "Our poet was sent to Glasgow College, after studying for some time under his father – – – – and it does not appear that the young man's conduct, whilst at College, or after it, was very satisfactory to the Rev. gentleman; and it appears, on that account, that Alexander's studies were interrupted. After leaving College, he remained for some time at home, and here he first began to devote himself to the muses". It is significant that there is no reference to an early marriage. Reid says that about this time, or soon after, the poet became a Catholic, and went to live on Canna, as ground officer to Clanranald. "The date of this residence seems to have been 1725, or perhaps some years before". He refers to "the bacchanalian potations of her (i.e. the poet's Muse's) Canna entertainer", and suggests that many of the poems in the 1751 book were composed in Canna "for the amusement of a private gentleman". Reid is very vague about the poet's teaching career, and this reinforces the impression of guesswork in his general account.

Finally, after a passage praising the poet's natural endowments, his excellence as a poet and his erudition as a scholar, there comes Reid's famous physical description of him: "In person, Macdonald was large and ill-favoured. His features were coarse and irregular. His clothes were very sluggishly put on, and generally very dirty. His mouth was continually fringed with a stream of tobacco juice, of which he chewed a very great quantity. His manner of composition was, to lie on his back in bed, in winter, or on the grass in summer, with a large stone on his breast, muttering to himself in a low whisper his poetical aspirations".

Commenting on this description, and on a statement attributed to Dr Scott that the poet took excessively to opium and died in a lunatic asylum, Fr. Charles Macdonald emphasises that the Moidart tradition was quite different. The opium reference he describes as "wild fiction", and he says that "Those who ought to be good judges of his personal appearance and habits know nothing of such objectionable details. At any rate all memory of them has vanished, if it ever existed" (*Moidart* – – –, 157).

In a letter written by the Rev. Duncan MacCallum, of Arasaig Manse, dated 21st December 1820, he makes a tentative approach to the Highland Society of Scotland to support his proposed collection of Gaelic poetry and song. The Society made a contribution to his costs, and the volume first appeared in 1821. Near the end of the 1820 letter MacCallum writes "I have also an account of the life and writings of the celebrated Highland poet McDonald, Allastair Mac: Mhaighistir Allastair, collected here, his native country, in the course of last two years" (Archives of the Royal Highland and Agricultural Society of Scotland, A. i. 19, No. 41). This account does not seem to have survived, and was apparently not known to Fr. Charles MacDonald, who was appointed as priest in Moidart in 1860. It may, however, be legitimate to speculate that MacCallum knew of the collection of songs which Mac Mhaighstir Alasdair's son Ranald claimed in 1808 to have been collecting for over forty years, and which he hoped to publish. A proposal for publishing by subscription was issued from Edinburgh in June 1808 (Ingliston Papers, A. i. 1, No. 10), at which time it is said that Ranald is "nearly eighty years of age". He seems to have died not long afterwards, and the collection did not appear.

It may well be that we have to give some place to the very varied assessments of the poet, and that they represent, to some degree, different aspects of his character and life-style. For example, he may on occasion have tried the ancient style of composition, lying on his back with a stone on his chest, but it was not in that position he wrote some of his poems in the old Gaelic script. There seem to have been wild and ungovernable aspects of his life-style, but at other times he appears as a caring family man. In spite of his extravagant satirical writings we see him often treated with respect and admiration. This mixed response continued with his later editors, as for example Donald Macpherson in 1874, often influenced by John Mackenzie's editorial work, and the MacDonald editors of 1924, who bring much tradition and learning to their work, and allow their admiration to dampen their moral disapproval, producing a positive assessment overall.

2. *The 1741 Vocabulary*

A brief note on this work may be appropriate as part of the poet's biography. The work is not, in itself, being treated here in any detail.

Discussions on the need for a Gaelic-English Vocabulary were already under way in the SSPCK in the mid-1720s. It was apparently hoped that the Rev. John Maclean, minister of

Kilninian, would undertake this work. Ronald Black suggests (1986, p.25) that Maclean may have encouraged Mac Mhaighstir Alasdair to take up the task when he temporarily lost his school in 1736. The Rev. David Malcolm of Duddingston had published a specimen of such a vocabulary in 1732, and a letter A section in 1738, and had been encouraged to proceed with his work on Gaelic vocabulary by both the Faculty of Advocates and the General Assembly, at various times between 1733 and 1737. Yet in 1738 the SSPCK decided not to proceed with Malcolm's proposal, possibly because they knew that Mac Mhaighstir Alasdair's was ready by that time. He went to Edinburgh in November 1738, and got general approval from the SSPCK committee for publication of the vocabulary, and the promise of £10 sterling, to be paid in the following Spring. Black, quoting SRO GD. 95/2/5, pp.411, 424, 429 says that arrangements for printing were settled in March and April, 1739, though the book did not appear until 1741. Again according to Black (*Ibid.*, 27), the poet made his way north from Edinburgh between 20th November, 1738, and 5th January, 1739, meeting Duncan Kennedy and Duncan Cameron at Loch Rannoch-side. The evidence for these encounters is in a MS which the poet apparently had in his possession at the time, with notes in his hand. The MS was apparently left behind him in Rannoch, and later came into the hands of James Macpherson. It is now in the National Library of Scotland (MS 72.1.39).

The poet does not seem to have made himself available when the Vocabulary came to be printed, and an 'Advertisement' at the end refers to "The Author's Absence from the Press, and the Difficulty of reading his Manuscript, together with the Want of a constant Corrector, who understood the Galic Language" causing several "Errata's". The Vocabulary is a strange work, arranged in the main thematically rather than alphabetically (with sections on e.g. God, air, water, parts of Man's Body, diseases, ranks, magistrates, women servants, plants and herbs, animals, household furniture etc.), though with an alphabetical Appendix of words that occur in Divinity, collected from the Irish Confession of Faith, Catechism, Book of Common Prayer in Irish etc. The orthography is somewhat variable, but not excessively so, and there is a little evidence of word-coinage, but also a wealth of native terminology. Dr J. L. Campbell, who published an article on the Vocabulary in the *Scots Magazine* in 1937, regards it as basically a translation of a Latin-English word-list.

There is evidence that the poet had refined to some extent his writing of Gaelic by 1751, but the 1741 text also confirms some of his usages e.g. the use of alternative dialectal forms. He gives 'Tombachce no Tombace' for Tobacco (p.62), but on p.82 has

'Bocse Thombaca' for A Tobacco-box and 'Píob Thombaca' for A Tobacco-pipe. In a number of other instances he gives only the *chc* form. His spelling sometimes indicates pronunciation eccentrically e.g. *Ni bhuinis do Ghiolaire* 'Belonging to an Eagle' (p.138). For 'Hellebore' he gives 'An Elibair, non Fudair Sron' (p.60), whereas in 1751 the form he uses is *elebor*.

It may be relevant to link with the 1741 publication some of the texts copied by Mac Mhaighstir Alasdair, now in Glasgow University MS Gen. 9. Mr David Weston, of the Special Collections Department there, informs me that the MS is mentioned in the University Senate minutes for March 16th, 1773, as having been presented to the Library by Dr Thomas Reid, the philosopher, who had strong Jacobite sympathies. Besides several of Mac Mhaighstir Alasdair's poems, the MS contains a copy, apparently in the poet's hand, of O'Molloy's Irish Grammar, transcribed from Lhuyd's *Archaeologia Britannica*, pp.299-309, a copy of McCurtin's Irish Grammar (which was printed at the end of Conor O'Begly's and Hugh MacCurtin's *The English Irish Dictionary* in Paris (1732), and copies of several prayers from the *Book of Common Prayer* in Irish, published in 1712. It seems likely that MS Gen. 9 dates from the later 1730s, though some of the author's poems in it would no doubt have been added a little later, some in the mid-1740s. Clearly he regarded Irish printed sources as a useful quarry, perhaps particularly for ecclesiastical vocabulary, and he was naturally interested in Gaelic's sister-language.

His whole involvement with the SSPCK, with its early hostility towards Gaelic and Catholicism, has been viewed sceptically and cynically by later commentators, with some good reason. Perhaps the strong need to support a wife and family, and the failure of his relationship with the Clanranald chief in the mid-1720s, drove him into accepting this work. Perhaps he hoped to influence the SSPCK to adopt more civilized policies, and perhaps he had some success in that. But he was capable of adopting conflicting roles: making conciliatory gestures to the inhabitants of the Lowlands of Scotland and at the same time castigating them for their persecution and intolerance of the Gaelic language (see Preface to the 1751 collection).

Another conflict appears, between his percipient account of the ancient spread of Celtic peoples in that same Preface, and passages in his poem in praise of Gaelic, which refers to it as the language of Eden and the progenitor of other languages. This can only be explained as a form of banter, including banter of the Rev. David Malcolm, whose publications of 1732 and 1738 probably inspired the poem.

3. *The Language of the Poetry*

Mac Mhaighstir Alasdair's *Vocabulary* of 1741 and his *Ais-eiridh* of 1751 come quite early in the history of reformed Scottish Gaelic spelling. The Classical literary language had a prestige that was not easily supplanted. We see early, misguided attempts to replace that system, particularly its orthography, in the manuscripts of the Dean of Lismore's Book and the Fernaig Collection, but the old system was basically retained by Carswell and by the authors of most of the ecclesiastical books published before 1741. The production of verse in the older literary language was in its final decade by that date. Somewhat older MSS, such as the Ardchonaill MS of c. 1690, do show a definite move towards a more vernacular norm, though retaining many classically influenced forms such as *ni bfhuil, fagfuidh, chunarc, na gcléus* (as quoted in *Leabhar na Fèinne*, 211). By contrast, the Rev. Alexander Pope's collection of ballads, made c. 1739, has much fewer Classical forms but uses many unhistorical spellings, such as *ghag* for *dh' fhàg*, *hug shin* for *thug sinn* etc. Even Donald MacNicol's collection of MSS, some of it dating from the 1750s, has similar unconventional spellings.

The Rev. John Maclean, minister of Kilninian in Mull, had contributed a poem, in praise of Gaelic and of Edward Lhuyd, to Lhuyd's *Archaeologia Britannica* in 1707. He writes in the Scottish vernacular, retaining occasional usages of the literary language (*air feadh na ccríochsa, do rinn* etc.), and his orthography is on the whole careful and consistent. Mac Mhaighstir Alasdair borrowed some phrases from this poem, and is thought to have admired John Maclean, and maintained contact with him. It has already been suggested that this minister may have pushed the poet's claims to prepare the *Vocabulary*, and it seems likely that there may have been continued consultancy during its preparation.

The orthography of the Vocabulary shows a fair degree of consistency, but it has a good number of aberrations also (e.g. *Piuar* twice on p.10 for 'sister', but *Piuir* twice on p.12). The rule of 'broad to broad and slender to slender' is not an important one to the author, so that spellings such as *lenabh* 'child', *banis* 'wedding', *peitag* 'waistcoat', *brisgaid* 'biscuit', *saorse* 'freedom' occur throughout, as do duplications of consonants (*dornn* 'fist', *peaccadh* 'sin') and various other 'irregularities' as they would now be regarded. There are other oddities such as 'An Tone, a Más *The Arse or Breech*' (p.15), but the general impression is of a job conscientiously done in a ground-breaking fashion.

This contrasts sharply with some of the poet's usage, for example in the Adv. MS 72.2.15 version of 'Oran an t-Samhraidh', where the orthography is much rougher.

A more consistent standard is maintained in the 1751 *Ais-eiridh*, though it has a fair input of inexact spellings, some of them no doubt misprints but others intentional (*doannan* for *daonnan*, *seallamh* for *seallaibh* probably giving an example of each). Certainly the 1751 text does not justify John Mackenzie's comment in the 1839 edition, that "the very incorrect state of the text in the old editions, rendered the book almost unintelligible". We have to bear in mind that systematisation of Scottish Gaelic orthography was an ongoing process, recently given a sharper definition by the Rev. Alexander MacFarlane in his translation of Richard Baxter's *Call to the Unconverted.* This translation appeared in 1750, and the translation of the New Testament was to come seventeen years later. The decades from 1750 to 1770 were crucial to the stabilisation of the orthography, but a degree of credit can be given to Mac Mhaighstir Alasdair for helping to open up the access to the printed Gaelic word.

In his Preface to the 1751 text he explains some innovations in his spelling: "And in order to make the force and sound of the syllables approach as near as possible to that of the English, and to the more usual pronunciation of the generality of the highlanders, some quiescent letters formerly used in the Galic are thrown out: and some are changed, especially in words whose terminations are *bh*, instead of which, *n* and *on* (leg. *an*) are commonly used."

With regard to borrowings, usually from Scots and English, Mac Mhaighstir Alasdair in his poetry is very ready to use these, though in his poem on the Gaelic language he asserts that Gaelic needs no borrowings. Occasionally he retains an English plural as in *crambos* (1.99), *matins* (1.867: the MS 72.2.15 reading), *hymns* (1.963) and perhaps *drais* (drawers?) in 1.1288, while sometimes he uses a Gaelic plural e.g. *òirseidean* (1.232), *òrainsean* (1.312). The borrowings range from proper names (*Cancer*, 834, *Capricorn*, 922, *Aeolus*, 987, *Neptiun*, 989, *Brittinn*, 1011n, *Antrum*, 1257, *Lùth*, 1377) to common and unusual words (*ceap* 'cap', *cèidse* 'cage, gage', *ranc* 'rank', *act* 'act', *loidhn* 'line', *dreass* 'dress', and the less common *suibseic* 'subject', *eileabor* 'hellebore', *flanigat* 'planxty'(?), *bhalet* 'valet', to quote only a few examples). We can see him moving from earlier readings such as *matins* and *feispar* in the Adv. MS 72.2.15 text to *maidnen'* and *feasgurrain* of the 1751 text. (Here an interesting point may arise: the poem in which these words, for 'matins' and 'vespers', occur is thought to have been composed about 1743, while his official conversion to Catholicism was in the next or the next but one year. He may have adjusted to more Gaelic forms of these Catholic terms by the end of the decade.)

There do not seem to be many outright coinages (*dastram*, 325, and *beusadh* 'singing bass', 743, may be such), but plenty of adaptations of existing Gaelic words, as in the rich series of *-ach* epithets in his descriptive poems. Nor are there many instances of English/Scots calques (one possibility is raised in 1322*n*). He appears to use a Scots pronunciation of *Whitehall*, to rhyme with *tàmh* (11.1448-50*n*). There may have been a degree of editing out, or down, some of his borrowing. At any rate there is quite a rash of borrowing in the poem 'Tha Clannach ainmeil' in MS 63 (e.g. *beatadh* 'beating', *ratreut* 'retreat', *bhomit* 'vomit', *register*, *histori*, *sentens*, *charters*).

By contrast, a fair number of Classical Gaelic (or semi-Classical) usages survive, and occasional archaic usages. These are commented on in the notes to individual poems, but a selection of examples may be usefully brought together here. He uses *Naoi*, 13, for 'Noah', *sgol*, 113, for *sgoil*, and some older spellings such as *athlamh*, 370, 1054, *fathrom*, 372, *dh'aimhdheòin*, 640 (also used in the Rev. Malcolm's Glossary), *sgàileadh*, 872, *taith-* rather than *ath-*, 978, and *oirceanach*, 1446, rather than *uirceanach*. He uses some old plural forms e.g. *smuainti*, 551, *prionnsaidh'*, 591, and *slèibhti*, 858, and the old type of genitive singular of the verbal noun e.g. *sàraichthe*, . The negative *nìor* surfaces in 1.247, and an assortment of older verbal forms such as *ghlacas*, 137, *fuair*, 172, 574, *facas*, 247, *togbhar*, 1171, *triallfaidh*, 1198, *cuirfeamaid*, 1234, 1241, *togbhail*, 2051, *do bhà*, a confusion of older *do bhí* and *bhà* (*Birlinn*, Section 16 *n*).

There are some instances of preferences which may be orthographical or may reflect dialectal usage, in the 1751 text. These are commented on, but not always retained in our text here. Examples are *go 'm* as against *d'am*, 7, *do* against *de*, 9, *go ba* against *ge bu*, 12, *go – – – go* against *ge – – – gu*, 55, *chugam* against *thugam*, 77, *na* against *nan*, 218 etc. The poet has a preference for equative forms such as *cho-mhòr*, 127, *choi '-mìn*, 361-2, *choi '-dílis*, 1026.

There is a good deal of dialectal evidence in the texts, but it is sometimes difficult to be sure whether this reflects the poet's preferences or those of editors or the writers of MS versions. The poet's own usage seems to have fluctuated, perhaps reflecting different degrees of Mainland and Island usage at different points in his career. The following selection of instances can only suggest some of the possibilities which a dialect scholar could profitably investigate.

There are several instances of words where the rhyme required the Mainland pronunciation of *ìo* to rhyme with *ì* (rather than the Island *ia*) e.g. *dìolaibh*, 68, *shìos*, 203-4, *blìon*, 212, *mìodachadh*, 702. Certain vowel variations suggest dialectal usage e.g. *niod*, 33 (though the rhyme requires *nead*), *gaigheadh*, 51 (reflecting a pronunciation of *gidheadh* that survived well into the twentieth century), *eochraichean*, 79, *iunaidh*, 244 (rather than *iongnaidh*), *siumrag*, 2028-9 (rather than *seamrag*), and *iumraich*, 2051 (rather than *iomraich*). The variation between *c* and *chd* probably reflects Mainland versus Uist usage e.g. *ghlachdas*, 137, *sochdair*, 205, 473, 1735, *plochdach*, 1636-7, *piochdaid*, 2084, and *glachdach*, 2210, as against the common *-c-* usage in the texts. There are instances of gender variation e.g. *com*, 84, as feminine (as in earlier usage), or *greann*, 953 (feminine as in North Argyll), of a dative in *-idh* e.g. *chruinnidh*, 410, and a genitive in *-idh*, e.g. *beinnidh*, 523, and of a plural form *naimhde*, 1319. There are instances of noun endings in *-ein* rather than *-ean* e.g. *soillsein* --- *coirein*, 959, and *stuibein*, 1208(?), which again suggest Island influence.

It is probably fair to allow some of this diversity of usage to survive in the poet's texts, but it is extremely difficult to know exactly where to draw lines or make choices.

4. *The Metrics*

This brief discussion of the metrics is confined to the poems in this volume. While it is clear that Mac Mhaighstir Alasdair regarded stanzaic patterned verse as the norm, and was acquainted with a range of metrical forms, it is not to be expected that he would practise these in the more-or-less rigorous fashion of the trained classical poet, though he was aware of such ideals. There is evidence, also, that for certain purposes he preferred an extended stanza, and perhaps sometimes extended 'paragraphs' that are composed of a succession of quatrains. Such an easing of structural rigidity would seem to suit his general temperament, and allows a ranging discussion or argument such as the one he conducts in the poem of 1746 in which he is concerned with the history and philosophy of the Jacobite rising as well as with the specific events of that year.

It is clear from a passage in his address to the Muses, 'Guidhe no Urnaigh an Ughdair don Cheòlraidh', that he was wary of verse which comes to rely overmuch on its sound-pattern, a temptation which many Gaelic poets were unable to resist, and a temptation made stronger by the rich range of phonemes which the language has. He appeals to Minerva to offer him a dozen words and he will not seek more, and he then asks the Muses generally not to give him a product/work that rattles in the ear and is empty of meaning, like nuts without kernels that make a noise as they are piled together:

A Mhinerbha, oide nan sgol
'S a chèidse nam fil,
Cuir aon dusan facal am char
'S tuilleadh cha sir.
Na tugaibh dhomh saothair nì glagan sa' chluais
'S do thuigse bhios fàs
Mar chaoch-chnuasaich chruinn a nì fuaim
Gun eitean 'na làr.

He did not stick to the principle of using few words, but for the most part he is not seduced merely by the sound-patterns.

It is normal for poets to experiment with a range of metres, and one would expect a young poet, learning his craft, to do this. The elegy for a Pet Dove, 'Marbhrainn do Pheata Coluim', is presumably an early poem. W. J. Watson, in *Bàrdachd Ghàidhlig* xlii draws attention to its basic metrical model, the metre known as *Cummasc etir rannaigheacht mhór agus leath-rannaigheacht*, with stanzaic pattern $2(7^1 + 5^1)^{2+4}$, but here handled rather freely, with lines 1 and 3 of the quatrain rhyming as well as 2 and 4, and with the second line of the couplet reaching a syllable count as high as twelve instead of the regulation five. (Rhyme in these discussions is usually of the assonantal kind rather than the more rigidly defined classical rhyme.)

There is a similar mixture of regulation and licence in the metre of the poem to the Muses, again with quatrains rhyming 1 + 3 and 2 + 4, with the second line of the couplet always shorter than the first, but with syllable counts ranging from seven to ten syllables for the long lines, and four to six for the short lines.

Again, the poem in praise of the Gaelic language, 'Moladh an Ughdair don t-seann Chànain Ghàidhlig', is in quatrains metrically, but divided into thematic paragraphs. The quatrains are basically a mixture of *rinnard* (using 6^2 lines in 11. 1 and 3) and *leath-rannaigheacht mhór* (using 5^1 lines in 11. 2 and 4), with 1 + 3 and 2 + 4 rhyming pattern. But the sequence of longer and shorter lines tends to be switched in the different verse paragraphs, or even within paragraphs, and again the syllable count is not strictly observed.

A few poems use a much more regular metrical pattern. 'Smeòrach Chlann Raghnaill' is one such, using generally eight-syllable, four-stress lines rhyming 1 + 3 and 2 + 4, and scarcely deviating from this pattern throughout. The formal, traditional nature of this poem does not seem to encourage metrical variation. A different regular pattern appears in 'Cuachag an Fhàsaich', which has a basic seven-syllable line, with two stresses, with 11. 1, 2 and 3 of each quatrain rhyming, and with a matching internal rhyme in 1. 4, while the end-rhyme of 1. 4 is maintained throughout the poem. Again the metre of 'Imrich Alasdair -- ás Eigneig do dh' Inbhir-aoidh' is very regular as regards syllabic line-length, using eight syllables in most lines, but in its end-rhyming pattern alternating irregularly between *a a a a* and *a b a b*, with an occasional *a b c b*. It is hard to say whether this reflects the turmoil in the poet's mind, or a less rigorous attitude to verse technique in his later years – more probably the latter.

Two of our poems use couplets. The 'Oran d'a Chèile' is presumably a fairly early poem (c. 1727). Its metre is very regular, with the first line of the couplet having eight syllables and the second seven, with very few exceptions, with internal rhyme in each couplet, and with the end-rhyme of the couplet maintained, in trisyllabic words or phrases, throughout the poem. 'Fàilte na Mòrthir', which may have both early and late sections, is also regular, with eight syllables in 1. 1 and six in 1. 2, internal rhyme in each couplet and couplet end-rhyme maintained throughout, with the rhyme falling on the penultimate syllable.

Another group of poems uses an eight-line stanza. This type of stanza had become a popular one in the late seventeenth and in the early eighteenth centuries, often used in formal praise-songs. Mac Mhaighstir Alasdair's versions of it do not strictly match the norm of these. In 'Oran an t-Samhraidh' for example he was clearly influenced by the metre of Allan Ramsay's song 'As early I walked', although he sets his stanzas in eight lines as against Ramsay's five. He deviated slightly from Ramsay's pattern after stanza 1, often using for example six-syllable rather than five-syllable lines for the third-last lines of stanzas. The pattern of end-rhymes settles after a verse or two to the sequence *a b c c c b d b*, with internal rhyme normally between 11. 1 and 2, 5 and 6, and 7 and 8. 'Oran a' Gheamhraidh' also uses an eight-line stanza, but has a different, more sombre rhythm, with a high proportion of nine-syllable lines, and a scatter of eight- and ten-syllable ones. The end-rhyme structure is less rigid, the first half of the stanza usually following the pattern *a b c b*, but the second half varying (e.g. *d e f e*, *d b e b*, *a b a b* etc.), and with internal rhyme in each couplet. 'Oran nam Fineachan Gaidhealach' is another variation on the eight-line stanza, with a good deal of variety in syllable-count, but with the stanza generally closing with a longish line of eight or nine syllables, followed by a short one of five or six. The end-rhyme pattern is usually *a b a a a b c b*, and internal rhyme occurs between 11. 1 and 2, 5 and 6, and 7 and 8. We can see that even in the poems using eight-line stanzas there are considerable variations in general pattern and within individual poems.

'Oran a rinneadh a' bhliadhna 1746' uses a ten-line stanza

throughout. The syllable-count follows a general but not rigid pattern, with the second, sixth and ninth lines longer (eight or nine syllables) and the others generally having five or six syllables. The rhyme pattern is often *a b a a a c a d e d*. The larger clusters of rhymes give a swinging movement to the verses, which are clearly designed to have popular appeal, although their doctrinal content is very serious.

'Moladh Mòraig' has a special place in Gaelic metrical history. Its metre, based to a degree on the rhythms and overall construction of classical pipe music or *ceòl mòr*, appears to have been Mac Mhaighstir Alasdair's invention, at least in as developed a form as it has here. For a brief commentary on this metre, see the introduction to the poem. The metre was also used by the poet in his 'Mì-mholadh Mòraig', the Dispraise of Morag, and was further developed a little later in the century by Duncan Bàn Macintyre, and used briefly by Rob Donn also.

The *Birlinn* is Mac Mhaighstir Alasdair's longest and most elaborate poem, and a good deal of thought went into its preparation, including the planning of its metrical structure. Some of the source material was existing verse (see introduction to the poem) whose metrical shape is retained, and some rhetorical 'runs' were used in part, this also affecting the metrical choices. The different aspects of the poem, such as blessing, description of the crew's functions, and the description of the storm, call for different metrical carriages. The *Birlinn* is a re-working and extension of the poet's earlier 'Iorram', which uses a strophic metre as was apparently the common practice for rowing-songs, and he reverts to this kind of metre in Section 4, using three-line stanzas, with the three lines connected by means of end-rhymes on dissyllabic words, while l. 3 has an additional three syllables which carry a separate rhyme which is held throughout the poem. His metre has a syllabic base $7^2\ 7^2\ 7^2\ 3^2$, but as often this is elastic, the seven-syllable line often being replaced by a six- or eight-syllable one. The other introductory sections of the poem also use syllabic metres. Section 1 is based on the *séadna* metre, with basic syllabic structure $2(8^2 + 7^1)^{2+4}$, but the syllable count is not strictly observed, nor are some other requirements, e.g. alliteration, of the classical metre. Section 2 begins with a stanza in *séadna*, but moves to other syllabic patterns as it proceeds. It is difficult at times to believe that all these variations are metrically planned; it seems more credible that they are dictated by the language the poet is using. Section 3 moves to a different metre again, this time one that has had a long history which continued into modern times. This is *sneadhbhairdne*, with its short second line of each couplet. The stanza formula for this is $2(8^2 + 4^2)^{2+4}$, and the poet holds the syllabic structure quite strictly through this longish section of sixty-six lines. Section 5 begins with *sneadhbhairdne* metre, for six lines, and for the last four abandons the four-syllable part of the structure. End-rhyme is maintained through this short section on the even lines. Section 6 is again consistently in *sneadhbhairdne*, as are Sections 7, 8, 9, 10, 11, 12, 13, 14 and 15. Section 16 is mainly in the same metre, with a couple of instances where multi-syllable words have to be split between the two lines of the couplet to preserve the syllabic formula. Section 16 also has a four-line sequence (11. 1988-91) where each line has eight syllables: this sequence drives home the point about how all the parts of the ship were bent and battered by the storm.

The impression may be justified that the poet began with the idea of switching metres progressively through the poem, but found the *sneadhbhairdne* one so attractive and pliable that he stayed with it for most of the latter part of the poem.

It is clear, at any rate, that Mac Mhaighstir Alasdair exploited a good range of metres, showing his ability to observe some of them quite strictly, within the conventions of his times, to handle some of them individually and creatively, and to create some novel metrical structures.

5. *A Note on Tunes and Airs*

It is not proposed to discuss the topic of tunes and airs in any detail in this edition. Some reference has already been made to the surprisingly large number of instances in which poems in the 1751 edition refer to Scots and English airs. There is some argument as to whether some of these may already have been in circulation in Gaelic communities, but the weight of evidence seems to point to Mac Mhaighstir Alasdair having been strongly influenced by his non-Gaelic reading, and no doubt his city friends and experience, in choosing a number of airs which were featuring in publications of the early decades of the eighteenth century, such as William Thomson's *Orpheus Caledonius* and Allan Ramsay's *Tea-table Miscellany*, to name two of the most popular of these.

It is reported in a book published in 1822 (W. M. Wade) that it had for long been the custom to play a different air for each day of the week on the chimes in the Tolbooth Steeple at Glasgow Cross, and two of the airs mentioned are 'Tweed-side' and 'The Lass o' Patie's Mill', both referred to by Mac Mhaighstir Alasdair (see Murchison, 1952). I am not aware of any evidence that these airs were played at the time the poet was a student at the Old College nearby, but the long-lasting popularity of these two airs is worth considering, and this may have influenced him in choosing a number of non-Gaelic songs as his 'airs'. Also we have clear evidence from one of his drinking-songs, 'Oran rìoghail a' bhotail', that he had memories of Glasgow musical bells, for he links the sound of whisky being poured to the sound of bells:

> *'S binne no cluig-chiuil ad Ghlas'cha*
> *T fhuaim le bastul dol 's a chorn*

to quote the couplet as it appears in 1751, p.80 ('Sweeter than these musical bells of Glasgow is the sound you make very audibly going into the drinking-cup').

Some of his songs have retained their popularity as sung performances down to the present. These are, in the main, campaign songs connected with the '45, such as 'Hì ri rì, tha e tighinn' and 'Hùg ò lathaill ò' and 'Dealachadh a' Phrionnsa 's nan Gaidheal' and 'A Mhòrag chiatach a' chùil dualaich'. Others survived more selectively in the oral tradition. There has been no systematic collection of the airs, but J. L. Campbell gives the notation for nine airs used with the political songs in *Highland Songs of the Forty-five*, pp.295-302.

Pipers do not seem to have identified any work of *ceòl mòr* which is linked clearly to 'Moladh Mòraig'. John Macinnes of South Uist told Ronald Morrison of a tune said in that island to correspond to the Urlar of 'Moladh Mòraig' (reported in the *Oban Times*, 16.2.95), but it is perhaps unlikely that there ever was a close correspondence between the whole poem and a specific piece of *ceòl mòr*.

6. *The Poetry*

The introductions to individual poems in this collection attempt to set them in their literary context, but here a more general view is developed of the poet's overall achievement, and its relation to literary landscapes. The present selection is intended to include the core works, but it is more selective in the area of political verse, since this has been largely collected by Dr J. L. Campbell in his *Highland Songs of the Forty-five*. In the area of satirical verse there are several examples included, but some of the more extended, and the more savage, of these are not. They can at least be brought into our general discussion of the poet's surviving work. It seems clear that his total *ouvre* was a good deal more extensive than the surviving one, but it will be useful to indicate the extent of surviving work, and to place labels, giving the number of lines, on some aspects of it.

The present selection has two poems closely connected with the

'45 Rising. Besides these Dr Campbell has included another thirteen poems, with a total of 1004 lines. The total of political poems (using that term somewhat loosely to include poems about Clan Donald, dispraise of the Mackenzies etc.) is much larger, with 'Diomoladh Chabair-fèidh' for instance (with its references to the '15 Rising) running to 360 lines, and 'An Airc', with much satire of the Campbells, running to 392 lines. Here we cross the fragile border between political verse and satire. Satire forms another high-profile sector of Mac Mhaighstir Alasdair's work, with poems ranging from 'Mì-mholadh Mòraig' (The Dispraise of Morag) to his anti-Campbell verse, his attacks on the Oban poetess, and his poems on the outbreak of sexual disease in Ardnamurchan. Some of these are quite lengthy, the 'Mì-mholadh' running to 224 lines, and 'Oran nam Bodach' (The Song of the Old Men) to 240 lines.

The 1924 edition has 2927 lines not included in the present selection or in Campbell's *Highland Songs ---*. In addition there are 608 lines in the 1751 text not included in these three collections (1924, Campbell, the present one), and another 136 lines in MS 63 in the National Library of Scotland, not included in these or other earlier collections. Altogether, a total of just under 6000 lines has been ascribed to the poet, so that the present selection represents a little over a third of his surviving work. It can be argued, however, that this selection gives a fair representation of his range (except in the scatalogical verse) and includes much of his finest work.

He clearly had developed a tremendous facility in versifying, and no doubt this raises the danger of producing facile work at times. Some of the political verse can be classified as facile, though it was probably pitched at too wide an audience to tolerate overmuch literary sophistication. Some of the political poems clearly were designed to arouse and maintain enthusiasm among the troops. This probably explains his use of less elaborate stanza forms for some of these poems and songs. The drinking songs associated with the '45 campaign fall into this category, as do some of the songs of welcome to the Prince. The same technical facility shows in his post-campaign poems. He is said to have composed a good deal while he and his family were on the run after Culloden, and probably some of his anti-Campbell satire dates from this period. Here he may be supposed to have been driven by anger and bitterness rather than by literary urge or ambition. The versifying facility was securely in place, and at times he forgot his earlier appeal to the Muses not to give him a product that rattled in the ear and was rather empty of judgement.

There seems, as yet, to be no way of pin-pointing the dates of his earlier poems, and we have to rely on general impressions regarding choice of subject-matter and style, together with such clues as early provenance provides. This leaves a good deal of room for differences of opinion. For example, 'Cuachag an Fhàsaich' has often been regarded as an early poem, and may have early components, but the reference to Morar, and the late appearance (not in 1751) may point to a later composition or revision. The date of the 'Oran d'a Chèile Nuadh-phòsda' (Song to his Bride) is most probably c. 1727, if we accept the date of his son's birth as 1728. I have argued elsewhere (*Alasdair Mac Mhaighstir Alasdair: his Political Poetry*, 3-6) that two poems, 'Moladh an Leòghainn' (Praise of the Lion i.e. of the MacDonalds) and 'Diomoladh Chabair-fèidh' (Dispraise of the Deer's Antler i.e. of the Mackenzies) probably date from about 1725. It is likely that the poet was practising his craft well before this time, whether he was born early or late in the decade 1690-1700. Two poems which seem to fit naturally into an early, exploratory and learning period are the rather formal Elegy for a Pet Dove and the carefully researched and structured Address to the Muses, both with echoes of his early education in the Classics, and both having a strongly literary orientation. These two poems may well date from before 1720, but in any case are probably earlier than the c. 1725 poems, in which some political urgency is already apparent. Already by 1727 we are probably justified in seeing the poet as having set out his poetic stance, both theoretically as in the Address to the Muses, and more politically with the c. 1725 poems, while at the same time showing his acquainance with Classical (Latin and Greek) literacy, with Classical (Gaelic) metrics, and with the less complicated couplet of his Bride Song.

Some aspects of this early literary apprenticeship show up in poems which are probably a decade or more later. The 'Moladh an Ughdair – – –' (The Author's Praise of Gaelic) may belong to the later part of the 1730s (1738 in particular), but it is still involved with early Gaelic traditions, and harks back to Lhuyd's *Archaeologia Britannica* of 1707. Other poems of the 1730s or early 1740s probably include the Morag ones and the poems on Summer and Winter, again carrying Classical (Latin and Greek) references, and also showing an acquaintance with Scots and English poetry of the time and of earlier periods.

Yet already in the group of poems mentioned we see quite a wide range of attitudes and styles, and some clear experimentation with metrics. Political poetry combined with satire has begun to appear in the poems of c. 1725. The scatalogical and obscene strains show clearly in the Dispraise of Morag and in the poems on the Ardnamurchan sexual scandals and diseases, which probably all date from the 1730s. His interest in Gaelic legend appears in the Praise of Gaelic poem, and his intense observation of natural phenomena, lighting up the Praise of Morag at times, is fully exploited in his poems on Summer and Winter, and his 'Allt an t-Siùcair' (The Sugar Brook), these three evidently associated with his period as schoolmaster in Ardnamurchan. The metres range from near-Classical ones to simple couplets, and the more intricate eight-line stanza is used in some, while the Praise of Morag launches his fairly intricate experimentation with metrics associated with pipe music. Much of this body of work suggests a poet exploiting the inherited tradition, and developing new emphases of his own. With the possible exception of the satirical poems, it shows a dedicated poet consciously developing an individual body of work, whatever influences play a part in that development.

Some of these influences may be briefly grouped together at this point. His religious background shows up in his vocabulary generally as well as in the instance of the Elegy for a Pet Dove. That poem probably reflects acquaintance with Catullus's poem on a Sparrow, and his Classical reading also shows in the range of references to Phoebus, Venus etc. His acquaintance with the Muses may come both from Classical and from earlier Scots writing, and perhaps observation of artistic motifs. He shows acquaintance with Allan Ramsay and James Thomson, his contemporaries, and very probably with Gavin Douglas's Scots poetry. The influence of earlier Gaelic verse is pervasive e.g. the Harlaw Brosnachadh (11.1016-8*n*), 'An Duanag Ullamh' (1.1511*n*), and the various clan songs. His acquaintance with the saga 'Gaisgeach na Sgèithe Deirge' shows in the *Birlinn*.

The years 1744 to 1748 or 1749 mark a period of intense commitment to political ideals. This does not entirely dampen his creative and literary drive (as we can see in the 1746 poem especially), but that drive seems to be subordinated to the political one. After this short period we can see some return to literary ambition, with such structured poems as 'An Airc' (The Ark). This was included in the 1751 edition. It purports to describe a dream which a certain gentleman had of a flood which was to submerge the land of Argyll, and it goes on to urge Alexander Campbell of Ardslignis (referred to in the poem as the Campbell Noah) to build an Ark, and to admit certain people to it, excluding many of those who took the Hanoverian side in the '45. This poem has its moments of bitterness, but is full of fun also, and gives a detailed listing of those who deserve to be saved and those who do not. It is significant that a fair number of Campbells appear in the former category. The metre here is a straightforward quatrain, but the overall structure and concept shows a return to political sobriety and to literary inventiveness. It uses Biblical imagery alongside more nautical concepts. Presumably it was not long after this that the *Birlinn* poem was conceived, with its more elaborate structure and metrical mix.

It is not possible to date many poems closely after 1751. The Eigneig and Morar poems are the ones that fit most neatly into this period, and they show us the opposite extremes of the poet's temperament, the highly-charged bitterness of the farewell to Eigneig, and the joy and serenity of the 'Welcome to Morar'. His vivid descriptive powers are brought into play in both, but it is the Eigneig one that makes the sharpest impact. This reinforces the impression that recurs in reading his work, that intense emotion produces his most intense, linguistically inventive language.

Although there are many instances of poems which are structured in a detailed and inventive way, it is probably the linguistic richness and idiosyncracy that leaves the deepest impression. He achieves this richness in a variety of ways. Sometimes he achieves it by building a detailed structure on a relatively simple framework, such as the description of the seasons, where he explores weather, vegetation, insect animal fish and bird life, music, and food; or the description of the Allt an t-Siùcair countryside which is even more detailed. An instance from the political poetry is the Song for the Highland Clans, in which earlier models are re-worked and refined, and the *Birlinn* exploits in a similar way the potential of sea-movements and of the men who battle with them. The richness is a lexical one on an important level, showing his deep knowledge of Gaelic on both the oral and the literate planes. But it also has the vital ingredients of inventiveness and exciting juxtaposition. The Winter months are brosy, trousered, stockinged, the Summer wood becomes an organ producing a marvellous musical medley, the Eigneig countryside is waspish and adder-like. The denizens of the sea, sometimes imaginary, come into clear view at the surface. Jacobite legitimacy is given historical and philosophical depth. A girl's beauty is described with lyrical fervour and a touch of mischief, and vices can be exaggerated almost beyond belief. The appropriate language is always to hand for these multifarious purposes. And in addition, the rhythm changes fluidly, so that somnolence is warded off, even in lengthy passages. But it requires some richness of linguistic knowledge to keep pace with all this.

Mac Mhaighstir Alasdair has not infrequently been accused of exaggeration or overkill, particularly in his descriptive passages. Sometimes these accusations have arisen from misunderstanding of his intentions. The storm-scenes in the *Birlinn* are a case in point: lurid exaggeration is of their essence, for the poet is indulging in a fantasy that has some basis in fact but also in fiction (Gaelic saga fiction). It is not intended as a sober report to an insurance company. He has often been accused of excess in his Nature descriptions, and of following uncritically the fashion of piling up banks of adjectives etc. It is easy to find good examples of mere piling up in Gaelic verse before and after his time, and no doubt some can be identified in his work also, but the passages of packed adjectival description in the seasonal songs, for example, have a fine detail and mobility and inventiveness that is highly impressive. There are inherited traditional elements in such passages, but the verve and incisiveness of the seasonal poems, the skilful intermix of themes and motifs, and the careful development of themes (e.g. the musical progression from lute to chanter to bird music to organ music in the Song to Summer) have never been equalled in such verse in Gaelic. Clearly these poems made a deep impression on the poet's contemporaries and successors, many of whom attempted work in this genre.

The accusation of overkill may more credibly be applied to some of the satirical verse. The poem about the libidinous octogenarians of Ardnamurchan ('Oran nam Bodach') has its moments of fun, but it may be doubted if the search for salacious detail there is governed by literary sensitivity. The man of extremes could go off the rails when the mood took him.

It is fair to judge him by his core work, and to distance that from some of the hack-work associated with Jacobite recruitment or community entertainment, although some of that work has his stamp of genius on it too. In his work openness to outside influence and loyalty to traditional values are fruitfully brought together in what may well be regarded as the prime literary *ouvre* in Gaelic in the eighteenth century.

SOURCES AND EDITIONS

The sources and editions of the poems in this volume are set out here in their chronological order, insofar as this is ascertainable, and the abbreviations or dates are indicated which will be used to identify these. Dates are used in many instances, but not in the cases of the Eigg and Gillies Collections (of 1776 and 1786 respectively) nor in the case of MS versions.

Adv. MS 72.2.15 :	MS in the Advocates Library Collection, in the National Library of Scotland
1751 :	*Ais-eiridh na Sean chánoin Albannaich; No, An nuadh Oranaiche Gaidhealach*
1764 :	*Ais-eiridh* – – – (a reprint of part of 1751)
McD :	MS anthology by Ewen MacDiarmid, dated c.1770
MS Gen 9 :	MS in Glasgow University Library, dated a.1773
Eigg :	*Comh-chruinneachidh Orannaigh Gaidhealach,* le Raonuill MacDhomhnuill (1776)
R.I.A. :	Royal Irish Academy MS E ii 1 (746)
McL 2 :	MS in the McLagan Collection, in Glasgow University Library
McL 15 :	” ”
McL 33 :	” ”
McL 120 :	” ”
McL 126 :	” ”
McL 148 :	” ”
McL 187 :	” ”
Campbell Coll. :	Campbell Collection A, in Edinburgh University Library
P. Campbell MS :	P. Campbell MS in Argyll and Bute District Archives DRI/67/17
Gillies :	*Sean Dain, agus Orain Ghaidhealach*, Published by John Gillies (1786)
1802 :	*Orain Ghaelich. An nuadh Oranaiche Gaidhealach*
1806 :	*Co-chruinneachadh Nuadh do dh' Orannibh Gaidhealach* (often referred to as the Inverness Collection)
1809 :	*Comh-chruinneachadh Orain Ghaidhealach* (i.e. Eigg, revised Turner)
1813 :	*Co'-chruinneachadh de dh' orain agus de luinneagaibh thaghta Ghae'lach* – – –, le P. MacPharlain

1839	:	*The Poetical Works of Alexander MacDonald*, ed. John Mackenzie
S.O.	:	*Sàr-obair nam Bard Gaelach*, ed. John Mackenzie
1874	:	*Eiseirigh na Seann Chanain Albannaich*, ed. Donald C. Macpherson
1892	:	Reprint of 1874
1908-09	:	'Unpublished Poems by Alexander MacDonald', ed. Donald Mackinnon, in *The Celtic Review*, Vols. 4 and 5 (1908-09)
1910	:	George Henderson, *The Norse Influence on Celtic Scotland*
1918	:	W. J. Watson, *Bàrdachd Ghàidhlig* (rev. ed. 1959)
1924	:	*The Poems of Alexander MacDonald*, ed. A. and A. MacDonald
1933	:	*Sàr Orain*, ed. Angus MacLeod
1934-35	:	'Gaelic MS 63 of the National Library', ed. J. L. Campbell, in *Scottish Gaelic Studies*, Vol. IV, Pts. 1 and 2
1961	:	The R.I.A. text of the *Birlinn*, ed. J. L. Campbell, in SGS, Vol. IX, Pt. 1
1984	:	*Highland Songs of the Forty-five*, ed. J. L. Campbell (first published 1933)
1993	:	*Gaelic Poetry in the Eighteenth Century*, ed. D. S. Thomson

The 1751 edition, edited by the poet, must naturally take precedence, and Eigg, edited by his son and presumably based in many instances on the poet's papers, is another primary source, although editorial idiosyncracies or lapses can be observed in both these sources. Adv. MS 72.2.15 is apparently earlier than 1751, while MS Gen 9, R.I.A. E ii 1 (746), and McL 15 may pre-date Eigg. The datings of MSS in the McLagan and Campbell Collections are not precise, but probably fall in the sixth, seventh and eighth decades of the eighteenth century.

There was a partial reprint of 1751 in 1764, with some new printer's errors and with some of the more prurient items excised, and there was another reprint in 1802, which follows 1751 very closely. John Mackenzie produced a new edition in 1834, and re-issued it with a new title, additional poems and a memoir in 1839 (with a reprint in 1851), while he included some of the poems in his *Sàr Obair* of 1841. There is some evidence of Mackenzie using a variety of sources, and imposing some editorial emendations, partly influenced by Eigg rev. Turner (1809) and MacPhàrlain

(1813). The 1874 edition, organised by Donald C. Macpherson and with a memoir supplied by Donald Mackinnon, often follows the 1839 readings, and introduces other editorial emendations. The 1892 reprint is a close copy. George Henderson edited the *Birlinn* text in 1910, and W. J. Watson has a small selection of Mac Mhaighstir Alasdair's poems in his *Bàrdachd Ghàidhlig* of 1918. The most complete edition is that of 1924, but it is very deficient in apparatus; it often follows the editorial preferences of 1874, and introduces its own, while the translations are often a little too free although often discerning also. Angus MacLeod's edition of the *Birlinn* (1933) is the first meticulously edited version of this poem to be published. J. L. Campbell edited a good selection of the political poems (1933, rev. 1984), and also produced an edition of the R.I.A. MS of the *Birlinn.* I included a short selection of passages in the 1993 publication.

As the discussions of individual poems will demonstrate, a wide range of editorial decisions has to be taken when all these variant sources are brought into the reckoning. The sources appear to reflect revisions and expansions of certain poems, made by the poet himself, probably some variants which arose in early transmission of some poems, the poet's editorial idiosyncracies, and the linguistic preferences of later editors. It is scarcely possible to resolve all these problems, and produce a text that mirrors exactly the poet's original intentions (even allowing for fluidity at that source), but that is the optimistic aim of the present edition.

Though the 1751 versions of poems must be given priority, and a lesser priority is given to versions in Eigg, the idiosyncracies of both these sources have to be carefully assessed. There is a good deal of evidence of authorial variants and additions to individual poems. This shows up very clearly in the cases of 'Oran an t-Samhraidh' and 'Oran a' Gheamhraidh', and may well be reflected in the MS versions of other poems, some of these MSS earlier than Eigg.

Textual variants are not exhaustively quoted, since many of these reflect idiosyncracies of copyists and editors, and printer's errors. Variants are sometimes quoted to illustrate the methodologies of earlier editions, but usually only where they may throw some light on the original reading. Normalisation of spelling is not given full priority, as it might sometimes obscure the poet's usage, but accents are often supplied where 1751 omits them. Editorial decisions relating to particular poems are discussed in the introductions to these poems.

TABLE OF SOURCES/EDITIONS

Title of Poem	Adv. MS 72.2.15	1751 (Ais-eiridh)	McDiarmid MS	MS Gen 9	Eigg	R.I.A. MS E ii 1(746)	McL 2	McL 15	McL 33	McL 120	McL 126	McL 148	McL 187	Campbell Coll.	P. Campbell MS	Gillies	1802	1806	1809	1813	1839	Sàr Obair	1874	1892	1910	1918, 1959	1924	1933	1961	1984	1993
1. Marbhrainn do Pheata Coluim		150															162				129		122	122		102	16				16
2. Guidhe no Urnaigh an Ughdair don Cheòlraidh		7		1													19				5		5	5			10				
3. Oran d'a Chèile nuadh-phòsda		94															106				191		100	100			238				
4. Moladh Mòraig		11		4												212	23				8	106	8	8			212				34
5. Moladh an Ughdair do 'n t-seann Chànain Ghàidhlig		1															13				1	105	1	1		97	2				
6. Oran an t-Samhraidh	55	36		25	200												48				20	110	19	19			20				22
7. Oran a' Gheamhraidh	38	43		30	334												55		348		25	111	24	24			28				28
8. Oran nam Fineachan Gaidhealach		51		36													63	6			31	113	29	29			76			72	
9. Smeòrach Chlann Raghnaill					246				2												75	121	71	71			180				
10. Oran a rinneadh a' Bhliadhna 1746		116															128				111		103	103			118			94	52
11. Birlinn Chlann Raghnaill			92		146	125		1							5				160	1	156	136	166	166	221		370	37	39		
12. Imrich Alasdair MhicDhòmhnaill ás Eigneig do dh'Inbhir-aoidh					143					Item 9				3					157		88		81	81			270				
13. Cuachag an Fhàsaich					115		14					7	7	3		206		112			102	127	93	93			234				
14. Fàilte na Mòrthir			6		118						4										91	125	86	86			36				

MARBHRAINN DO PHEATA COLUIM

Sources and Editions:

1751, pp.150-53
1802, 162-5
1839, 129-31
1874, 122-3
1918 etc., 102-4
1924, 16-18

The full title given in 1751 is 'Marbhrainn a rinneadh do pheata Colum, a mharbhadh le aubhag'. Our text is of course firmly based on that of 1751. 1839 has occasional misprints, and both it and later texts have editorial emendations which do not generally carry sufficient weight to be quoted. The orthography of the 1751 text is normalised where this does not seriously distort the evidence of the author's dialectal, lexical or idiomatic usage. This involves, for example, interpreting his preferred form *go* as *gu* or *ge*, to clarify the meaning in different contexts.

W. J. Watson, in his *Bàrdachd Ghàidhlig*, p.xlii cites this poem as an example of the old metre *Cummasc etir rannaigheacht mhór agus leath-rannaigheacht* $2(7^1 + 5^1)^{2+4}$, remarking that the poet rhymes his odd lines as well as his even lines. It is even more of a *cummasc* or mixture, for the odd lines can range as to syllabic count from six to twelve syllables, and the even lines from four to six. For all that, its overall resonance is syllabic and classical.

We are probably justified in regarding this as an early poem by Mac Mhaighstir Alasdair. It is unusually formal and sober, with an uncharacteristic touch of sentimentality, but the poet's gift of wry, slightly off-beat reference appears in the passage about Noah's Ark, with its punning instances.

MARBHRAINN DO PHEATA COLUIM

'S tùrsach mo sgeul ri luaidh
'S gun chàch d'ad chaoidh
Mu bhàs an fhir bu leanbail tuar
'S bu mheanbh ri chlaoidh.

'S oil leam bàs a' choluim chaoimh
Nach b' anagrach gnàths:
A thuiteam le madadh d'am beus
Dòbhran nan càrn.

'S tu as truaigh leinn de bhàs nan eun;
Mo chràdh nach beò,
Fhir a b' iteagach, miotagach triall
Ge bu mheirbh do threòir.

B' fheumail do Naoi na càch
An àm bhàrcadh nan stuadh,
Bu tu 'n teachdair' gun seacharan dà
Nuair thràigh an cuan.

A dh' fhidreachdainn 'do dh' fhalbh an tuil,
Litir gach fear,
Dùghall is Colum gun chuir
Deagh Naoi thar lear.

Ach chaidh Dùghall air seacharan-cuain
'S cha do phill e riamh,
Ach phill Colum le iteagaich luath
'S a fhreagra 'na bheul.

Air thùs, cha d' fhuair e ionad d'a bhonn
A seasadh e ann
Gus 'do thiormaich dìle nan tonn
Far mullach nam beann.

'S an sin, an litir sin leugh an duine bha glic,
Gun thiormaich a' bhailc,
'S gu faigheadh a mhuirichinn cobhair 'nan teirc'
Agus fuasgladh 'nan airc.

Le neart cha spùillte do nead
Ge do thigte d'ad shlad;
Bhiodh do chaisteal fo bhearraibh nan creag
Ann an daingnichibh rag.

Bha do mhodh-sìolaich air leth o chàch:
Cha togradh tu suas
Ach a' durrghail an taca ri d' ghràdh
A' cur cagair 'na cluais.

Cha do chuir thu dùil an airgead no sprèidh,
No fèisd am biodh sùgh
Ach spioladh is criomadh an t-sìl le d' bheul
'S ag òl a' bhùirn.

Aodach no anart, sìoda no sròl,
Cha cheannaicheadh tu 'm bùth,
Bhiodh t' èididh de mhìn-iteacha gorm
Air nach drùidheadh an driùchd.

Cha do ghabh thu riamh paidir no creud
A ghuidhe nan dùl;
Gidheadh, chan eil t' anam am pèin
O chaidh tu nùnn.

Chan e gun chiste no anart bhith còmhdach do chrè
Fo lic anns an ùir
Tha mise, ge cruaidh e, 'n diugh 'g acain gu lèir,
Ach do thuiteam le cù.

NOTES

Title: *Marbhrainn* is the form used in the 1751 title, although Mac Mhaighstir Alasdair uses *marbhrann* in other places. He probably uses this form deliberately here. The terms *marbhrann/marbhrainn* do not occur in early Gaelic, where *marbhnadh* (<*marbh* + *nath* 'poem, elegy') is preferred.

5 *Choluim* 1751 *Cholum*

6 *anagrach* This is probably to be taken as a compound of intensive *an-* and *agrach* 'quarrelsome', the sense being literally 'whose disposition was not very quarrelsome' and actually '– – – – not quarrelsome at all'.

7 *d'a*, 1751 *go 'm*
The sense of 11. 7-8 is 'His falling (i.e. killing) by a cur whose characteristics were those of the otter among the rocks'. W. J. Watson (note to 1918 etc., 1. 2740) took the meaning to be '– – – – cur whose proper due is – – –'. This seems less convincing.

9 *de* 1751 *do*

11 *miotagach* The usual senses of this word are 'gloved, mittened' and perhaps 'frightened' (<*miotag* terror). The latter seems possible, but Watson suggested the sense 'mincing (of step)', which fits well with the following *triall.*

12 *Ge bu* 1751 *Go ba*

13 *Naoi* The older Gaelic form for Noah.

14 *bhàrcadh* The aspiration of the 1751 text is retained, the expression *bhàrcadh nan stuadh* being regarded as a bound phrase. A similar usage occurs in Donnchadh Bàn's *An àm chur ghearran an èill.*

17 *'do dh' fhalbh* 1751 *do dh' fhalbh*. This is a speech contraction for *an do dh'*

fhalbh, cf. also l. 27 below. Later edd. emend to *an d' fhalbh.*

18–20 The reference is to the Biblical story (*Genesis*, 8, 11). Noah did not of course send letters with the dove and the raven, but he got a leaf back via the dove, and read it as though it were a letter, telling that vegetation was surfacing after the Flood. The poet here is probably punning on *litir/leitir*, where *leitir* could refer to the slopes of Mt. Ararat: Noah, as it were, sends the dove over the sea (*thar lear*) to reconnoitre one slope, and the raven another.

19 *Dùghall* The poet's name for the raven, which is black. Watson makes the interesting suggestion that he was recalling the raven imagery used on the galleys of the Norsemen (who were known as *Dùbhghaill*, 'black strangers': Watson, 1918, 289).

21–2 The Bible (*Gen.*, 8, 7) says simply that the dove went to and fro until the waters dried off the surface of the earth.

24 *fhreagra* The 1751 form is retained.

26 *a seasadh e ann* In more usual speech this would be *anns an seasadh e.*

27 *'do* See note on l. 17 above.

28 *Far* Later edd. *Bhàrr.*

29 *an litir sin* 1751 *a litirsin.* Subsequent editors (1839, Macpherson, Watson, MacDonalds) have *a litir-san.* The sense 'that letter' (which can refer to the leaf) seems marginally more credible than 'his letter', and since the poet has an instance of *sin* earlier in the line we might expect a different form for *-san.*

31 *muirichinn* The sense here seems to be 'family, brood'. Armstrong (1825) has *muirighinn* in the senses of 'burden' and 'family', and earlier forms are attested in older Gaelic (cf. *muirigin* 'burden etc.' in RIA Dictionary, which also has the form *muirgein* 'sea-birth, sea-child', sometimes occurring as a personal name). Probably Mac Mhaighstir Alasdair is playing with similar ideas, thinking of Noah's brood as a sea-brood, and perhaps allowing a looser pun, between *airc* 'scarcity' and *àirc* 'ark' in the next line.

33 *nead* 1751 *niod.* A closer rhyme with *creag* in l. 35 seems desirable.

37–40 Watson omits these lines from his edition.

40 *A' cur cagair* 1751 *'G cuir cogair.*

47 *èididh* The 1751 form is retained, against the more standard *èideadh.*

50 *dùl* The usual senses of *dùil* are 'element, creature', but the poet appears to be using the plural here to refer to 'heavenly beings'.

51 *Gidheadh* 1751 *Gaigheidh* The spelling, with initial *gai-*, signals clearly the pronunciation the poet knew: it is one still heard from ministers in the second half of the twentieth century.

55 – – – – *ge* – – – – *gu* 1751 – – – *go* – – – – *go.*

GUIDHE NO URNAIGH AN UGHDAIR DON CHEOLRAIDH

Sources and Editions:

1751	7-10
MS Gen 9	1-3
1802	19-22
1839	5-8
1874	5-7
1892	5-7
1924	10-14

The basic text is provided by the 1751 edition, the 1802 edition being mainly a straight reprint. The version in MS Gen 9 is almost identical, the only significant differences occurring in 11. 69, 72 and 125. The first and third of these may indicate authorial revision, and the second either that or a lapse of attention in copying. Mackenzie's 1839 edition introduces some unacceptable editorial revisions, most of which are not recorded in the following notes. Later editors, up to the 1924 edition, make minor editorial and orthographical changes which often obscure what was clearly the poet's own usage.

This is likely to be a fairly early poem, concerned as it is with the fostering of the author's own poetic talent. Its central theme is the appeal to the nine Muses to help him develop various aspects of his art, and he suggests, late in the poem, that he is as yet something of a novice, needing guidance. Though there is a degree of false modesty in this, he was probably thinking of his lack of the formal training which Classical Gaelic poets had in the past. The appeal to the Muses is of course in the other Classical tradition, that of Latin and Greek verse, widely developed by medieval poets in various languages. A notable Scottish example is in Part 2 of Gavin Douglas's 'The Palice of Honour', a poem which was composed c. 1501. Douglas introduces us to the court of Venus, which is also the "court rethoricall", the celestial well, the fountain and original from which the well of Helicon flows. He refers to Thespis, mother of the nine Muses, and proceeds to name them one by one. Mac Mhaighstir Alasdair also deals with the nine Muses in a group, although in a different order (though both begin with Cleo/Clio, the eldest), and he comments in a rather different way on each of them. He then goes on to address Apollo and Minerva, whereas Douglas follows up with repeated references to Calliope and Venus, various Latin poets and authors, Chaucer, Gower, Kennedy, Dunbar etc. Douglas refers to his own poetic work in a mock-modest way, as Priscilla Bawcutt notes in her *Gavin Douglas* (1976), 56-7.

Thomas Ruddiman published an edition of Douglas's *Aeneados* in 1710, and Mac Mhaighstir Alasdair was probably familiar with that publication, and this may have led him to read Douglas's other poetry also, while he would be aware of other references to the Muses, and may have seen artists' representations of them. His Entreaty to the Muses is on a less elaborate and ambitious scale than Douglas's, but it has its own sharp focus. It seems rather likely that he knew Douglas's poem but typically did not produce a clone of it.

Guidhe no Urnaigh an Ughdair don Cheòlraidh

A Cheòlraidh mhòr tha 'n tàmh gu h-àrd,
Seallaibh a-nìos,
Nach cluinn sibh ur daltan air làr
Ag atach a chìos?
E lùthadh a ghlùn ris a' phàirc,
'S a shùilean a-suas
Ag asnachadh uireasan bàird
Gun chàird a-nuas;
Laoigh a bheòil le cridhe tiom
Dan ìobairt gu cruaidh:
Freasdlaibh don altair san tìm,
Dìolaibh dha duais.
A naoinear, inghinn' Iupiter àird
'S Mhenemhosene chaoimh,
Sèidibh m'aignidh ler pìobanaibh àigh
'S deilbhim meadrach nach claon.
A Chlio mhaiseach, thaobh barrachd t'aois,
'S do bhreith roimh chàch,
Chan iarram d'ad bhuadhan-s' ach braon
'S bidh m'athchuinge pàight.
Urania, tilg chugam d'ad stòr
Na dh'fhosglas mo bheul,
Sgaoil mo ghlasan le t'eochraichean òir;
Taisbein do dhèirc.
Chailiope, a rèil-iùil nan duan,
Rèitich mo shnaoim,
'S cuir facail thaghte gheur chruaidh
Gu luath 'nam chuim.
Euterpe, a bheairteis nan rann,
An amalaidh ghrinn,
Locair gu snasda gach siolladh d'am chainnt,
M' fhaobhar 's mo rinn.
Erato, a chiste na maoin,
Fileanta deas,
Gleus mo mheomhair 's thoir dhomh d'ad thaisg
Na dh'fhòghnas treis.
A Mhelpomene, air m'uireasaibh fòir
As t'ulaidh làn mhaoin;
On dh'fhòghnas leam pàirt do na th'agad do chòrr
Cha bhi m'athchuingean daor.
A Therpsicore, a mhuime nan duan,
'S pàirt do chuilidh na frìth,
Cuir *crambos* taitneach 'nam chluais

Am bi cruas agus brìgh.
A Phoilihimnia 's geal-chraicneach cruth,
Ge tu 's òige san t-sreath,
Do chomradh milis, fileant seach stuth,
Sirim gu seth.
A Thalia, le t'ola ro-thlàth
Suath rothan mo ghlèis,
Leig siubhal is gluasad le t'fhaobhar 's le t'àgh
Gu labhairt d'am bheul.
Apollo, tha m'inntinn cho rag
Ri speilg do chreig;
Fàg-s' i gun dàil, so-lùibte mar ghad
Coineallach bog.
A Mhinerbha, oide nan sgol
'S a chèidse nam fil,
Cuir aon dusan facal am char
'S tuilleadh cha sir.
Na tugaibh dhomh saothair nì glagan sa' chluais
'S do thuigse bhios fàs
Mar chaoch-chnuasaich chruinn a nì fuaim
Gun eitean 'na làr.
Gabhaidh sibh-pèin, ge h-àrd ur staid,
Ri ìobairtean beag,
Nochdaidh mise mo chomas ge lag
'S eugcoir mur creid.
Tha speuran mo chomais cumhang nas leòr
Ge farsaing mo mhiann,
Gu balla thogail air stèidh cho-mhòr
'S clach-shnaighte d'am dhìth:
Cainnt-shnasda d'am dhìth, ge stracte mo thoil
Tha mi falamh do sgil;
'S nì gun susbaint ealain gun sgoil
Air suibseic mar mhil.
Gur h-aimhgheur mo pheann, 's neo-sgaiteach mo bhil,
Mo cheann cha mhol,
Mo phàipear is m'inc tha iad làn do chron,
'S uireasaibh sin.

NOTES

The title in the 1751 edition and in MS Gen. 9 is 'Guidhe, no urnaigh an ughdair, do 'n Cheolrai, etc.'. The etc. is to be explained by the fact that he refers to more than the traditional *nine* Muses. These are traditionally listed as the nine daughters of Zeus and Mnemosyne: Clio, Calliope, Erato, Euterpe, Melpomene, Polyhymnia, Terpsichore, Thalia and Urania. Greek sources, especially the writings of Hesiod, appear to be a primary source. In Douglas's 'Palice of Honour' Thespis is given as the mother of the Muses, while Mac Mhaighstir Alasdair gives Jupiter as the father.

57 Mac Mhaighstir Alasdair glosses *A Cheolraidh* in the 1751 book as 'the muses'. This may be the earliest recorded instance of this usage. Armstrong in his Dictionary quotes the line 'Sguir na ceolraidhean Greugach o'n dàn' from Peter MacFarlane's *Collection of Poems* (1813). MacFarlane in his *English and Gaelic Vocabulary* (1815) gives *Ceòlairidh* for Muse. Irish does not use this term, having *ceólaidh* and *ceólaire* in the sense of 'musician'. One is tempted to credit Mac Mhaighstir Alasdair with the invention of this Gaelic term.

58 *a-nìos* Here clearly the sense is 'down', and the rhyme with *chìos* confirms the form. The normal sense is 'upwards', as see 1. 1908n.

59 *air làr* on the ground, here 'on Earth'.

60 *ag atach a chìos* 'requesting his wages'. *Cìos* is quite common in earlier Gaelic, alongside *cìs*. The usual senses are 'tax, tribute, rent', but the sense of 'wages, return' seems more appropriate here: the poet's reward for his obeisance to the Muses.

61 *lùthadh* 1751 *lúdhadh*, MS Gen 9 *lūđađ* bending cf. *lùdag* hinge, little finger.

62 *shùilean a-suas* MS Gen 9 *ṡuilib˙ suas*.

63 *Ag asnuchadh* All sources *'G*; 1874, 1892, 1924 *aslachadh*. The form with *l* is the standard one, in both Gaelic and Irish.
uireasan 1839 *ur-fasan*

64 *Gun chàird* The primary sense of *càird* is 'pact, covenant', but the other sense, 'delay, respite' is the appropriate one here.

65 *Laoigh* The poet is punning here on the words *laoigh* 'calves' (appropriate as sacrifices) and *laoidh* 'lay, poem', an appropriate offering from a poet.
tiom timid, fearful. 1874, 1892 and 1924 give *tìom/tìom'*

66 *Dan 1874ff. give 'G an*

67 *Freasdlaibh* MS Gen 9 *Freisdabh*

68 *Dìolaibh* Note the rhyme with *tìm* in 1. 67, indicating the poet's mainland pronunciation of *dìolaibh*.

69 *A naoinear, inghinn'* – – – The punctuation, and the form *inghinn'* (short for *inghinnibh*) used in the 1751 and 1802 sources, suggests the sense 'O nine, daughters of – – –', while the reading of later editions (*A naoinear inghean*) has the sense of 'O nine daughters of – – –'. The Muses are here given as parents Jupiter (as alternative to Zeus) and Mnemosyne. Mac Mhaighstir Alasdair would be familiar with the Greek form of the mother's name, but he gives it a Gaelic colouring.

71 *Sèidibh* 1839 *Sèinibh*
aignidh This was presumably the poet's usage, rather than the *aigne* of later sources.

72 *meadrach* 1874 ff. *meadrachd*

73 *Clio* She is addressed first, as the eldest of the Muses. She was the Muse associated with history, tradition, the past etc.
t' aois 1751, MS Gen 9 *t aos*

76 *m' athchuinge pàight* 1751, 1802 *m' achoini páit*, 1839 *m' achanaich*, 1874 ff. *m' achainean*

77 *Urania* the Muse of Astronomy
chugam This form, used in 1751, MS Gen 9 and 1802, changed to *h-ugam/thugam* in later sources.

79 *ghlasan* MS Gen 9 *ġlasab˙*
eochraichean The 1751 form is retained, as reflecting the poet's pronunciation.

81 *Cailiope* The Greek *Kalliope* was the Muse of Eloquence and of Epic poetry.

82 *shnaoim* 1751, 1802 *shnuim*, MS Gen 9 *ṡniúim*, rhyming with *chuim* in 1. 84, q.v. The sense of the line is 'tease out my knot' i.e. 'solve my problems', referring to the poet's versifying problems.

83 *thaghte* 1751, MS Gen 9, 1802 *thoite*

84 *chuim* Later sources (post-1839) read *chom*. The word is a masculine noun in

modern Gaelic, but was feminine in earlier usage (cf. Irish *coim*). The poet's usage was as a feminine noun. Later sources destroy the rhyme between 11. 82 and 84, by substituting the forms *shnaim* and *chom.*

85 *Euterpe* the Muse/Goddess of Music
nan 1751 etc. *na*

86 *An amalaidh* 1924 *'S an amhlaidh*

85–6 Probably the logical order of these lines is 'Euterpe an amalaidh ghrinn, a bheairteis nan rann' (E. of the delicate interweaving, O richness of verses), but requirements of rhyme have moved *ghrinn* to the end of 1. 86.

85–8 The poet is concerned here with verse technique, the planing of syllables, the honing of language, the polishing of rhyme. In his use of the word *rinn* he puns on the senses of 'point' and 'rhyme'.

89 the Muse of lyric and amorous poetry.

90–92 The 1751 and 1802 sources, no doubt showing the original printer's choice, distort the logical line order by the setting *Fileonta deas, gleus mo mheobhair,/'S thoir dhomh d'a d' thaisg.* MS Gen 9 is similar, underlining the likelihood that it is a copy of the 1751 text.
d'ad thaisg out of your store
treis 1839 ff. *greis*

93 *Melpomene* 1751 *Mhelpimone*, where the *i* is probably a printer's error. MS Gen 9 has *o*. Melpomene the Muse of Tragedy.
uireasaibh 1751 *uireasbh*, 1839 *uireasaidh.* Later sources have *uireasbhuidh*, but the original reading presumably is the dative plural in *-(a)ibh.* The lines 37-8 mean 'M., bring relief to (me in) my needs from your treasure which is full of wealth'. The aspiration in *mhaoin* may reflect the poet's usage

95 The poet's own usage is retained in *do na th' agad do chòrr* (1751 etc. *do'n th' agad do*), while later sources change to *de'n th' agad de*, or, in the case of the 1924 ed., *pàirt de do chòrr.*

97 *A Therpsicore* 1751, MS Gen 9, 1802 *A Herpsicore* Terpsichore was the Muse of Dancing.

98 *chuilidh* 1751 etc. *chuile.* It is difficult to make sense of the phrase *cuilidh na frìth* if we take *frìth* in the commoner sense of 'deer forest'. More likely is the sense of 'divination, incantation', suggesting that Terpsichore here has some connection with the 'treasure-house of incantation'. She is being asked to let him hear pleasant *crambos: crambo* was the name of a game in which one player spoke a word or line and the other players had to match the rhyme. Note that the poet retains the English plural in *-s* here.

99 *crambos* See above.

101 *Phoilihimnia* 1751 etc. *Pholihimnia* The youngest of the Muses.

102 *Ge* 1751 etc. *Go*

103 *chomradh* 1751 etc. *chomoradh* The 1751 Glossary includes 'Comaradh, aid, assistance, help'.

104 'Let me likewise seek (?)'. I take this expression to be derived from older Gaelic *co se*, literally 'to/with this' i.e. along with this, also. The later sources emend to *gu sèamh*, but this breaks the rhyme, which is unthinkable.

105 *Thalia* the Muse of Comedy and Idyllic Poetry.

106 *rothan mo ghlèis* 'the wheels of my invention/preparation'. Here he is probably referring to his mental processes rather than to the technicalities of verse-composition.

109 *Apollo* the sun-god

111 *Fàg-s'* = *Fàg-sa* = *Fàg thusa* 'do you leave/make it'.

112 *Coineallach* Also *coingheallach* 'accommodating, pliable'. The 1751 Glossary gives the senses of 'flexible, pliable'. 1839 emends to *Caoin-iallach.*

113 *Minerbha* A Roman goddess of wisdom.

modern Gaelic *sgoil* is historically the dative case. It is used here in one of its older senses too, e.g. learned people, writers.

114 *cèidse nam fil* 1751 etc *na. cèidse* is a borrowing from English, as is recognised in the 1874 and 1892 version which italicises the word. The 1924 ed. changes the word to *chèile.* Presumably it is a borrowing not of *cage* but of *gage*, in the sense of 'pledge'. *fil* is a short form of the commoner *filidh*, poet (especially a learned, highly-trained poet).

116 *sir* Later sources alter this to *shir.*

117 The poet now addresses the Muses and gods collectively, having made separate appeals to each of them. He makes it clear that his ambition is not simply to compose jingling verses that sound good but have no kernel in them. And then (11.125 ff.) he adopts an apologetic stance, saying that he lacks the training and language to fulfil his ambition. He is probably thinking here of the lengthy and detailed training that professional Gaelic poets had to undertake, but also there is no doubt an element of playful false modesty in this passage.

119–20 *Mar chaoch-chnuasaich – – – – cnuasaich* is often used with *cnò* 'nut' to mean 'gather nuts', but here it seems to be used of the nut itself, or of the collection of nuts: these nuts have no kernel, so they are empty or *caoch. cnuasach*, which is also used of 'fruit', is usually masculine, but here the poet seems to use the dative (after *mar*) of a feminine noun. The lines translate 'like a round empty nut that makes a noise, having no kernel within it'.
eitean 1751, 1802 *eitiunn*, MS Gen 9 *eitiañ* may suggest that the poet's pronunciation was *eiteann.* Older forms of the word are *etne/eitne.*

125–6 *speuran* 1924 *spéirid* 'The orbit (lit. skies) of my capacity is restricted enough, though my desire is expansive'. MS Gen 9 has *sreinib'* instead of 1751's *spérin.* Is this a rare authorial revision?

127 *cho-mhòr* An older usage than the modern *cho mòr.*

128 *clach-shnaighte* MS Gen 9 has *claċ-ṡnasda.*

129 *Cainnt-shnasda* This developes the image of *clach-shnaighte* 'a chiselled stone' in 1. 128. His words should be as skilfully shaped for his verse as the mason's stones for his wall.

131–2 'A matter of no substance is art without schooling, (even) on a subject like/sweet as honey'.
The poet gives a Gaelic pronunciation to English 'subject'.

133 *mo bhil* my lip i.e. mouth (is not cutting/sharp-tongued)

134 *Mo cheann cha mhol* This can be taken in two senses: (1) 'my brain does not praise', (2) 'I shall not praise my brain', and probably both are intended.

135–6 To complete the exaggerated dismal picture, he says that his paper and ink are defective (and his pen is blunt, as he says in 1. 133).
uireasaibh The more standard *uireasbhuidh* undergoes a form of metathesis here. The later sources restore the standard form. See also 93n. Angus Matheson (1951) suggested that the final two lines of the poem should be printed *mo phaipeir is m'ink – is uireasbhuidh sin –/tha iad lan de chron*, so as to preserve the usual rhyme sequence.

ORAN D'A CHEILE NUADH-PHOSDA

Sources and editions:

1751 94-8
1802 106-110
1839 (in the Supplement) 191-3
1874 100-103
1892 100-103
1924 238-43

The title of the poem, in the 1751 source, is 'Oran a rinn duin'-uasul árrait, d'a chèile nuadh phosda. Air fonn, Dh' fhalbh 's an easgar an t-óg ba deise, &c.' The use of *duin'-uasal àraid* may be simply a distancing by the poet from personal matters, but just as probably a playful formality, in which he refers to himself, the recent quarry of Hanoverian blood-hunters, as 'a certain gentleman'.

The metrical model, or tune to which it was to be sung, is given as 'Dh' fhalbh san fheasgar an t-òg bu deise'. This is not listed in Ó Baoill and MacAulay, *Scottish Gaelic Vernacular Verse to 1730*, but it must have a date earlier than 1730. It is likely that the poet married about the year 1727, and his wife, Jane MacDonald of Dalness, was presumably still in her teens at the time, judging by his reference to her as a *pàisde* (1. 172). The reference to Parliament in 1. 156 may just possibly suggest she was born in 1707. The song, despite its formal aspects, sounds as if it was composed at the very start of the marriage. It begins with the reference to catching this lovely salmon at Allt Ghartan, quickly transferring the beauty of the salmon to the girl, breaking briefly into the extended praise sequence to refer to her father, the Rhymer, and to the girl's native locality, placed between Loch Etive to the south-west of Dalness, and Coire Cheathaich to the south-east (if this is the correct restoration of 1. 157). There are classical references, to Phoenix, Dido and Venus, which are characteristic of Mac Mhaighstir Alasdair's verse, especially in his earlier period.

The main concern of the poem is to give a detailed complimentary description of Jane, concentrating on her physical attributes, but not neglecting spiritual aspects and traits of personality. The poet's eroticism surfaces in a controlled way at several points, and an emotional high point occurs near the centre of the poem, in 11. 175-8. An element of dutiful formality in the poem may be minimally betrayed by the repetition of various descriptive nouns and adjectives (*leug, faite, fonnmhor*), but it would be more appropriate to comment on the richness and variety of the descriptive language used. The poem would seem to have been completed before the couple settled in Moidart, as he looks forward to seeing her settled there.

Oran d'a chèile nuadh-phòsda

Air Allt Ghartan ghlacas bradan,
Bain-iasg gasda làn-mhaiseach.

Am breac as ciataich ann mo bheachd-sa,
'S dreach mìn sneachd-gheal sàile dhi.

Bean ghlan bhas-bhàn chaoin shèimh chas-chruinn
Nan calg-rasg donn gàireachdach.

Chaidh na dùilean chum an dùbhlain
Dh'fheuchainn dùrachd ceàirdeadh oirr'.

Air a sòinneadh do sgèimh glòrmhor,
'S cloch-iùil mhòr ghaol-thàirneach i.

Dreach an aingil, fiamh na h-ainnir,
Chuir am anam gàirdeachas.

'S ann on Reumhair fhuair mi 'n euchdag,
Phènix, eud na Gàidhealtachd.

Araichdinn prìseil nam bas mìngheal
'S beusach mìnneil càileachdan.

Fuaras leug air bhruachaibh Eitibh,
'S faodail cheutach àlainn i.

Leug na foindeal 's feàrr no 'n daoimean,
An gabh loinn á Pàrlamaid?

Dèideag shoitheamh E[*itibh*] 's C[*heathaich*]
Gur neamh-dhoitheamh m'àilleagan.

Beul as binne, deud as gile,
Cùl as finne fàinnichean.

Maoth mar shioras dearg bhermilion,
Briathrach milis mànranach.

Geal mar ìbhri, deud cruinn Dìdo,
Pàirc na[n] spìsridh fàileanach.

Dà lèig bhuadhach mheallach ghuamach
Sùil as buairich fàitichean.

Ruisg neamh-luaineach 's mòdhar gluasad,
'S staideil suairce t'àbhaistean.

Modhail cùirteil 's baindidh 'giùlan;
'S làn bain-diùc o 'pàirtinnibh.

Geug nam mìog-shùl, 's mòr mo phrìs dìot,
Fhuair mi fhìn nad phàiste thu.

Thàrr mi 'n ulaidh, 's cha b'i 'm munar,
'S feàrr no tuillidh saidhbhireis.

Fhuair mi mòran, mo thoil mhòr leat,
Fhuair mi òr na h-Asia.

Fhuair mi òg thu, fhuair mi 'd òigh thu,
Fhuair mi bòidheach àlainn thu.

Mo thaip dhreachmhor shona thlachdmhor,
Mhaiseach ghlac-gheal làn-ghasda.

Aignidh fonnmhor banail tromdha,
'S lìonmhor conn f'a pàirtinnibh.

Caomhag mhaoineach 's cha b'i 'n fhaoineag,
'S caoin ciùin faoilteach fàiltichean.

'S rèimeil rùmail, ciallach grùnndail
Mo shonn sùnndach sàr-thuigseach.

Beul dearg tosdach, làn de shoistinn,
Nach geàrr focal eàrr-loisgeach.

Do chùl peucach òr-bhuidh peurlach
'S ainglidh ceutach clàideagan;

'S dalladh lèirsinn sealltainn geur orr'
'S gathain ghrèine a' deàrrsadh air.

Amladh teudach fann-bhuidh' seudach:
Cùl na gèige blàth-mhaisich.

Tùir gheal chriostail, plùir-mhìn stòite,
Cìochan tòicte bàn-chraicneach.

'S sgapach glèidhteach, ùirneach dèirceach,
Traisgeach beusach cràbhach i.

Coltas Vènuis, snuadh na h-[Eighpheit];
'S geanmnaidh èagsamhail tàlantan.

Muineal mìngheal gloine-thrìdeach,
Chìte fìon a' teàrnadh leis.

Gairbhe 's mìne shuas is shìos oirr',
'S donna-gheal mìnneach nàrach i.

'S briathrach sìobhalt socair fìnealt
Bean as mìogach fàitichean.

'S i gu tosdach fìor-shaor socair,
Gun dad moit no àrdain innt'.

'S fonnmhor mùirneach ceòlmhor cùirteach
A' gheal-ùiseil làmh-ghnìomhach.

Slàn gu faic mi fhìn mo leannan
Ann am M[ùideart] àird-chreigich.

NOTES

137 *Allt Ghartan* a small stream in the vicinity of Dalness
ghlacas 1751, 1802 *ghlachdas* presumably indicates the poet's pronunciation, which seems to have fluctuated between the *-c-* and the *-chd-* forms. This verbal form is used as a past passive, cf. Uilleam Ros's *Leughas litir naidheachd leinn*; see Calder, *Grammar*, 245.

138 *bain-iasg* Salmon-fishermen traditionally referred to their catch as either female or male.
gasda The gender of *iasg* apparently determined for the poet the form of the adjective. Later editions, e.g. 1874 onwards, have *ghasda*, taking *bain-iasg* as a feminine noun.

139 *ann mo* 1839 *ann am*, 1874 etc. *ann an* (the *an* a misprint), 1924 *ann am*.

140 sàile dhi 1874 to 1924 *sàil' oirre*.

141–2 The poet is fond of compound adjectives, and here adds the ornament of internal rhyme between *bhas* and *chas*, and between *chas-chruinn* and *-rasg donn*.

143–4 *dùbhlain* The older form of this word was the compound *dubh-shlàn* 'defiance, challenge'. The couplet might be translated 'The elements did their level best, aiming to perfect their skills in making her'.
ceàirdeadh oirr' 1751, 1802 *ceardadh orra*, 1839 *cearda*, 1874 to 1924 *cèaird'/ceaird' oirre*.

145 *sòinneadh* 1839 *foinneamh*, 1874 to 1924 *foinneadh*. The form of the early sources was unfamiliar to the later editors, and they substitute a word which breaks the normal internal rhyming sequence. Older Gaelic has the word *soinmech*, often with long *o*, in the sense of 'favourable, prosperous'. Thurneysen (*RIA Dictionary*, S, 330) analyses this as a compound of *so* and

gnímach. The verb *soinmigidir* has the sense of 'makes prosperous'. If the poet's word is related, as seems likely, its sense may be 'excellently fashioned'.

149 *Reumhair* 1751, 1802 *reamhair*, 1874 to 1924 *Réumhar/Reumhar*, with the note in the 1924 ed.: 'Thomas the Rhymer, of Erceldoune, Berwickshire, a romancer who flourished in the 13th century'. 'Tòmas (an) Reumhair' is used at times of the Lowland poet/seer, but the reference here is to another rhymer, MacDonald of Dalness, Jane's father.

150 *Phènix* The phoenix was a marvellous, many-coloured bird in classical and Arabian mythology.

151 *Araichdinn* 1751, 1802 *Airrichdin* The Highland Society Dictionary (1828) has *àraichdin*, diminutive of *àraichd* 'a present, gift; a fit, or deserving object'.

152 *mìnneil* 1874 to 1924 *mèineil*. The word means 'affable, tender'. The form with *ì* is required for internal rhyme.

153 *Fuaras* 1924 *Fhuaras*
bhruachaibh 1751, 1802 *bhruachamh*, 1839, 1924 *bruachaibh*

153–4 This couplet is missing from 1874, 1892 – this seems to be due to oversight.

155 *foindeal* 1751, 1802, 1839 *foineal*, 1874 to 1924 *foidhneul*. The form *foindeal*, which rhymes internally with *daoimean*, is probably to be related to older Gaelic *foíndel* 'wandering'. The sense here may be of a jewel which the poet found on his wanderings.

156 There is no question-mark in the earliest sources, but it is difficult to interpret the line without one. The sense may be 'Can (even) Parliament add lustre to her?' Has the poet momentarily forgotten a natural hostility to the Union Parliament? Or can this be an odd reference to Jane's year of birth, which might be 1707?

157 1751, 1802 *Deideag shoithibh, E---- is C----;* The missing words, not restored in previous editions, are likely to be place-names, and the second of them must rhyme internally with *shoithibh* and with *-dhoithibh* in l. 158. The place-names *Eitibh* and *Cheathaich* are of places to the south (Loch Etive) and the east (Coire Cheathaich) of Dalness, which is itself in Glen Etive.

160 *fàinnichean* 1751, 1802 *fàinichion*, 1839 *fainichean*. The later editions have *fàinneachan*.

161 *shioras* The form *siris* is commoner for 'cherry'.

162 *mànranach* 1751, 1802 have the pronunciation spelling *márranach*.

163 *ibhri* 1751, 1802 *íbhi*, presumably a printer's error, as the references to whiteness and teeth are conclusively in favour of 'ivory'.

164 *na[n] spìsridh fàileanach* 1751, 1802, 1839 *na spísri fáileneach*, but 1874ff. *na spìsridh' fàileinich'*, where the spice is singular. Mac Mhaighstir Alasdair's common usage of *na* rather than *nan* allows for the more generous interpretation: Jane was a 'park of sweet-smelling spices', not a single spice.

166 *buairich* 1839 to 1924 *buaireach*
fàitichean faite 'smile' usually has a short *a*, but long *a* is required for end-rhyme here.

168 *staideil* 1751, 1802 *staiddeil*. The *dd* may be taken to underline the short vowel; the form with long *à* is commoner.

170 *bain-diùc o 'pàirtinnibh* 1874 to 1924 *bhan-diùc bho 'pàirtean i*. The couplet translates 'Her deportment is mannerly, courtly and womanly; she is a complete duchess because of her accomplishments'.

172 *Fhuair* 1751, 1802 *Fuair*, and similarly in ll. 175-8.
nad 1874 to 1924 *ad*
'I won you when you were still a youngster'. The use of *pàiste* suggests that Jane was still in her teens when she married the poet.

174 *feàrr – – – – tuillidh saidhbhireis* 1751, 1802 – – – – *saibhiris*, 1874 to 1924 *fhéarr/fhearr na tuilleadh saibhiris*

175 *mo thoil mhòr* 1839 *am thoil mhoir*

175–8 The lyrical warmth of the poem reaches its high note in these lines.

179 *thaip* 1751, 1802 *thaipp. taipe* in the sense of 'fragment, portion' is meagrely attested in Old Gaelic (see RIA Dictionary). The Highland Society Dictionary has *taip*, with this reference but with the unsuitable sense of 'a clumsy person'; it quotes another instance from Gillies' Collection (1786), 294, in the sense of 'lumber' (see *MacDiarmid Anthology*, 1. 743*n*). The sense of 'portion' (i.e. the portion he has fallen heir to) is much more appropriate here.

181 *tromdha* 'dignified'. The word is commoner in Irish than in Scottish Gaelic. It is not included in the Highland Soc. Dict. nor in Dwelly.

182 *conn* The 1751 Glossary gives 'regulator'
pàirtinnibh 1874 to 1924 *pàirteanna.* 'with plenty of sense [showing] in her attributes'.

185 *rùmail* 1751, 1802 *rummoil.* The exact sense of this adjective is elusive. Literally 'roomy', but here perhaps 'using her space well, well-positioned'.

187 *soistinn* High. Soc. Dict. gives *soistean* with the sense of 'sense, meaning: intelligentia', referring to 1751, p.108, perhaps mistakenly for p.96, as the word does not occur on p.108.

189 *peucach peuc* meant 'a long tail', so 'long-tailed', perhaps with a hint of colour and show as in *peucag* 'peacock'. The poet also uses the word in his 'Oran luaidh no fùcaidh': *'Do chùl peucach sìos 'na dhualaibh'* (1751, p.99).

191–2 *orr'* refers back to *clàideagan* in 1. 190, and *air* to *cùl* in 1. 189

193 *Amladh* 1751, 1802 *Amaladh*

194 *Cùl na gèige* The *geug* here is Jane, whose head of hair (*cùl*) is lovingly described.

196 *tòicte* 1751, 1802 *toite*, 1839 *taghte* 1874 to 1924 interpret this as *tighte*, evidently regarding it as the plural form of borrowed English 'tight'. But we need a rhyme with *stòite*, and *tòicte* 'swollen' fits in all respects.

197 *sgapach* and *glèidhteach* are opposites. Perhaps he means that Jane is generous to others, careful as a housewife.
ùirneach 1874 to 1924 expand this to *ùrnaigheach*, but it is better to accept the poet's choice, rhythmically determined.

199 *h-[Eighpheit]* 1751, 1802 *h---- bh---t.* The later sources leave these gaps, an idiosyncracy of the author. Is this a comment on Jane's complexion, or on her beauty generally?

200 *èagsamhail* is a syllable too long for the rhythm, and was probably contracted in pronunciation.

201 *gloine-thrìdeach* 1751, 1802, 1839 *glain(n)e-triodach.* The sense is evidently 'transparent as glass'.

203–4 Internal rhyme on *ì* seems indicated, involving a Mainland pronunciation of *shìos*, and changing 1751, 1802 *mheinneach* to *m[h]ìnneach.* The sense of this last word is 'affable, affectionate'. l. 203 seems to refer to Jane's shape and skin.

205 *socair* 1751, 1802 *sochdair.* This example like others in 1751, shows that the poet often used the *chd* pronunciation of *c*. So also 1. 207

206 *mìogach* 1751, 1802 *miogach.* The later versions change this to *mìogaich*, the comparative rather than the positive form of the adjective.

208 *moit no àrdain* The later versions change to *'mhoit no dh' àrdan.*

209 *cùirteach* 1751, 1802 *cúirdeach*

210 *làmh-ghnìomhach* 1751, 1802 *laimh-ghnìomhach*

212 *M(ùideart)* 1751, 1802 *m-----*

This line seems to suggest the poem was composed before the couple settled in Moidart, i.e. very soon after the marriage.

MOLADH MÒRAIG

Sources and editions:

1751	11-25
MS Gen 9	4-16
Gillies	212-22
1802	23-37
1839	8-20
1841	106-10
1874	8-19
1892	8-19
1924	212-30

The 1751, Gillies, 1802 and MS Gen 9 versions are very closely related. The 1802 version is a virtually straight reprint of 1751, although there are a few small variations, noted below. The MS Gen 9 is a copy either of 1751 or of its MS original, with lenition dots over consonants usually replacing *h*, and again with a small number of variants, noted below. Gillies follows 1751 very closely. The 1839 and 1841 texts are close to the 1751 text, but introduce some editorial changes, often being followed in these by later editions, especially the 1924 one. The 1924 edition is also influenced strongly by Donald Macpherson's 1874 edition, and both of these omit the final stanza which they regard as improper (Macpherson does not in fact refer to it, but the 1924 editors indicate their disapproval).

This edition tries to stay closer to the 1751 original than any previous edition does, retaining what are clearly the poet's usages and preferences in many cases, though imposing some orthographical uniformity also.

It may be added that the 1924 translation is something of a mixed bag. Its use of rhyme leads to various approximations and inaccuracies, but there are many instances of sharp understanding of the sense.

This is a rich and complicated poem, employing a torrent of language, with frequent adjectival runs and quite frequent use of synonyms and near-synonyms. Its plot seems deliberately constructed to allow for this kind of expansiveness and variety. The traditional explanation of the poem's origin is set out, and probably elaborated, by John Mackenzie in a note at the end of his 1841 edition (*Sàr Obair*, 109-10), where he says "Morag was a common country girl; and it is said that the poet's wife became jealous of her rival. The bard had talked of the marriage ties with the greatest contempt, and regretted that he was fettered with the bonds of wedlock. This raised a storm, and the bard sacrificed the mistress to appease the wife, and composed his *"Mi-mholadh"*. Here is an instance of his disregard to truth and common decency, as well as of moral and poetical justice. As the praise was exaggerated and extravagant, the censure was cruel, unmanly, and undeserved. He first raised the object of his admiration to the skies, with the most hyperbolical praise – and then, without any provocation, he suddenly wheels round and overwhelms his goddess with the most slanderous, foul-mouthed and unfeeling abuse".

This is a simplistic judgement. Whether or not the poet was guilty of any extra-marital activity, this poem is certainly not a naive account of it, nor an emotional response. It is much too complicated and structured for that. An 'alternative explanation' is given by the poet himself in the final two sections of the poem (11. 517-48), where he says that the beautiful and erotic scenes and experiences described earlier were dream sequences, and that he wakens to find his wife Sìne lying beside him. In a further elaboration of this explanation he says that Sìne, dissatisfied with his sexual performance, had induced the sleep and the dream it produced, and they both enjoyed the enhanced love-making which followed.

In a real sense, then, it appears that the poem is a deliberate construct, whatever actualities of experience it may contain. There is a link between the final explanation and the opening words of the poem, where he says that it is a pity he was not in the wood when Morag was there. Had he been there, he says, they *would* have ranged and romped through it. Then from the second section onwards, at least intermittently, he describes Morag and their activities, and his feelings, as though they were actual.

There are passages, however, in which his attention seems to become fixed on topics not wholly relevant to the one of Morag. In particular, the sections from ll. 469-84 and 485-500, although they ostensibly refer to the music Morag makes (whether that is instrumental, vocal or sexual) concentrate clearly on an enthralling description of pipe-music: the physical movements associated with it, its rhythms and its musical divisions. This of course ties in neatly with the choice of metre, based however loosely on the rhythmical sequence of *ceòl-mòr* music, and may also suggest that the piping theme was a central one in the original conception of the poem. In the following section (11. 501-16) he describes a sequence of events and activities that would probably be typical of a courting episode in a fairly sophisticated society: wine, conversation, draughts/chess, a dram. He may be recalling earlier experience here, perhaps at the home of the Dalness MacDonalds.

The greater part of the poem is taken up with detailed, often lyrical descriptions of the lady and her natural surroundings. It is useful to observe the way the poem is organised, and this will reinforce the impression that it was very much a deliberate construct. The poem runs to 336 lines, divided into twenty-one verse paragraphs. Each of these has sixteen lines. A brief summary of the dominant topics of these paragraphs follows:

(1) He wishes he was in the wood with Morag, where they could rove about and enjoy its beauty and variety.
(2) A general description of Morag's beauty, with reference to the sun, a star, mirror of Nature's beauty.
(3) A comparison with four other girls who all had faults. Morag has none.
(4) There is no one like Morag in Mull or Lewis (one way of saying 'in the world'): she is educated, lovely, chaste, shapely, kindly etc.
(5) She inspires feelings of lust in the poet, in contrast to the formalities of marriage.
(6) A closer description of Morag's body, especially her breasts.
(7) In the woods, on a sunny day, chasing each other like buck and doe.
(8) Description of Morag's cheeks and teeth, with comparisons with Venus and Dido.
(9) Were he not married, he would place his heart on Morag's altar. This frenzy has struck him since early on Sunday.
(10) She is the finest of girls, in complexion, skin texture, figure, movement, personality.
(11) He wishes he were freed from marriage ties, then recognises this as foolishness, then returns to his obsession.
(12) Her lovely breasts attract him, but he is tied in marriage. Her lips are described. Cupid's arrows have struck him.
(13) He is stricken by grief since he saw Morag. Her golden curls are described in detail.
(14) Further description of Morag's skin, character, dress, conversation, with a further reference to seeing her in the crowd on Sunday.
(15) Moral reflections: the world is full of temptations, but none

so divine as Morag.

(16) The poet asks for advice. There is no one like Morag. This must be hidden from his wife Jane. There is not enough water in Loch Shiel, nor enough snow on Cruachan to cool his passion.

(17) Developing a passing reference in (16), he develops the theme of the music Morag provides: it appears to be a kind of *ceòl mòr*, and some of its movements and sounds are described.

(18) Further close detail of the musical movements and the sounds they produce.

(19) An interlude in polite society: a glass of wine, civilized talk, draughts/chess, a dram of whisky; ending with a quick description of the lady.

(20) His head is buzzing, and he is generally confused. When he thinks he is about to win Morag, he wakens.

(21) He finds himself lying beside Jane. This is the Morag of his dreams. She had induced the dreams to liven him up, so he turns to her and makes her his Morag.

One can detect a strong element of playfulness in this sequence. It may be that some of the sections get out of hand, but this is probably deliberate also.

The fact that the poem was given a prominent position in the 1751 publication suggests strongly that it was not an indiscretion. It is followed there by the *Mì-mholadh Mòraig* (Dispraise of Morag). This begins with a sixteen-line section ostensibly by his wife, addressed to the 'bold black Moidart-man of the sharp words', telling him to stop his nonsense and mockery, and threatening to go to Alan the Bard and other poets she knows in Edinburgh; they will make short work of him. There follows a detailed debunking of Mòrag, now portrayed as ugly, unclean, a notorious prostitute, and so on. This whole poem runs to fourteen sixteen-line stanzas, many of them scurrilous and of interest mainly because of their rich inventive language.

The difficulty remains of arriving at conclusions on biographical or moral grounds. It is much easier, and more satisfactory, to reach a conclusion on artistic or literary grounds. This must give a clear precedence to the *Moladh Mòraig*, for its variety and artistry, and its overall construction. It takes a high place in Mac Mhaighstir Alasdair's surviving work, rivalling in some ways his *Birlinn Chlann Raghnaill*, and probably surpassing it in its lyrical quality.

We do not have any precise information as to when *Moladh Mòraig* was composed, but it seems likely that it was during the

1730s, perhaps in the first decade of his marriage. It may well have been influenced, marginally at least, by Thomson's *Seasons*, in which passages of eroticism formed one of the great attractions that that work had for the reading public.

The poem is notable also as being the first detailed example of a poem whose metrics attempt to mirror some of the movements of classical pipe music or *ceòl mòr*. The various sections are given piping names: *Urlar, Siubhal* and *Crùn-luath*, with clear rhythmical differences between them, culminating in the trisyllabic rhymes of the first part of the *Crùn-luath*: these are intended to echo the increasing complexity of piping grace-notes, though they can only go a short distance in that direction. This metrical scheme was later to be taken up, and further developed, by Duncan Bàn Macintyre in his Praise of Ben Doran. The poet's detailed interest in piping technique also shows up in entries in his Glossary to the 1751 book.

MOLADH MÒRAIG Air fonn Pìobaireachd

Urlar

'S truagh gun mi sa' choill
Nuair bha Mòrag ann,
Thilgeamaid na croinn
Cò bu bhòidhch' againn;
Inghean a' chùil duinn
Air a bheil a loinn,
Bhiomaid air ar broinn
Feadh na ròsanan;
Bhreugamaid sinn fhìn
Mireag air ar blìon,
A' buain shòbhrach mìn-
bhuidh nan còsagan;
Theannamaid ri strì
'S thadhlamaid san fhrìth
'S chailleamaid sinn fhìn
Feadh na strònagan.

Urlar

Sùil mar ghorm-dhearc driùchd
Ann an ceò-mhaidinn,
Deirg' is gil' nad ghnùis
Mar bhlàth òirseidean,
Shuas cho mìn ri plùr,
Shìos garbh mo chulaidh-chiùil,
Grian 'na planaid-cùrs'
A-measg òigheannan,
Reula glan gun smùr
Measg na rionnag-iùil,
Sgàthan-mais' air flùthar
Na bòidhchid thu,
Ailleagan glan ùr
A dhallas ruisg gu 'n cùl;
Mas ann do chrèadhaich thù
'S adhbhar mòr-iongnaidh.

Urlar

On thàinig gnè de thùr
O m' aois òige dhomh
Nìor facas creutair dhiùbh
Bu cho-glòrmhoire:
Bha Maili 's dearbha caoin
'S a gruaidh air dhreach nan caor,

Ach caochlaideach mar ghaoith
'S i ro òranach;
Bha Peigi fad an aois –
Mur bhith sin b' i mo ghaol;
Bha Marsaili fìor aotrom
Làn neònachais;
Bha Lili a' taitne rium
Mur bhith a ruisg bhith fionn;
Ach cha bu shàth bùrn-ionnlaid
Don Mhòraig-s' iad.

Siubhal

O, 's coma leam, 's coma leam
Uil' iad ach Mòrag:
Rìoghainn dheas chulach
Gun uireasaibh fòghlaim;
Chan fhaighear a tiunnail
Air mhaise no bhunailt,
No 'm beusaibh neo-chumant
Am Muile no 'n Leòdhas,
Gu geanmnaidh, deas, furanach,
Duineil, gun mhòrchuis,
Air thagha na cumachd
O 'mullach gu 'brògaibh;
A neul tha neamh-churaidh
'S a h-aignidh ro-lurach
Gu brìodalach, cuireideach,
Urramach, seòlta.

Siubhal

O guiliugag, guiliugag,
Guiliugag Mòrag!
Aice ata 'chulaidh
Gu cuireadh nan òigfhear;
B'e 'n t-aighear 's an sulas
Bhith sìnte ri t' ulaidh
Seach daonnan bhith fuireach
Ri munaran pòsaidh.
D'am phianadh 's d'am ruagadh
Le buaireadh na feòla,
Le aislingean connain
Na colna d'am leònadh:
Nuair chithinn mu m' choinneamh
A cìochan le coinnil
Theid m' aigne air bhoilich
'S 'na theine dearg sòlais.

Siubhal

O fairigean, fairigean,
Fairigean Mòrag!
Aice ata 'chroiteag
As toite san Eòrpa;
A cìochan geal criostail
Na faiceadh tu stòit' iad
Gun tàirneadh gu beag-nàir
Ceann-eaglais na Ròimhe;
Air bhuige 's air ghile
Mar lili na lònan;
Nuair dhèanadh tu 'n dinneadh
Gun cinneadh tu deònach;
An deirgead, an grinnead,
Am mìnead 's an tinnead,
Gum b' àsainn chur spionnaidh
Agus spiorad a feòil iad.

Urlar

Thogamaid ar fonn
Anns an òg-mhaidinn,
'S Phèbus 'dath nan tonn
Air fiamh òrainsean;
F' ar cèill cha bhiodh conn
Air sgàth dhoire 's thom,
Sinn air dàireadh trom
Le 'r cuid gòraileis,
Dìreach mar gum bìodh
Maoiseach 's boc a frìth
Crom-ruaig a chèile dìan
Timcheall òganan;
Chailleamaid ar clì
A' gàireachdaich leinn fhìn
Le bras mhacnas dìan sin
Na h-ògalachd.

Siubhal

O dastram, dastram
Dastram Mòrag!
Rìoghainn bhuidh', bhasdalach,
Leac-ruiteach, ròsach;
A gruaidhean air lasadh
Mar an lasair-chlach dhathte
'S a deud mar a sneachda,
Cruinn-shnaighte 'n dlùth òrdugh;

Ri Vènus chomh-tlachdmhor
An taitneachdainn fheòlmhoir,
Ri Dìdo chomh-maiseach,
Chomh-snasmhor 's chomh-còrr rith';
'S e thionnsgain dhomh caitheamh
'S a laoghdaich mo rathan,
A' bhallag ghrinn laghach
Chuir na gathan-sa 'm fheòil-sa.

Siubhal

'S mur bithinn fo ghlasaibh
Cruaidh-phaisgte le pòsadh
Dh' ìobrainn cridhe mo phearsan
Air an altair-se Mòraig,
Gun lìobhrainn gun airteal
Aig stòilibh a cas e,
'S mur gabhadh i tlachd dhiom
Cha b' fhad a sin beò mi.
O! 'n t-urram, an t-urram,
An t-urram do Mhòraig!
Cha mhòr nach do chuir i
M' fhuil uil' ás a h-òrdugh,
Gun d' rug oirr' ceum-tuislidh
Fo imeachd mo chuislean
Le teas is le murtachd
O mhochthrath DiaDòmhnaich.

Siubhal

'S tu reula nan cailin,
Làn lainnir, gun cheò ort,
Fìor chòmhnard gun charraid,
Gun arral, gun bheòlam;
Cho mìn ri cloimh eala
'S cho geal ris a' ghaillinn
Do sheang-shlios sèimh fallain
Thug barrachd air mòran.
'S tu bainrigh nan ainnir –
Cha sgallais an còmhradh –
Ard, foinnidh nad ghallan,
Gun bhallart, gun mhòrchuis;
Tha thu coimhliont nad bhallaibh,
Gu h-innsginneach, athlamh,
Caoin, meachaire, farasd,
Gun fhathrom, gun ròpal.

Urlar

B' fheàrr gum bithinn sgaoilt
As na còrdaibh-sa,
Thug mi tuilleadh gaoil
Is bu chòir dhomh dhuit;
Gun tig fo dhuine taom
Gu droch-ghnìomh bhios claon –
Cuireadh e cruaidh-shnaoim
Air o 'n ghòraich sin.
Ach thug i seo mo chiall
Uile uam gu trian:
Chan fhaca mi riamh
Tiunnail Mòraig seo.
Ghoid i uam mo chrìdh
'S shlad i uam mo chlì,
'S cuiridh i san chìll
Fo na fòdaibh mi.

Siubhal

Mo cheist agus m' ulaidh
De 'n chonnairc mi d' sheòrs' thu,
Le d' bhroilleach geal-thuraid
Nam mullaichean bòidheach;
Chan fhaigh mi de dh' fhuras
Na nì mionaid uat fuireach
Ged tha buarach na dunach
Gam chumail o d' phòsadh.
Do bheul mar an t-sirist
'S e milis ri phògadh,
Cho dearg ri bhermilion
Mar bhileagan ròsan;
Gun d' rinn thu mo mhilleadh
Le d' Chupid dam bhioradh,
'S le d' shaighdean caol biorach
A rinn ciorram fo m' chòta.

Siubhal

Tha mi làn mulaid
On chunnaic mi Mòrag,
Cho trom ri cloch-mhuilinn
Air lunnaibh da seòladh;
Mac-samhailt na cruinneig
Chan eil anns a' chruinnidh,
Mo chrìdh air a ghuin leat
On chunnaic mi t' òr-chùl

'Na shlamagan bachallach,
Casarlach, còrnach,
Gu fàinneagach, cleachdagach,
Dreach-lùbach, glòrmhor,
'Na reulagan cearclach
Mar usgraichean dreachmhor,
Le fùdar san fhasan
Grian-lasda, ciabh-òrbhuidh.

Siubhal

Do shlios mar an canach,
Mar chaineal do phògan,
Ri phènix cho-ainneamh
'S glan lainnir do chòta;
Gu mùirneineach, banail,
Gun àrdan, gun stannart,
'S i còrr ann an ceanal,
Gun ainnis, gun fhòtas.
Na faicte mo leannan
Sa' mhath-shluagh DiaDòmhnaich
B' i coltas an aingil
'Na h-earradh 's 'na còmhradh,
A pearsa gun talach,
Air a gibhtean tha barrachd,
An Tì a dh' fhàg thu gun aineamh
A rinn de thalamh rud bòidheach.

Urlar

Tha 'n saoghal làn de smaoint-
innean feòlmhor,
Mammon bidh dar claonadh
Le 'ghòisnichean,
A' cholann bheir oirnn gaol
Ghabhail gu ro-fhaoin
Air strìopachas, air craos
Agus stròdhalachd.
Ach cha do chreid mi riamh
Gun do sheas air sliabh
Aon tè bha cho ciatach
Ri Mòraig seo;
A subhailcean 's a ciall
Mar gum biodh bain-dia,
Leagh i 'n crìdh am chliabh
Le 'cuid òrrachan.

Siubhal

Ur comhairle na ceilibh orm
Ciod eile their no nì mi
Mun rìoghainn bu tearc ceilearadh
A sheinneadh air an fhìdeig.
Chan fhaighear a leith'd eile seo
Air tir-mòr no 'n eileanaibh,
Coimh-iomlan is coimh-eireachdail,
Coimh-teiridneach 's coimh-bìogail.
'S nì cinnteach gur nì deireasach,
Mur ceilear seo air Sìne,
Mi thuiteam an gaol leth-phàirteach
'S mo cheathrannan am dhìobhail:
Chan eil de bhùrn an Seile siud
No shneachd an Cruachan eilidneach
Na bheir aon fhionnachd eiridneach
Don teine ata 'nam innsginn.

Siubhal

Nuair chuala mi ceòl leadanach
An fheadain a bh' aig Mòraig
Rinn m' aignidh dannsa beadarach
'S e freagra dha le sòlas:
Sèimh ùrlar socair, leadarra
A puirt, 's a meòir a' breabadaich,
B' e siud an oirfeid eagarra
Do 'n bheus na creaga mòra.
Ochòin! a feadan bailleagach,
Cruaidh, sgailleagach, glan, ceòlmhor,
Nam binn-phort stuirteil, trileanta,
Rèidh, mion-dhìonach, bog, rò-chaoin;
Am màrsal còmhnard, staideil sin,
'S e lùthmhor, gràsmhor, caismeachdach,
Fìor chruinn-lùth brisg, spalparra
F'a cliath-lùth bras-chaoin, spòrsail.

Siubhal

Chinn pròis, is stuirt, is sprachdalachd
Am ghnùis nuair bheachdaich guamag
A' seinn an fheadain ioraltaich,
B' àrd iolach ann am chluasaibh;
A suain-cheòl sìthe, mireineach,
Mear-stoirmeil, pongail, mionaideach,
Na b' fhoirmeile nach sireamaid
Air mhireid ri h-uchd tuasaid.

O! 'm buille meòir bu lomarra
Gu pronnadh a' phuirt uaibhrich,
'S na h-uilt bu lùthmhoir cromaidhean
Air thollaibh a' chrainn bhuadhaich;
Gun slaoidmheoirich, gun ronnaireachd,
Brisg, tioram, socair, collaideach;
Geal-lùdag nan geàrr-chollainnean
'Na crap-lùth loinneil, guanach.

Urlar

Chaisgeamaid ar n-ìot
Le glainn' fhìon a sin,
'S bhuaileamaid gu dìan
Air glòr shìobhalta;
Tuilleadh cha bhiodh ann
Gus an tigeadh àm
A bhith cluich air dàm
Air na tìthean sin;
Dh' òlamaid ar dràm
Dh' fhògradh uainn gun taing
Gach nì chuireadh maill
Air bhith mìogchuiseach;
Maighdean nan ciabh fann,
Shnìomhanach nan clann,
Mala chaol, dhonn, chàm,
Channach, fhìnealta.

An Crùn-luath

Mo cheann tha làn de sheilleinibh
O dheilich mi ri d' bhrìodal,
Mo shròn tha stoipt' a dh' eileabor,
'Na deil le teine dìombais,
Mo shùilean tha cho deireasach
Nach faic mi gnè gun teileascop,
Is ged bhiodh meudachd beinnidh ann
'S ann theirinn gura frìd e.
Dh' fhalbh mo chèidse corporra
Gu docharach le bruadar,
Nuair shaoil mi fortan thorchairt domh
'S mi 'm thorraichim air mo chluasaig;
Air dùsgadh ás a' chaithream sin
Cha d' fhuair mi ach ion-faileis deth
An ionad na maoin bearraidich
A mheal mi gu seachd uairean.

Ach ciod thug mi gu glan fhaireachadh
Ach carachadh rinn Cluanag,
'S cò seo, o thùs, bu Mhòrag ann
Ach Sìne 'n òr-fhuilt chuachaich;
Nuair thùir i gun do lagaich mi
'S gu feumainn rag-chur stalcaidh ann,
Gun d' rinn i draoidheachd cadail domh
Rinn cruaidh fìor-rag d' am luaidhe.
Bha 'chleasachd-sa cho fìnealta,
'S cho innleachdach mun cuairt di,
Nach faodainn fhìn thaobh sìobhaltachd
Gun dligheadh crìon thoirt uam dhi;
Gun thionndaidh mi gu h-òrdail rith'
'S gun shaoil mi gum b' i Mòrag i,
'S gun d' aisig mi na pògan di
'S cha robh d'a còir dad uaithe.

NOTES

The heading in 1751 is 'Moladh Moraig. Air fonn Piobaireachd', and this, with the headings of sections using 'Urlar', 'Siubhal' and 'An crúnluath' show clearly that the poet had constructed the poem influenced by the model of classical pipe music or *ceòl mòr*.

213 *mi sa'* 1751, MS Gen 9 *me 's an*, 1839 *mì 'san*, 1841 *mì 's a'*, 1874 to 1924 *bhi 's a'*

214 *Morag* 1751, MS Gen 9 *Moraig*

215 *croinn* All edd. except 1839, 1841, 1874, 1892 *crainn*

217 *Inghean* 1751, MS Gen 9 *Inghinn*

218 *a bheil a* 1841 to 1924 *am beil an*. The poet's usage is followed here, and in similar contexts, e.g. 1. 220, where he has *na ròsanan*, while editors from 1874 restore the 'correct' *nan*.

222 *blìon* 1924's *blian* is inappropriate, as an *i*-rhyme is needed. Here, as often, the poet uses the Mainland pronunciation.

224 *Nan còsagan* 1751, 1839 have *Na*, and MS Gen 9 *Na'n*

228 *na strònagan* 1839 *na strōineagan*, 1841 *nan sròineagan*, 1874 to 1924 *nan srònagan*

230 *mhaidinn* 1751, MS Gen 9 *mhaidin*, 1839 to 1924 *mhadainn*

232 *òirseidean* 1751, MS Gen 9, 1841 *óirseidin*, 1874, 1892 *òrainsean*, 1924 *òr-sheudan*. The poet is probably using *òirseid* here in the sense of 'orange'.

233 *cho mìn* 1751 *choi'-min*

'the upper part (skin) as smooth as a flower'. *plùr* is used both of 'flower' and 'flour', but the former seems more poetic.

234 *garbh mo chulaidh-chiùil* 1924 *searbh mo chuisle chiùil*. There seems to be no warrant for the 1924 reading. The reference is surely a sexual one, disguised as a musical instrument.

235 *planaid-cùrs'* 1751 *plaineid coúrs*, 1874 *plaineid cùrs'*, 1924 *planaid cùrs'*. Taking *planaid-cùrs'* as a compound may give the best sense: 'A sun on its progress among the planets'.

237 *Reula* 1751 *Réulla*, 1874 *Réulta*, 1924 *Reul tha*

238 *-iuil* 1751 *-uill*

flùthar 1751 *flour*, 1839 *flùr*, 1841, 1874, 1924 *flùra*. It may be better to take *flour* as a singular noun, but the rhythm requires a dissyllable here. I take the

sense of 11. 239-40 to be 'You are a mirror reflecting the loveliness of the flower of beauty'.
244 *mòr-iongnaidh* 1751 *móir-iunaidh* suggests a dialectal pronunciation in *-u-*.
247 *Nìor* 1751 *Nir.* An old form of the negative used with a past tense.
facas 1874 to 1924 *fhacas*
248 *cho-glòrmhoire* an equative, 'equally glorious'
249 *'s dearbha* Used as an equivalent to modern *gu dearbha*, 'indeed, certainly'.
254 *Mur bhith* 1839 *Mar be.* So too 1. 258
257 *taitne* 1841 to 1924 *taitin(n)*
263 *Rìoghainn* 1874 *Rìmhinn*, 1841, 1924 *Rìbhinn*
culach This can refer either to fullness of figure or stylishness of dress.
264 *uireasaibh* 1751 *uireasabh*, 1839 *uireasaidh*, 1841 to 1924 *uireasbhuidh*
265 *tiunnail* 1839 *siunnail*, 1841 *siunnailt*
266 *bhunailt* 1924 *mhunaidh*
273 *neamh-churaidh* 1751 Glossary gives '*Neamhchurri*, tenacious of beauty'.
274 *aignidh* 1839, 1841 *aghaidh*, 1874 to 1924 *aigne*
277 *guiliugag guileag* is commoner, in the sense of a bird's warble; here the word is used as an expression of rapture.
279 *culaidh* The word has various senses such as 'dress', 'instrument'. Here it is probably used in a more general sense e.g. 'means, qualities'. 'She is well equipped to welcome young men'.
282 *ri t' ulaidh* 1874 to 1924 *riut, ulaidh.* The poet's sense is more direct, *ulaidh* referring to a precious part of the body, rather than in the sense of 'sweetheart'.
284 *munaran* 'trifling, playing about'. The poet seems to be making a distinction here between dalliance and lust.
285 *D'am* This form is retained, against the more standard *'Gam*, as the poet's clear preference.
286 *buaireadh* 1751 *buairidh* may just possibly have indicated a plural form.
287–8 *aislingean connain/Na colna* 'the lustful dreams of the flesh'. The High. Soc. Dict. quotes this phrase under *connan*, giving the sense of 'lust' which is clearly appropriate, but the word is poorly attested. The 1751 Glossary gives *aisling-chonnain* 'a libidinous dream'. The poet's gen. form *na colna* is retained, rather than the form *na colla* adopted by later editors.
289 *chithinn* 1839 *chidhinn*, 1841 *chidh mi*
290 *coinnil* Gillies *coinneal.* It is difficult to be sure how to interpret this line. *coinneal* was used of the stick on which tweed was rolled: the sense of 'roundness' is perhaps possible. Or we might regard the word as the plural of *coinneal* 'candle', referring to the swollen nipple of the breast.
291 *bhoilich* Gillies *bhoille*, 1874 *bhoilidh*, 1841, 1924 *bhoile.*
289–92 We would expect close rhyme between *choinneamh*, *coinnil*, *bhoilich* and *theine*, and this suggests that the first three approximate in pronunciation to that of *theine.*
295 *croiteag* The more common sense is 'hillock, small eminence'. The sense here is '*pudenta*, woman's genitals'.
296 *toite* English 'tight' given a Gaelic plural ending.
299–300 'It (they) would draw to shamelessness the head of the Roman church'.
301 1841 *Air bhuigead 's air ghilead*
302 lònan 1841 *lòintean* Plural of *lòn*, which can mean 'meadow' or 'brook', probably the latter here, making the reference one to water-lilies.
303–4 'When you squeezed them you would grow willing'.
308 *a feòil* 'in flesh'.
311 *Phèbus* Phoebus, the sun-god.
312 *òrainsean* 1751, 1839, 1841 *órensin.* Contrast *òirseidean* in 1. 232.
313–4 The sense of these lines is hard to pin down exactly. Perhaps 'prudence did not underlie our reason as to (our movements over) woods and knolls'.

315 *dàireadh* 1751, 1841 *daradh*. The common sense is 'rutting', but more appropriate here would be 'in a sexual frenzy'.
317 *bìodh* Here a stressed monosyllable, to rhyme with *frìth* and *dìan*, the latter having its Mainland pronunciation.
318 *a frìth* = *am frìth* 'in a deer-forest'.
319 *crom-ruaig* Literally 'bent-chasing'. This may refer to the shapes of the doe and the buck, or to the crooked paths they follow.
320 *gàireachdaich* 1839 *gaireadaich*
325 *dastram* Apparently the poet's coinage, used as an exclamation of wonder etc., perhaps designed to fit into the end-rhyme scheme of this section.
334 *fheòlmhoir* 1751 *fheolor*
337–8 'What began my decay and reduced my good luck'. This looks like an admission of trouble following an affair.
338 *rathan* 1751, 1839 *raithin*
339 *ballag* The 1751 Glossary gives 'a shell of an egg etc.; also a spruce, neat little woman'.
340 *gathan-sa* 1751 *gaithionsa*
343 *phearsan* 1751 *phearsann*, 1841 to 1924 *phearsa*
344 *altair-se Mòraig* 1839 to 1924 *altair se [,] Mòrag*. The poet's use of the genitive is surely justified: 'on this altar of Morag's'.
345 *lìobhrainn* 1751 *liobhrain*, 1839 *liudhrain*, 1841 to 1924 *liùbhrainn*. If this word is a borrowing of Eng. *deliver*, which seems as likely as MacBain's derivation from Latin *libero*, Eng. *liberate*, the poet's form is closer to its origin.
349–50 *t-urram* 1751 *urrum*
352 *òrdugh* 1751 *órdo*
353 *oirr'* 1751 *orra*, 1839 *orradh*
351–6 'She practically upset my whole blood-stream; it (i.e. my blood) stumbled with the rush of my (i.e. through my) veins caused by heat and sultriness since early on Sunday'. The image of stumbling does not work particularly well, though the overall upheaval is well conveyed. Probably we should read *mhuchthrath* in 1.356, for internal rhyme.
357 *reula* 1874 to 1924 *réulta/reulta*. The poet's form, a variant of the singular *reul*, is more appropriate than the plural *reulta*.
359 *Fìor chòmhnard còmhnard* can be either a noun, 'plain', or an adjective, 'smooth etc.'. The adjectival sense is more appropriate here. 11. 359-60 may be translated 'Very level-headed, not given to strife, insolence or censoriousness'.
360 *arral* The 1751 Glossary glosses this 'a bairnly pride, self-conceit'.
361–2 *Cho mìn – – – – cho geal* 1751 *Choi' min – – – – choi'-geal*. The poet's usage seems to fluctuate between the older *chomh/choimh*, followed by lenition, and the modern *cho*, not leniting.
cho geal ris a' ghaillinn 'as white as the snow-storm/white ground left by snow'. Dwelly quotes information from Alex Henderson, of Ardnamurchan, giving these senses, rather than the more standard 'storm'.
367–8 If we take *gallan* too literally, in the sense of a young tree, the imagery sits uneasily. The sense may be 'Tall, comely as a young tree, not given to boasting or pride'.
370 *athlamh* The poet uses the older form of the word, now *ealamh* 'ready'.
372 *fathrom* The poet again retains the older spelling. Modern *farum/faram*.
373 *gum* 1751 *go*.
377 *Gun tig* 1751 *Go d'thig*. 1874 to 1924 interpret this as *Ged thig*. Either interpretation is possible.
381–2 'This one took my sense all away from me down to a third part'. This is the interpretation of the 1924 editors, and seems reasonable.
384 *Tiunnail* 1839, 1841 *Siunnailt*
Mòraig seo 1751 *Móraigs'*, which might be interpreted as *Mòraig-sa*, as in 1841.

386 *shlad* Gillies *shlaid*.
390 *chonnairc* The 1751 form, an older one, is retained, though *u* is needed for rhyme. 1839 to 1924 *chunnaic*. The line translates 'You, of all I have seen of your kind'.
393–4 'I cannot find enough patience to stay away from you for a minute'.
399 *Cho dearg* 1751 *Choimhdearg*.
400 *bileag* usually means a little leaf; here 'petal'.
403 *shaighdean* 1751 *shoidion*.
406 *chunnaic* 1751 *chonnaig*. See note on 1. 390. The modern form, however, suits the rhyme here.
407 *Cho trom* 1751 *Chomhtrom*.
410 *chruinnidh* This is the 1751 form, presumably a natural dative feminine in the poet's usage.
412 *chunnaic* 1751 *chonnaig*. See 1. 406*n*.
417 *reulagan* 1751 *reullagan*, 1874 ff. *reultagan*
420 *ciabh-òrbhuidh* The syntax requires a compound adjective here.
423–4 Although 1751 has *Phcnix* with a capital, the reference here is to the many-coloured bird. 1874 has *phoenix*. Morag's coat i.e. skin has a similar gleam.
428 *ainnis* In the older language *aindeis* can mean both 'awkward, ungainly' and 'poor, wretched'. The pairing here with *fòtas* 'blemish' suggests the former of these senses.
430 *Sa'* 1751 *'S an*
431 *B'i – – –* She was like an angel (lit. the appearance of an angel).
437 *Tha 'n* 1751 *Tha* All edd. before 1924 present 11. 437-8 as one line. 1924 makes the break after *làn*.
448 *Mòraig seo* 1751 *Móraigs'*.
451 *Leagh i 'n crìdh* 1751 *Leugh i crí*, 1802 and MS Gen 9 *Leugh an crí*.
It is unusual to find these three sources differing. 1839 *Leagh an crī*.
452 *òrrachan* It is difficult to be sure of the intended sense here. One possibility is *òrraichean* 'ornaments', but perhaps more likely is *òrthachan* pl. of *ortha/òrtha* 'charm, enchantment'.
454 *their* 1751 *a h eir*, MS Gen 9 *a d' eir*, 1802 *a h deir*.
456 *fhìdeig* The 'whistle' here is presumably Morag's voice.
457 *leith'd* 1751 *lei't leithid* needs to be reduced to a monosyllable for rhythmical purposes.
459–60 *Coimh-* 1839 *Cho*
Coimh-teiridneach teiridneach is probably a variant of *eiridneach*, from *eiridinn* 'healing etc.'
464 *cheathrannan am* 1751 *cherenion am*, 1874 to 1924 *cheathramhnan de m'*. The line may be translated 'and my quarters/thighs causing me distress' i.e. in a state of physical collapse.
455 *Seile siud* 'Loch Shiel over there'. This confirms the location of the poet at the time of writing this poem.
468 *ata 'nam* 1751 *a 't' ann am*, 1839 *thann*.
469 *leadanach* 1751 *leudanach*. The end-rhyming words in 11. 469-76 are mostly spelt with *eu*, probably indicating the poet's pronunciation, although some internal rhymes are spelt with *ea* e.g. *fheadain*, *freagra*. There is probably a pun intended in *leadanach* which means both 'melodious' and 'having long locks of hair'.
473 *socair* 1751 *sochdair*. So too 1. 498. 1841 *sochrach*.
475 *an oirfeid* 1841 *òr-fhead*, 1874 to 1924 edit to *an t-oirfeid*, making the word masculine. Dinneen gives it as a feminine noun in Irish.
476 'to which the great rocks provide a base'.
477 *bailleagach* 1839, 1841 *baill-eughach*.
478 *sgailleagach* 1839 *sgal-eugach*, 1841 *sgal-eughach*.
479 *binn-phort* 1751, MS Gen 9 *bionn-phort*.

480 *Rèidh* 1751 *Ré*, 1839 *Ri*
mion-dhìonach mion 'detailed, careful' + *dìonach* 'not allowing air to enter or escape at random'. This is part of the poet's detailed description of playing the pipes. He has virtually forgotten, for the moment, that he is writing about Morag.
482 *caismeachdach* 1751 *caismichdeach*, 1839 *caiseamachd*
483 *chruinn-lùth* 1751 *chruinnlúath*, 1839 *chrunnlùath*, 1841 to 1924 *chrùnluath*. This line seems a syllable short, unless the poet used a svarabhakti syllable in the middle of the word.
484 *F'a cliath-lùth* 1751 *Fa clialú*, MS Gen 9 *Na clialū*. The exact significance of *F'a* lit. 'under its/her', is uncertain, but the poet may here be returning to a reference to Morag.
486 *bheachdaich guamag* Presumably the poet (i.e. his face: *gnùis*) is himself the subject of the verb: 'when I observed/watched the neat girl'.
487 *ioraltaich* MS Gen 9 *ioroltrich*. This MS misses the following two lines, presumably a copying fault.
490 This line is missed out in 1874 and 1892, but re-appears in 1924.
491–2 '(a music) than which we would not seek a more stirring one when roused by the prospect of battle'.
492 *Air mhireid* 1751, 1802, MS Gen 9, 1841 *Ar mhirid*, 1874 to 1924 *Air mhiread*. High. Soc. Dict. has *miread* as a feminine noun, quoting this instance from the 1802 ed.
493 *'m buille meòir* 1874 to 1924 *bhuille-mheòir*. *buille* is a fem. noun in modern Gaelic; it occurs as both masc. and fem. in early Gaelic. Is this a genuine survival of the masc. version?
493 *lomarra* Perhaps this can be taken as connected with *lomadh* 'fleecing', in the sense of the finger-strokes on the chanter being closely defined.
494 *uaibhrich* 1751, 1839 *uairich*
495 *cromaidhean* 1839 *cromainin*
496 *a' chrainn* The *crann* here is the pipe chanter.
497 *slaoidmheoirich* 1874 to 1924 *slaodmhiaraich*
504 *glòr shìobhalta* civilized talk. The 1924 editors' translation of 11. 503-4 hits the mark: 'and cultivate with zest conviviality'.
512 *mìogchuiseach* This sometimes has the sense of 'flirtatious', as well as 'genial', and the former sense may link more naturally with the following lines, though the sense of 'genial' may be more in accord with this passage as a whole.
514 *Shnìomhanach* 1874 to 1924 change to *Snìomhanach*, but the poet's intention was probably to begin a fresh description of the maiden, so that the lenition goes with that feminine noun rather than with the gen. pl. *ciabh*.
517 The heading of this section is given as *An crúnluath*, in contrast to an earlier reference in 1. 483 to *cruinn-luath*.
519 *stoipt a dh' eileabor* 1751 *stoipte a dh' elebor*, 1874 to 1924 *stopt' le hellebore*. hellebore, ultimately from Greek *helleborus*, applied to plants that were supposed to cure madness. The 1751 Glossary gives '*Elebor*, a kind of snuff that occasions much sneesing'.
519–20 'My nose is stuffed with hellebore, aflame with the fire of lasciviousness'.
522 *teileascop* 1751 *telescop*
523 *beinnidh* This is 1751's form, and it is retained rather than the later, and more standard, *beinne*.
524 *gura* 1751 *gur a*, 1839 to 1924 *gur h-e*
frìd This can mean various tiny insects, or 'wart' or 'pigmy'. Perhaps the latter senses are intended here.
525 *chèidse* 1751, 1802 *chédsi* (with the old form of *s* which resembles *f*), MS Gen 9 *ċeidsi* (with modern *s*), Gillies *chéudfa*, 1839, 1841, 1874 *chéudfaidh*, 1924 *cheudfadh*.

525–6 'My corporal cage disappeared/went away, hurtfully, in a dream'.
527–8 *thorchairt* Gillies *tha chairt* 'When I thought good fortune was happening to me, as I dozed on my pillow'.
530 *faileis* 1751 *failéus*, 1839 *aon failēas*
531 *bearraidich* 1751 etc. *bearraideach*
532 *gu seachd uairean* 'till seven o'clock'
533 These sixteen lines appear in 1751, 1802, MS Gen 9, 1839 and 1841; they are ignored in 1874 and 1892, and the 1924 editors omit them, adding the comment 'In the Bard's 1st Edition 16 lines appeared which are scarcely publishable'. At this late stage in the twentieth century we may feel freer to let the Bard have his say.
534 *Cluanag* The Deceitful Woman (used playfully here).
537 *thùir* 1751 etc. *thúr*. This verbal form seems to be related, unusually, to the noun *tùr*, and to mean 'sense'. 'When she sensed that I had weakened'.
538 *rag-chur* 1751, 1802, 1841 *rag chuir*, MS Gen 9 *pog ċuir*. The MS Gen 9 emendation is ill-judged, since the next lines make it clear that it was the dream rather than a kiss that produced the desired effect. The line translates 'and that I needed resolutely to stiffen it'.
540 *luaidhe* 1751 etc. *luaidh'*, Gillies *luaidh'ibh*. 11. 539-40 translate 'she produced a magical sleep for me that turned my lead into absolutely hard steel'.
541 *finealta* 1839 *ionolta*, 1841 *innealta*
544 'not to pay her a trifling duty'.
547 This line is missing from MS Gen 9.
548 *uaithe* 1751 *uaith'*. The 1839, 1841 reading *uaipe* emphasises the feminine form, justifiably perhaps.

MOLADH AN UGHDAIR DON T-SEANN CHÀNAIN GHÀIDHLIG

Sources and Editions:

1751	1-7
1802	13-19
1834-39	1-5
1874, 1892	1-5
1918, 1959	97–102
1924	2-8

The 1751 text is basic. Later editions provide small clarifications in the main.

It seems likely that this poem was written after the publication of the Rev. David Malcolm's letters etc. in 1738. The poet visited Edinburgh about that time, and may have become acquainted with Malcolm's work then. Mac Mhaighstir Alasdair had been involved for some time in preparing his Gaelic Vocabulary which finally appeared in 1741, so his interest in language had that dimension in addition to his verse writings. Genuine pride in the ancient history of Gaelic in Scotland is combined here with claims of antiquity and pre-eminence which were very probably made tongue-in-cheek, and partly in response to Malcolm's exaggerated claims on behalf of Gaelic.

The paragraph arrangement of the 1751 edition is followed here, though each paragraph consists of a variable number of quatrains. The paragraphs are carefully and logically planned, beginning with a short philosophical discussion of the place language has in the world, and which has been determined by God. The second paragraph indulges at first in the myth of Gaelic supremacy from prehistorical, indeed antedeluvian times, moving then to a more historical summary of its Scottish history. The third paragraph reverts to the ancient history and supposed supremacy of Gaelic, exalting it above Latin, Greek and French. The fourth and longest paragraph discusses the uses made of Gaelic by poets and satirists, battle-inciters and lawyers, and goes on to describe and praise its virtues of rhythm, sound, depth, complexity, sweetness etc., ending with a reference to the mythical and legendary ancestors of the Gaels, and what may be a gently mocking reference to the Rev. Malcolm.

We would not be justified in regarding many of the statements in this poem as representing Mac Mhaighstir Alasdair's beliefs, except in the case of Paragraph 4's descriptions. It is more a mixture of propaganda and playfulness. It is also in the tradition of the Rev. John Maclean's address to Edward Lhuyd, printed in the Preface to Lhuyd's *Archaeologia Britannica* in 1707. This includes a reference to Gaidheal Glas (see 1. 676 of Mac Mhaighstir Alasdair's poem) and the line *'S i labhair Pádraic 'n Inse Fáil na Ríogh* is echoed in 11. 605-6 here.

Moladh an ùghdair don t-seann chànain Ghàidhlig

Gur h-i as crìoch àraid
Do gach cainnt fon ghrèin
Gu ar smuainti fhàsmhor
A phàirteachadh ri chèil',
Ar n-inntinnean a rùsgadh
Agus rùn ar crìdh
(Le 'r gnìomh, is le 'r giùlan)
Sùrd chur air ar dìth,
'S gu laoigh ar beòil
A dh' ìobradh 'Dhia nan dùl;
'S i a h-àrd chrìoch mhòr
Gu bhith toirt dò-san cliù.
'S e 'n duine fèin
'S aon chreutair rèasant' ann:
Gun tug toil Dè dha
Gibht le bheul bhith cainnt;
Gun chùm e seo
On uile bhrùid gu lèir –
O, 'ghibht mhòr phrìseil-s'
Dheilbh 'na ìomhaigh fèin!
Nam beirte balbh e
'S a theanga marbh 'na cheann,
B' i 'n iargain shearbh i,
B' fheàrr bhith marbh na ann.

'S ge h-ioma cànain
O linn Bhàbeil fhuair
A' sliochd sin Adhaimh
'S i Ghàidhlig a thug buaidh.
Don labhradh dhàicheil –
An t-urram àrd gun tuairms',
Gun mheang, gun fhàillinn
As urra càch a luaidh –
Bha a' Ghàidhlig ullamh,
'Na glòr fìor ghuineach, cruaidh,
Air feadh a' chruinne
Mun d' thuilich an Tuil-ruadh.
Mhair i fòs
'S cha teid a' ghlòir air chall
Dh' aindeoin gò
Is mì-rùin mhòir nan Gall.
'S i labhair Alba
'S galla-bhodaiche fèin,

Ar flaith, ar prionnsaidh',
'S ar diùcanna gun èis.
An taigh-comhairl' an rìgh,
Nuair shuidheadh air binn a' chùirt,
'S i 'Ghàidhlig lìomhtha
Dh' fhuasgladh snaoim gach cùis.
'S i labhair Calum
Allail a' chinn mhòir,
Gach mith is maith
Bha 'n Alba, beag is mòr.

'S i labhair Gaill is Gaidheil,
Neo-chlèirich is clèir,
Gach fear is bean
A ghluaiseadh teanga am beul,
'S i labhair Adhamh
Ann a phàrras fèin
'S bu shiùbhlach Gàidhlig
O bheul àlainn Eubh.
Och, tha 'bhuil ann!
'S uireasach, gann, fo dhìth
Glòr gach teanga
A labhras cainnt seach ì.
Tha Laideann coimhliont,
Torrach, teann nas leòr,
Ach 's sgalag thràilleil
I don Ghàidhlig chòir.
San Athen mhòir
Bha 'Ghreugais còrr 'na tìm,
Ach b' ion di h-òrdag
Chur fo h-òirchrios grinn.
'S ge mìn, slìom, bòidheach,
Cùirteil, rò-bhog, lìomhth'
An Fhraingis lòghmhor
Am pailis mòr gach Rìgh,
Ma thagras càch oirr'
Pàirt d' an ainbhfheich fèin
'S ro bheag a dh' fhàgas
Iad do dh' àgh 'na crè.

'S i 'n aon chànain
Am beul nam bàrd 's nan èisg
As feàrr gu càineadh
O linn Bhàbeil fèin.
'S i 's feàrr gu moladh,

'S as torrannaiche gleus,
Gu rann no laoidh,
A tharraing gaoth roimh bheul.
'S i 's feàrr gu comhairl'
'S gu gnothach chur gu feum
Na aon teang' Eòrpach,
Dh' aimhdheoin bòsd nan Greug.
'S i 's feàrr gu rosg
'S air chosaibh a chur duain,
'S ri cruaidh uchd cosgair
Bhrosnachadh an t-sluaigh.
Mu choinne bàir
'S i 's tàbhachdaich bheir buaidh
Gu toirt a bhàis
Don eucoir dhàicheil chruaidh.
Cainnt làidir, ruithteach
As neo-liotach fuaim,
'S i seaghail, sliochdmhor,
Briosg-ghlòrach, mall, luath.
Chan fheum i iasad
'S cha mhò dh' iarras uath';
O! an t-sean mhàthair chiatach,
Làn do chiadaibh buaidh!
Tha i fèin daonnan
Saidhbhir, maoineach, slàn,
A taighean-taisge
Dh' fhoclaibh gasda làn.
A' chànain sgapach,
Thapaidh, bhlasda, ghrinn
Thig le tartar
Neartmhor á 'beul-cinn.
An labhairt shìolmhor,
Lìonmhor, 's mìlteach buaidh,
Shultmhor, bhrìoghmhor,
Fhìorghlan, chaoidh nach truaill.
B' i 'n teanga mhilis,
Bhinn-fhoclach san dàn,
Gu spreigeil, tioram,
Ioraltach, 's i làn.
A' chànain cheòlmhor,
Shòghmhor, 's glòrmhor blas
A labhair mòr-shliochd
Scòta 's Ghaidheil Ghlais,
'S air-rèir MhicComb,
An t-ùghdar mòr ri luaidh!,

'S i 's freumhach òir
'S ciad ghràmair glòir gach sluaigh.

NOTES

The title in 1751 ends --- *chánoin Ghailic.* This leaves no doubt as to the author's intention, although the 1874 to 1924 editions substitute *Ghaidhealaich.*

549 *àraid* 1924 *àraidh*
As Watson pointed out (*Bàrdachd Ghàidhlig*, 287) the opening is reminiscent of the first question in the Shorter Catechism: *ciod is crìoch àraidh do'n duine?*

550 *fon* 1751 *fa 'n*

551 *Gu ar smuainti* 1751 *Go 'r smuainti.* The poet's usage shows a closeness to Irish usage here cf. Early Modern forms such as *smuaintighthe* 'thoughts', *cridhe lán do smuaintighibh, Dánta Grádha*, 52, 1.

553–6 The syntax and thought sequence in these lines is complicated. He is saying here that the purpose of language is to lay bare/reveal our minds (1. 553), and to reveal the purpose of our hearts (1. 554), (which is) to bestir ourselves to supply what we lack (1. 556), by means of our action and our conduct (1. 555). This clarification was first supplied by Watson in his 1918 edition.

557 *laoigh ar beòil* 'the calves of our lips' are offered as a sacrifice to the Lord; this sacrifice can be in the form of poems or lays (*laoidh* a lay) – the poet was partial to punning. Angus Matheson (1951) draws attention to the Biblical origin of this phrase (*Hosea*, XIV, 2)

559 *a h-àrd* 1751 *h ard*

560 *Gu bhith* 1751, 1839 *Go bi*, 1874, 1924 *A bhi*
dò-san 1751 *dósan*, 1924 *dhàsan* (which ignores the internal rhyme required).

564 *cainnt* Evidently used as a verb/verbal noun here.

569 *beirte* 1874, 1892, 1924 *bheirteadh*

572 *na* 1751 *no*

574 *fhuair* 1751 *fuair*

575 *Adhaimh* 1751 *Adhamh*

575–84 The sense runs from *Don labhradh* to *Bha a' Ghàidhlig ullamh* and so to the end of 1. 584, with 11. 578-80 an interjection: 'For dignified discourse – high praise, without a doubt, with no blemish or failing that others can mention – Gaelic was ready/complete, a speech truly sharp and hard (?), throughout the world before the Red/Mighty Flood flooded'. *ruadh* has an older sense of 'strong/mighty' as well as 'red/ruddy'.

586 *a' ghlòir* 1751 *a ghloir.* All later editions *a glòir.* If the reference is to 'its (i.e. Gaelic's) sound/glory', the later editors are justified, but probably the poet means 'the sound/glory': he is not very consistent in using apostrophes.

588 *mì-rùin mhòir* 1751 *mio-rúin mhór*, 1874, 1892, 1924 *mi-rùn mòr.* The inflexion of *rùn* and lenition of *m* in 1751 show that the poet intended to show the genitive after *dh' aindeoin*, or just possibly the plural.

590 *galla-bhodaiche* 1874, 1892, 1924 *Gall-bhodacha*, 1918 *Is gallbhodaich.* The poet's apparent choice of plural is retained. The sense is 'lowland old men/Lowlanders'.

591 *prionnsaidh'* 1751 *priunnsai.* In older Gaelic, various forms of the plural of this word were used e.g. *prinnsaighi, prionnsaidhe, prionnsadha.*

595 *lìomhtha* 1751, 1874, 1892 *líobha*, 1924 *lìobhaidh*

596 *snaoim* 1751 *snuim.* This perhaps indicates a Hebridean rather than Mainland pronunciation.

597–8 *Calum --- mhòir* i.e. Malcolm Canmore, King of Scots, 1058-93.

602 *Neo-chlèirich* 1751 *Neimhchleirich*

606 *a phàrras* 1751 *a phárrais.* Presumably the sense is '(in) his (own) Paradise'.

Pàrras is a masculine noun, so one would not expect the dative ending *-ais*, unless it had become the nominative form in the poet's dialect. 1874, 1892, 1924 have *am Pàrras*, 'in Paradise.'

605–8 These lines, asserting that Gaelic was the language of the Garden of Eden, need not be taken at face value. The poet could speak with tongue in cheek. So too in ll. 613 ff., where Latin, Greek and French are given lower ratings than Gaelic.

615 *'s sgalag* 1751 *sgalog*

617 *Athen* The normal Gaelic for Athens is *An Aithne*, but the poet evidently made a different choice.

618 The line translates 'Greek was outstanding in its time'.

619–20 'it was fitting for it to place its thumb under its neat golden girdle' i.e. Greek had to bow the knee to Gaelic.

622 *lìomhth'* 1751 *líobh'*. See 1. 595 for another instance of this word.

626 *ainbhfheich feich* is an older plural of *fiach* 'debt', (modern *fiachan*). Though the poet refers here to 'others' being owed a debt by French, he is presumably referring mainly to Latin.

630 *èisg* 1751 *éisc* 'satirist'. Mac Mhaighstir Alasdair was well qualified to appreciate Gaelic's potential for satiric verse.

633–6 'It is the best for praising, and the one that has the most resounding potential, (the best) for stanza or lay, that wind (i.e. air stream/breath) has ever drawn through mouth'.

636 *tharraing* 1751 *tharraig*, no doubt indicating pronunciation, as in many modern dialects.

roimh 1751 *roi'*, probably to be taken as a variant of *throimh* 'through'.

640 *Dh' aimhdheòin* This form is common in older Gaelic, though replaced now by *dh' aindeoin*. Malcolm's Glossary uses this form.

641 *rosg* The common modern sense is 'prose', but here it is more probably used in an older sense, as in *rosg-catha*, a short poem inciting to battle.

642 'to set up a poem'.

644 *Bhrosnachadh* 1751 *Phrosnachadh*

645 *choinne* Modern form *choinneamh*.

bàir genitive of *bàr* i.e. legal bar.

648 *dhàicheil* The common modern sense is 'pleasant, handsome', but the senses of 'haughty, bold' also occur, and are more appropriate here, in reference to a criminal being sentenced to death.

649 *ruithteach* 1751 *rithteach*

651 *sliochdmhor* 1751 *sliochdor*

649–52 'A strong, flowing speech, its sounds not lispy, full of meaning, prolific, with swiftly-moving utterance, deliberate, fast-moving'. 1. 652 in particular mirrors in its language movement, the characteristics described.

652 *briosg-ghlòrach* 1751 Glossary gives 'having a prattling, chattering disposition'.

653–4 'It does not need to borrow, nor does it ask from them'. The 'them' presumably refers to other languages. 1. 654 seems redundant, and perhaps exists for metrical convenience. The sentiment in these lines is chauvinistic: Gaelic of course has borrowed e.g. from Latin, Norse, French and English, and the poet was very ready to use modern borrowings in his poems.

656 *chiadaibh* 1751 *chiadamh*

'full of hundreds of (good) qualities'.

661 *sgapach* 'scattering' i.e. in the sense of scattering richness or bounty.

663–4 'that comes with strong clamour from its mouth', as though the language itself had a mouth like its speakers.

664–7 The series of words ending in *-mhor* 1751 spells in *-or*. There is evidence of conscious spelling reform in the 1751 edition.

666 *mìlteach* This can be taken as an adverb/adjective based on *mìle* 'thousand', meaning 'numerous'.

670 *Bhinn-fhoclach* 1751 *Bhionfhoclach*

672 *Ioraltach* 'inventive, intertwined'. Watson, Glossary of 1918 ed., following MacBain, suggests a derivation from *air* + *alt.*

676 This refers to the Gaels' legendary descent from Scota, Queen of Egypt, and Gaidheal Glas.

677–80 The reference is to the Rev. David Malcolm, minister of Duddingston (Edinburgh). He wrote on antiquarian topics, and proposed connections between Gaelic and Latin, Greek, the Darien Indians' speech, Chinese etc. His *An Essay on the Antiquities of Great Britain and Ireland* includes letters etc. written mostly between 1732 and 1738. He died in 1748. There is a hint of mockery in the poet's reference to him in 1. 678, and the poet's linguistic exaggerations may be in part a taking-off of Malcolm.

ORAN AN T-SAMHRAIDH

Sources and Editions:

a.	1751	Adv. MS 72.2.15, pp. 55-7
	1751	36-43
	MS Gen 9	25-30
	Eigg	200-205
	1802	48-55
	1839	20-25
	1874, 1892	19-24
	1924	20-26
	1993	22-4

In the instances of 'Oran an t-Samhraidh' and 'Oran a' Gheamhraidh', we have the complication and bonus of versions in Adv. MS 72.2.15. These were described by Ewen MacLachlan (in his analysis of the contents of MSS belonging to the Highland Society) as 'Rude Sketch of Macdonald's Summar/ Winter'. Comparison with the 1751 versions of the poems on Summer and Winter suggests strongly that they are earlier versions, by no means 'rude' but later polished and sharpened considerably. Although we must regard the 1751 version of 'Oran an t-Samhraidh' as the authoritative one, it seemed essential to reproduce all the significant variant readings from MS 72.2.25, as they cast a most valuable light on the poet's re-working of parts of the poem. We see various rhythmical and syntactical awkwardnesses removed (e.g. 11. 691-2), imagery sharpened, and in some instances a more logical sequence of ideas and references introduced. But in other instances, notably in the long descriptive runs with *-ach* epithets, there is little change. The final three stanzas, describing birds and bird-song, are not in MS 72.2.15, and this would suggest that they were a late addendum to the poem.

It is significant that Adv. MS 72.2.15 (MS LXV in the old nomenclature) also includes the Kintyre poem 'Moladh Chinntìre', as does one of the Turner MSS (for the latter text, see Cameron, *Reliquiae Celticae*, Vol. 2, 315 ff.). This poem has passages of very detailed nature description and recurrent instances of *-ach* runs, one or two of these closely paralleled in

Mac Mhaighstir Alasdair's work. It seems very likely that he was familiar with this poem, and that it was one of several diverse influences that helped to shape his poetry of natural description.

The MS Gen 9 version is basically a copy of the 1751 version, and there is an unusual degree of agreement between later versions, with occasional variants from 1802, 1874 ff., and some evidence that the 1924 editors had used the MS 72.2.15 version, or a related one, spasmodically.

Keith Norman Macdonald (1900), p. 30, says that 'Oran an t-Samhraidh' was composed at Glen Scribisdale, on the south side of Loch Suinart, in the parish of Morven, and John Mackenzie, in his introduction to the poet's work in *Sàr Obair*, also has this tradition, with the more specific detail: "He came there on a visit the last day of April; and rising early next morning, and viewing the picturesque scenes around, was powerfully impressed with the varied beauties of nature, displayed in such ample profusion".

The poem is a very carefully planned one. It begins with a close paraphrase of the first stanza of Allan Ramsay's song to the tune 'Through the Wood Laddie' (*Tea-Table Miscellany*, 1724). The metre of the Ramsay song is closely followed, but after the first stanza no further use is made of the content of Ramsay's song. In that first stanza the chanter is substituted for Ramsay's lute, and this imagery is extensively developed later. Mac Mhaighstir Alasdair then develops a detailed description of the approach and burgeoning of summer, as illustrated by the development and movement and sound of plants, flowers, trees, animals, birds and their interactions. The human species is not given a specific place in this description, but the human reactions to nature are what give the description life and depth. The more mobile actors in this pageant, the birds, impinge on the senses at various points in the poem, helping to unify it.

At the first impression it might be thought that the stanzas consisting almost entirely of a series of descriptive adjectives would give a sense of overkill, but the imaginative montage, and the often unexpected creations and juxtaposition of words grip the reader's interest.

It is likely also that Mac Mhaighstir Alasdair knew Gavin Douglas's *Aeneados*, which had appeared in Ruddiman's new edition in 1710, and his planetary references may have been triggered by Douglas's Prologues, as some of Douglas's own planetary references probably owe something to Henryson's *Testament of Cresseid*.

For further detailed analysis, see my paper 'Mac Mhaighstir Alasdair's Nature Poetry and its Sources', in *Gaelic and Scots in Harmony*.

Oran an t-Samhraidh

Air fonn, 'Through the wood laddie'

An dèis dhomh dùsgadh san mhaidean
'S an dealt air a' choill,
Ann am maidean ro shoilleir,
Ann a lagan beag doilleir,
Gun cualas a feadan
Gu leadarra seinn,
'S mac-talla nan creagan
Da fhreagra bròn-bhinn.

Bidh am beithe deagh-bholtrach,
Urail, dosrach nan càrn,
Ri maoth-bhlàs driùchd Cèitein,
Mar ri caoin-dheàrrsadh grèine,
Brùchdadh barraich roi gheugaibh
San mhìos cheutach-sa Mhàigh:
Am mìos breac-laoghach buailteach,
Bainneach, buadhach gu dàir.

Bidh gach doire dlùth uaignidh
'S trusgan uaine umpa a' fàs;
Bidh an snodhach a' dìreadh
As gach freumhaich as ìsle
Roi na cuislinnean snìomhain
Gu mìodachadh blàth;
Cuach is smeòrach san fheasgar
Seinn a leadain 'nam bàrr.

Am mìos breac-uigheach braonach,
Creamhach maoth-ròsach àigh,
Chuireas sgeadas neo-thruaillidh
Air gach àite da dhuaichneachd,
A dh'fhògras sneachd le chuid fuachda
O gheur-ghruaim nam beann àrd
'S aig meud eagail roi Phèbus
Thèid sna speuraibh 'na smàl.

Am mìos lusanach mealach,
Feurach failleanach blàth,
'S e gu gucagach duilleach,
Luachrach dìtheanach lurach,
Beachach seilleanach dearcach,

Ciùthrach dealtach trom tlàth,
'S i mar chùirneanan daoimein:
'Bhratach bhoillsgeil air làr.

'S moch bhios Phèbus ag òradh
Ceap nam mòr-chruach 's nam beann,
'S bidh san uair sin le sòlas
Gach eun bionnfhoclach bòidheach
Ceumadh mear-bhuillean ceòlar
Feadh phreas, ògan is ghleann:
A' choireal chùirteach gun sgreadan
Aig pòr as beadarrach greann.

'S an àm tighinn don fheasgar,
Coi-fhreasgradh aon àm,
Nì iad co-sheirm shèimh fhallain,
Gu beilleach bionnghobach allail,
A' seinn gu lùth-chleasach daingeann
Am measg ùr-mheangain nan crann,
'S iad fèin a' beiceil gu foirmeil
Le toirm nan òrgan gun mheang.

Bidh gach creutair da laigid
Dol le suigeart don choill,
Bidh an dreathan gu balcant,
Foirmeil, talcarra, bagant,
Sìor chur fàilt air a' mhaidean
Le rifeid mhaisich bhuig bhinn,
Agus Robin da bheusadh
Air a' ghèig os a chinn.

Gur glan gaill-fheadan Richard
A' seinn nan cuislinnean grinn
Am bàrr nam bilichean blàthor
'S an dos nan lom-dharag àrda
Bhiodh sna glacagan fàsaich
As cùbhraidh fàileadh na fìon,
Le d' phuirt thrileanta shiùbhlach
Phronnor lùthor le dìon.

Siud na puirt as glan gearradh,
'S as ro-ealanta roinn,
Chuireadh m' inntinn gu beadradh,
Cliath-lùth t'fheadain mun eadradh,
'N àm don chrodh bhith da leigeadh

An innis bheitir san choill,
'S tu 'd lèig air baideal ri cianthar
An grianan aonchasach croinn.

Bidh bradan seang-mhear nam fìoruisg
Gu brisg, slinn-leumnach, luath,
'Na bhuidhne tàrr-ghealach lannach,
Gu h-iteach, dearg-bhallach, earrach,
Le shoillsean airgid da earradh
'S mion-bhreac lainnireach tuar,
'S e fèin gu crom-ghobach ullamh
Ceapadh chuileag le cluain.

A' Bhealltainn bhog-bhailceach ghrianach,
Lònach, lianach mo ghràidh,
Bhainneach, fhinn-mhèagach, uachdrach,
Omhnach, loinideach, chuachach,
Ghruthach, shlamanach, mhiosrach,
Mhiodrach, mhiosganach, làn,
Uanach, mheannanach, mhaoineach,
Bhocach, mhaoiseach, làn àil.

O 's fìor èibhinn ra chluinntinn
Fann-gheum laoigh anns a' chrò,
Gu h-ùrail, mion-bhallach, àlainn
Druimfhionn, geàrr-fhionnach, fàilidh,
Ceannfhionn, colgrasgach, cluaisdearg,
Tàrr-gheal, guaineiseach, òg,
Gu mogach, bogladhrach, fàsor,
'S e leum ri bàirich nam bò.

A shòbhrach gheal-bhuidh nam bruachag
Gur fanna-gheal snuadhor do ghnùis
Chinneas badanach cluasach,
Maoth-mhìn, baganta, luaineach,
Gur tu ròs as feàrr cruadal
A nì gluasad á h-ùir:
Bidh tu 't èideadh as t-earrach
'S càch ri falach an sùl.

'S cùbhraidh fàileadh do mhuineil
A chrios-Choin-Chulainn nan càrn,
Nad chruinn bhabaidean rìomhach,
Loinneach, fhad-luirgneach, sgìomhach,
Nad thuim ghiobagach dhreach-mhìn,

Bhàrr-bhuidh', chasarlach, àrd,
Timcheall thulmanan diamhair
Mam bi 'm biadh-eunain a' fàs.

'S gum bi froidhneasan boillsgeil
A thilgeas foidhneul nas leòr
Air gach lùbhghort, do neòinein
'S do bharraibh shaimirean lòghor,
Mar sin is leasachan soilleir
Do dh'fheada-coille nan còs
Timcheall bhoganan loinneil
As tric an eilid dan còir.

Nis trèigidh coileach a' ghucag
'S caitean brucach nan craobh,
'S thèid gu mullach nan sliabhchnoc,
Le chirc gheàrr-ghobaich riabhaich,
'S bidh da suirghe gu cùirteil
Am pillibh cùlghorma fraoich,
'S ise freagradh le tùchan:
"Pi-hu-hù, tha thu faoin."

A choilich chraobhaich nan geàrr-sgiath
'S na falluinne duibh,
Tha dubh is geal air am miosgadh
Gu ro-òirdheirc nad itich;
Muineal lainnireach, sgibidh,
Uaine, slios-mhìn, 's tric crom,
Gob nam pongannan milis
Nach faict' a' sileadh nan ronn.

Siud an turraraich ghlan loinneil
As àird' coilleag air tom,
'S iad ri burraras sèimh ceutach
Ann am feasgar bog Cèitein,
Am bannal geal-sgiortach uchd-ruadh,
Mala ruiteach, chaol, chrom,
'S iad gu h-uchd-àrdach earra-gheal,
Grian-dheàrrsgnaidh, druim-dhonn.

NOTES

1751 gives the air as 'Through the wood ladie', and Eigg quotes the same air, with the spelling *Laddie*. This air, set to the Allan Ramsay words referred to in the introduction to this edition, occurs in William Thomson's *Orpheus Caledonius*. It may be noted that in the 1725 edition of Thomson, Item 4, this is given as 'Thro' the Wood Laddie', and in the 1733 edition, p. 7, as 'Throw the wood Laddie'. John Purser, in his *Scotland's Music*, 179, refers to how Ramsay and Thomson kept pirating each other's publications.

681 *dèis* 1751, MS Gen 9 and Eigg all have *deis*. MS 72.2.15 has *Moch s me geirigh*, and 1924 has *Moch 's mi 'g éiridh*. The form *dèis* comes from Old Gaelic *éis* cf. *tar éis* 'after'. *an éis* › *an déis*.
san mhaidean 1751, Eigg *'s an mhaidin*, MS Gen 9 *'s a mhaidin*. The two forms *matan* and *maiten* co-exist in Older Gaelic (both deriving from Latin *matutina*). *Madainn* became the commoner form in Sc. Gaelic, but Mac Mhaighstir Alasdair seems to have preferred the form *maidin/maidean* (see also 11. 683, 741). MS 72.2.15 reads *sa mhaduinn*.

683 *ro* MS 72.2.15 reads *Ghlan*

685 *a* MS 72.2.15; post-1874 *am*. Early forms may point to the poet's pronunciation.

686 *leadarra* MS Gen 9 *leadarrbha*

687 *mac-talla nan* MS 72.2.15 *mac hall' as na*

688 *bròn-bhinn* MS 72.2.15 *gu binn*. So also 1924. 1874 *bròn, bìnn*. It is best to take the 1751 reading as a compound adjective, 'sweet-sorrowful', echoing Allan Ramsay's 'dolorous lay'.

689 *am beithe* The poet evidently used *beithe* as a masculine noun.

690 *Urail* MS 72.2.15 *iúrach*

691–2 MS 72.2.15 *mar re maidin ghlan driuchd ceituin re gaoithean(?) sre grein ghil*. These lines have been tidied up considerably in the 1751 text.

693 *Brùchdadh* MS 72.2.15 *sprutadh*
roi 1874 ff. *troimh*

694 MS 72.2.15 reads *a mios ceitach a mhaidh*, and this is apparently followed in 1874 ff.

696 The early sources lenite *bainneach* and *buadhach*, though not the adjectives in 1. 695. MS 72.2.15 reads *bladhur buadhach*. The poet normally uses *mìos* as a masculine noun.

697–8 The MS 72.2.15 reading looks like a first shot, carefully revised later. It reads

Bidh gach doire blath buadhach
S livery uain' orrth a fas.

The borrowed *livery* is a syllable too long.
umpa 1874 ff. *uim'*. The early sources have *ump'*, clearly referring to 'woods' (*gach doire*).

702 *mìodachadh* The early sources mostly have *meadachadh*, but MS 72.2.15 reads *míodachidh*. The *ìo* vocalisation fits the rhyme-scheme, and reflects Mainland usage.

699–702 Comparison of the MS 72.2.15 reading with that of 1751 shows how an earlier version was tightened and polished. The MS reading is

Bidh an Snodhach a cinntinn
as na Cuisinibh Snimhairr
S as na freimhich is ísle hun míodachidh blathis.

701 The 1751 Glossary gives *'Cuislinne-sníomhain* the twisted winding veins of trees'.

703 *smeòrach* MS 72.2.15 *cuag*

704 *Seinn a* MS 72.2.15 *a gabhail*

705ff. MS Gen 9 has the first line of this stanza, but then proceeds to give 11. 2 to 8 of the following one, which also begins with *A mios*. MS 72.2.15 again has what looks like an early passage which gained markedly from revision. It goes

mios breca braonach chremhoil metoil sa chár
cuiridh scedachd nemh thruaillidh ar gach aite da duaithnachd

708 *da dhuaichneachd* 'however gloomy/ugly it was'.

709 *A dh' fhògras* MS 72.2.15 *dfhogart*

710 *O gheur-ghruaim* MS 72.2.15 *a mac ar bruaich*
712 *Thèid* MS 72.2.15 *a rioth*
714 *blàth* MS 72.2.15 *tlá.* 1924 *tlàth.* MS 72.2.15 also has *tla* in end-rhyme position in 1. 718, but 1924 substitutes *blàth* there.
718 *Ciùthrach* MS 72.2.15 *diurach*
719 *daoimein* 1751, Eigg *diamond*
720 MS 72.2.15 *a mbrat is boiscent ar blar*
brat 'covering, mantle' is a more literal usage than *bratach* 'banner'
721 MS 72.2.15 *moch do phoebus si gorach*
722 *Ceap* MS 72.2.15 *ar bharr*, 1924 *Air bàrr.*
ceap in the sense of 'block' etc. is an old Gaelic word, but it is the English/Scots 'cap/kep' that is borrowed here to refer to the mountain top.
723–6 MS 72.2.15 reads
gach en binnfhoclach neónach ann sa nuair sin le solas
le ncuid notichibh ceolmhor – – – –
Again, the description is sharpened in the 1751 reading.
724 *bionnfhoclach* MS 72.2.15 and 1802 ff. *binnfhoclach.* The 1751 etc. reading is perfectly credible, deriving from Older Gaelic *benn* 'point'. The birds are seen to be shaping and pointing their musical notes.
725 *ceumadh* stepping. The birds walk like pipers according to this description, and *strike* their notes.
727–8 MS 72.2.15 reads
a chuirt is curr(aidh?) om binn ledan por is betarrach caint,
which seems to lack rhythm and flow.
1924 follows the MS 72.2.15 reading for 1. 728, with *Aig pòr is beadarraich' cainnt.*
coireal 'choir, chorale; music' is usually masculine. There is another word, *corrghuil*, used of 'chirping', but perhaps the more formal sense of *coireal* fits the context better.
greann This word has a range of meanings. 'hue, appearance' or 'noise' seem the most appropriate here, and the sense of 'noise' goes better with *beadarrach* 'frolicksome'.
729–30 MS 72.2.15 reads
re linn techt don caomh fescar a ncomhfregra na nam
1924 also has – – – *nan am* in 1. 730.
730 *Coi-fhreasgradh* co-serving, contributing. Day and night both contribute, as it were, to twilight.
731 *co-sheirm* MS 72.2.15 *consorth*, presumably a borrowing of 'consort, consorting'.
732 *beilleach* MS 72.2.15 *minoil*, 1751-1802 *bailleach*, 1839 *billeach*, 1874 ff. *bileach.* The sense is probably 'with moving lips', cf. *beilleag* a lip.
bionnghobach with pointed beaks. See 1. 724*n*.
733 *A' seinn gu lùth-chleasach* MS 72.2.15 *sengach dluchasach* 'lithe, with feet close together'.
735 *beiceil* 1751, Eigg *beichdil*
foirmeil MS 72.2.15 *sporsoil* (which misses the internal rhyme)
736 *toirm nan organ* MS 72.2.15 *foirm an orgain*
The poet here seems to visualise the wood, still not heavily draped with leafage, as a mighty organ, the tree-trunks presumably recalling the organ pipes, and the birds producing their medley of music.
737–8 MS 72.2.15 reads
Co neil creituir da laigid nach dteid le suigart an c – – –
The edge of the MS is frayed here.
740 MS 72.2.15 reads
foirmoil bagant dos(?)gon – – –

One possible reading may be *dorgonta*. Armstrong in his Dictionary has the form *dorganta* 'discourteous, surly', and this may just possibly fit in the context.

742 MS 72.2.15 reads
minuilt maisech b(h?)og b(h?)inn.
The 1751 reading improves on this with its reference to the wren's *rifeid* 'reed, musical note'.

743 *bheusadh* One of many examples of Mac Mhaighstir Alasdair's readiness to adapt words to Gaelic naturally. The Robin Redbreast sings *bass* to the wren's *tenor*.

745 *gaill-fheadan* 1874 ff. *gall-fheadan*. MS 72.2.15 has an intriguing reading: *S glan do flanginat a lisart (lidhsart?)*.
Is *flanginat* a lenited borrowing of *planxty*, used of an Irish dance to harp music? I am unable to make sense of *lisart*. The 1751 reading is *richard*, which seems to refer to the wren referred to in 1. 739. Its trilling music has, to the poet, a more Lowland flavour, but one associated with piping or playing the flute.

747 *bilichean* MS 72.2.15 *medhlane* i.e. *meanglana(n)* 'branches'. *bile* is an old Gaelic word used of a large old tree.

748 *dos* MS 72.2.15 *barr*

749 *Bhiodh sna glacagan* MS 72.2.15 *tiomall glaca*, 1839 *Bhi'dh's* 1874 ff. *Bhios --*

751 *thrileanta* MS 72.2.15 *fhilenta*. The *i* of *trileanta* should perhaps be long, if the word is connected with Older Gaelic *trírech, trílech*.

752 *Phronnor* MS 72.2.15 *loma*. *pronnor* and *le dìon* continue the image of the pipes, with notes *struck* by the fingers, and with no air escaping from the note-hole.

753 *puirt* 1751, Eigg *pairt*, an error corrected in 1802.
as glan MS 72.2.15 *budh cruinn*

754 *as ro-ealanta* MS 72.2.15 *a bealant*

756 *Cliath-lùth* MS 72.2.15 *triall*

757 *don chrodh bhith da leigeadh* MS 72.2.15 *a chruidh bhith ga nliginn*

759 *baideal ri cianthar* MS 72.2.15 *badan re cional*
Neither *cianthar* nor *cianal* is well attested. These forms must be related to such words as *cian* and *cianalas*, and the probable sense is 'singing plaintively'.

760 MS 72.2.15 reads *gu grianach aoncasach cruinn*, apparently describing the bird rather than its perch. The 1751 reading is much more vivid and convincing.

761–2 MS 72.2.15 reads
a mbradan seimh bharr an fhioruisc na mbrec litleimnech luath.
This reads awkwardly even if we take *na mbrec* as meaning 'or the trout'. The sense of *litleimnech* is obscure unless *lialeimnech* 'leaping over stones' is intended. The 1751 reading, by contrast, is packed with sharp observation.

763–4 The order of *lannach* and *earrach* is reversed in MS 72.2.15.

765 *shoillsean* 1751 *shoislein* indicating the poet's pronunciation.

765–6 MS 72.2.15 reads
soillsi nairgid ar erradh mhionbrec lannanach tuar.
Again the 1751 reading is crisper, more controlled.

770 *lònach lòn* can mean either 'pool' or 'meadow', no doubt the latter here, tying in with *lianach*.

772 *loinideach loinid* means a churn-staff or whisk, and *loinid-omhain* referred to a small whisk used for producing froth from whey.

773 *shlamanach* MS 72.2.15 *shlampanach*

776 *Bhocach, mhaoiseach* MS 72.2.15 *a muc sa maolsec*. The 1751 revision adds a final touch to the *-(e)ach* sequence.

778 *anns a' chrò* MS 72.2.15 *on a cro*

783 *mogach* MS 72.2.15 *mongac*. The earlier reading is very clear, and perhaps

refers to the long hair of a Highland calf, although *mong* is more usually associated with a horse's mane. The form *mogach* of 1751 could possibly be a printer's error, but it also makes sense: 'shaggy etc.'

785 *shòbhrach* MS 72.2.15 *sheorach* may indicate the poet's pronunciation: forms with palatal and non-palatal *s-* still co-exist.

787–8 MS 72.2.15 reads

chinnis badanach dualach maothbhuidh casarlach cluanach.

1874 ff. have *maoth-gheal* in l. 788, and 1924 has *dualach* rather than *cluasach* in l. 787. The use of *cluasach* refers to the shape of the primrose leaves: one variety was known as *an t-sòbhrach chluasach*. The second line was radically reworked in the 1751 version.

789 *ròs* MS Gen 9 reads *pór*. This is one of its rare deviations from the 1751 text. In using *ròs* here, the poet is thinking of the English name *primrose*.

790 *gluasad á h-ùir* MS 72.2.15 *gluasacht an tus*

791 *as t-earrach* MS 72.2.15 *sa nerrach*

794 *A chrios Choin-Chulainn* Both MS 72.2.15 and MS Gen 9 read *C(h)oin,* with variant forms *cuilinn* and *chuluinn*, while 1751 has *chomhchuluinn*. 1839 *chrios-cho-culainn*. 1874 ff. prefer forms with *Chu-*.

795 *Nad chruinn bhabaidean* MS 72.2.15 *led puirt bhabanach*. The 1751 version fits the context of flower description better.

796 *Loinneach* 1751 has *Lóinneach*, but in its Glossary has '*Loinneach*, downy, pappous, spungy'.

797 MS 72.2.15 *na ngiobaga drechmhor*

799 *thulmanan* MS 72.2.15 *cuilltega*, 1751, Eigg, MS Gen 9 *thulmasan*. The *-s-* form seems an aberration, perhaps originally a misprint.

800 *biadh-eunain* 1802 *diothain*

801 MS 72.2.15 *Sud na frinsinnib boiscent*

frinsinnibh can probably be regarded as a variant of the dative plural of *fraoidhneas/froidhneas* 'fringe'.

802 *foidhneul* 1802 *soilse*. Armstrong's Dict. gives *foineul* the senses 'a little cloud; a gleam'.

803–4 MS 72.2.15 *leis gach mingart driucht neoinain s bar semar an lonain shaimirean* 1751 *shaimmirin*, 1802 ff. *sheamragan*

805 *leasachan* 1802 ff. *liosachan/liosaichean*

807 MS 72.2.15 *mad brollac bog altach loinnoil*

808 *dan còir* MS 72.2.15 *ad chóir*

809–32 These stanzas are not in MS 72.2.15

810 *caitean* The catkin or blossom of the osier is an early blossom.

814 *pillibh* 1839 *pillein*, 1874 ff. *pìllean*

820 *itich* The poet apparently used *iteach* as a feminine noun.

826 *àird'* 1924 *binne*

828 *bog* 1924 *ciùin*

829 *geal-sgiortach* 1924 *mogant*

832 *Grian – – – – – druim-* 1751, Eigg, 1802, 1839 *Ghrian – – –dhruim-*

ORAN A' GHEAMHRAIDH

Sources and Editions:

a.	1751	Adv. MS 72.2.15, pp. 38-40
	1751	43-50
	MS Gen 9	30-35
	Eigg	334-9
	1802	55-62
	1809	348-53
	1839	25-30
	1874, 1892	24-9
	1924	28-34
	1993	28-30

As in the case of 'Oran an t-Samhraidh', we have a shorter version of the song on Winter in Adv. MS 72.2.15, which must be earlier than the 1751 text. It consists of eight 8-line stanzas, presented in the MS as sixteen quatrains, as against the eighteen 8-line stanzas of 1751. Seven of these 8-line stanzas are variants of those in 1751, and clearly the 1751 text is a revision and development of the earlier text. Stanza 3 (i.e. quatrains 5 and 6) in MS 72.2.15 is not represented in 1751. We must take this as a conscious editorial decision on the part of the poet, and it is not included in our text, but it is reproduced, in edited form, here:

Tuitidh duilleach gorm-uaine nan craobh
Ann an caochanaibh faoin-lagaibh glac,
Crìonaidh beith' agus calltainn r'a taobh
Darach, fraoch agus caorthainn nam bad,
'S cha chinn air an talamh den phòr
Nach atharraich còmhdach is dreach,
Gu meataich 's gun caolaich an sprèidh
'S bidh gach creutair gu h-èislinneach lag.

He may have felt that this stanza was too diffuse in its references.

The 1751 version is much more comprehensive, and develops separate aspects of the theme with a well-planned attention to detail, including three stanzas which make brilliant use of the technique of compressed description using a series of *-(e)ach* epithets (see Thomson, D. S. 1990). The MS 72.2.15 version of 'Oran an t-Samhraidh', and some earlier poets, used this technique, so it is not simply a development of the 1740s, but the instances in 'Oran a' Gheamhraidh' are perhaps the most arresting ones in the poet's surviving work. Interestingly, there is a poem in praise of Kintyre in MS 72.2.15 which has similar runs. There is evidence in Mac Mhaighstir Alasdair's political poetry of continued revision and addition of stanzas after the date of the original poem, but the two instances in MS 72.2.15 give us the opportunity to see in detail how the poet tackled revision and extension. This can only increase respect for his craftsmanship.

The Winter poem handles the season very much as the antithesis of Summer, beginning and ending with strong Summer locations and references, and frequently contrasting the two seasons. This supports the view that the Summer poem came first, but does not necessarily give it artistic precedence. The Winter poem has more intense and imaginative passages than the Summer one. They make a fine contrasted pair.

There is a small crop of references that the poem shares with Gavin Douglas's Prologue to the Seventh book of his *Aeneados*: prominent references to Phoebus and Capricorn may be significant, and also Douglas's lines *In double garmont cled and wyly coyt,/Wyth mychty drink, and meytis confortive,/Agayne the storme wyntre for to strive* may have helped to spark off the marvellous passages (11. 929-52) about winter clothing and gluttony.

The probable influence of James Thomson's *Seasons* on Mac Mhaighstir Alasdair's seasonal poems has been discussed in various articles and books. The dates of poems make such influence very likely, as do the poet's Edinburgh contacts. Thomson's *Seasons* began to appear in 1726, and a greatly expanded edition was published in 1738, almost certainly a few years before Mac Mhaighstir Alasdair's poems on Summer and Winter. The eroticism of Thomson's poetry may also have had a share in stimulating some of his work e.g. 'Moladh Mòraig'. Campbell, J. L. (1958) suggests that a passage in Thomson's *Autumn* (11. 834-41) may have influenced our poet in 11. 865-72 in this edition, and John MacQueen (1982) discusses other specific instances of likely borrowing or influence. Thomson, D.S. (1990) discusses the sources of his Nature poetry generally.

Apart from the signal differences between the texts of MS 72.2.15 and 1751, there are not many variations between the sources. MS Gen 9, as elsewhere, is a very close copy of the 1751 version, and there are only occasional deviations between 1751 and 1809, with a few editorial sharpenings or prejudices appearing in 1839 ff.

ORAN A' GHEAMHRAIDH

Air fonn 'Tweed side'

Tharraing grian, rìgh nam planaid 's nan reul,
Gu *sign* Chancer Diciadain gu beachd
A riaghlas co-throm mun crìochnaich e thriall
Dà mhìos deug na bliadhna mu seach,
Ach gur h-e 'n dara Disathairn 'na dhèidh
A' ghrian-stad shamhraidh, aon-deug an là 's faid,
'S an sin tionnd'aidh e chùrsa gu sèimh
Gu seas-ghrian a' gheamhraidh gun stad.

'S o dh' imich e nis uainn mun cuairt
Gum bi fuachd oirnn gu 'm pill e air n-ais,
Bidh gach là dol an giorrad gu feum
'S gach oidhche d'a rèir dol am fad,
Struidhidh luibhean is coill agus feur,
'Na fàis-bheò ion-eugaidh iad ás,
Teichidh snodhach gu freumhaich nan crann,
Sùghaidh glaodhain an sùgh-bheath' a-steach.

Seacaidh geugan glan cùbhraidh nan crann
Bha san t-samhradh trom-stràichte le meas,
Gun toirleum an toradh gu làr,
Gu sgriosar am bàrr far gach lios,
Guilidh feadain is creachainn nam beann,
Sruthain chriostail nan gleann le trom sproc,
Caoidh na fuarain ri meacainn gun cluinn:
Deoch-thunta nam maoiseach 's nam boc.

Luighidh bròn air an talamh gu lèir,
Gun aognaich na slèibhti 's na cnoic,
Grad-dhubhaidh caoin-uachdar nam blàr,
Fàl-rùisgte, 's iad fàillinneach bochd.
Na h-eòin bhuchallach, bhreac-iteach, ghrinn
Sheinneadh baisgeanta, binn am bàrr dhos,
Gun tèid a' ghlas-ghoib air am beul,
Gun bhogha, gun teud 's iad 'nan tosd.

Sguiridh bùirdeasaich sgiathach nan speur
D'an ceileireadh grianach car treis,
Cha seinn iad a maidnean gu h-àrd
Na feasgarain chràbhach sa' phreas;
Cadal clùmhor gun dèan anns gach còs,
Gabhail fasgaidh am frògaibh nan creag,

'S iad ri ionndrain nan gathannan blàth
Bhiodh ri deàlradh o sgàileadh do theas.

Cuirear daltachan srian-bhuidh' nan ròs
Far mhìn-chìoch nan òr-dhìthein beag,
Sinean gucagach lilidh nan lòn,
Na flùran 's geal-neòinein nan eag
Cha deòghlar le beachainn nam bruach,
Cròdhaidh fuarachd car cuairt iad 'nan sgeap,
'S cha mhò chruinnicheas seillein a mhàl
'S thar gheal-ùr-ròs chrann gàrraidh cha streap.

Teàrnaidh bradan is sgadan 's gach iasg
O t' iargain gu fèath-ghrùnnd nan loch,
'S gu fan air an aigeann dubh-dhonn
Ann an doimhneachd nam fonn is nan slochd;
Na bric tharr-ghealach, eàrr-ghobhlach shlìom
Leumadh meardha ri usgraichean chop,
'Nan cairtealaibh geamhraidh gun tàmh
Meirbh, sàmhach o thàmh thu fon ghlob.

Chas is ghreannaich gach tulach 's gach tom
'S dòite lom chinn gach fireach 's gach glac,
Gun d' òdhraich na sìtheinean feòir
Bu lusanach, feòirneineach brat;
Thiormaich maghannan 's ruadhaich gach fonn,
Bhèic an fhairge 's ro thonn-ghreannach gart,
'S gun sgreitich an dùldachd gach long,
'S thèid an càbhlach 'nan longphort a-steach.

Neulaich pàircean is meadair gu bàs,
Thuit gach fàsach 's gach àite fo bhruid,
Chiaraich monaidh nan ìosal 's nan àrd,
Theirig dathannan gràsmhor gach luig;
Dh' fhalbh am fàileadh, am musga 's am fonn,
Dh' fhalbh a maise far lompair gach buig,
Chaidh an eunlaith gu caoidhearan truagh:
Uiseag, smeòrach is cuach agus druid.

A fhraoich bhadanaich, ghaganaich, ùir,
D'am b' ola 's d'am b' fhùdar a' mhil,
B' e 'bhlàth-ghrian do bhalet 's gach uair
Gu giollachd do ghruaige le sgil;
Sa' mhaidean iuchair nuair bhoillsgeadh a ghnùis
Air bhuidhinnean driùchdach nan dril,
B' fhìor chùbhraidh 's gum b' èibhinn an smùid
Seo dh' èireadh far chùirnein gach bil.

Gun theirig sùgh-talmhann nam bruach,
Dh' fhalbh an cnuasach le 'n trom-lùbadh slat,
Thuit an t-ubhall, an t-siris 's a' pheur
Chuireadh bogh' air a' ghèig anns a' bhad;
Dh' fhalbh am bainne on eallach air chùl
M'am bi leanaba ri ciùcharan bochd,
'S gu 'm pill a' ghrian gu *sign* Thaurus nam buadh
'S treun a bhuadhaicheas fuachd agus gort.

Thèid a' ghrian air a thuras mun cuairt
Do *thropic* Chapricorn ghruamaich gun stad
On tig fearthainn chruinn mheallanach luath
Bheir á mullach nan cruaidhtichean sad;
Thig tein'-adhair, thig torrann 'na dhèidh,
Thig gailleann, thig èighre nach lag,
'S cinnidh uisge 'na ghlainneachaibh cruaidh
'S 'na ghlas-leugaibh mìn fuar-licneach rag.

Am mìos nuarranta, garbh-fhrasach dorch,
Shneachdach, cholgarra, stoirm-shìonach bith;
Dhìlseach, dhall-churach, chathach, fhliuch, chruaidh,
Bhiorach, bhuagharra, 's tuath-ghaothach cith,
Dheigheach, liath-reothtach, ghlìb-shleamhainn, gharbh
Chuireas sgiobairean fairge 'nan ruith;
Fhlichneach, phunntainneach, ghuineach, gun tlàths:
Cuiridh t' anail gach càileachd air chrith.

Am mìos cnatanach, casadach, lom
A bhios trom air an t-sonn-bhrochan dubh,
Churraiceach, chasagach, lachdann is dhonn,
Bhrìsneach, stocainneach, chom-chochlach, thiugh,
Bhrògach, mheatagach, pheiteagach bhàn,
Imeacach, aranach, chàiseach, gun ghruth,
Le 'm miann bruthaiste, mairt-fheòil is càl,
'S ma bhios blàth nach dèan tàir air gnè stuth.

Am mìos brotagach, toiteanach, sòigh,
Ghionach, stròthail, fhìor gheòcail gu muic,
Liteach, làghanach, chabaisteach, chòrr,
Phòiteach, ròmasach, ròiceil gu sult;
'S an taobh a-muigh ged a thugh sinn ar com
Air an àilidh gheur-tholltach gun tlus
'S fheudar dram òl mar lìnigeadh clèibh
A ghrad-fhadas tein-èibhinn san uchd.

Bidh greann dhubh air cuid mhòr den Roinn Eòrp
O lagaich sgèimh òrdha do theas,
Do sholas bu shòlas ro mhòr,
Ar fradharc 's ar lòchran geal deas,
Ach nuair thig e gu Gemini rìs
'S a lainnir 's gach rìoghachd gun cuir,
Is buidh' soillsein nan coirein 's nam meall,
'S riochdail fiamh nan òr-pheall air a' mhuir.

'S thèid gach salmadair ball-mhaiseach ùr
An crannaig chùbhraidh chraobh dlùth-dhuilleach cas,
Le 'n seòl fèin a sheinn *hymns* 's a thoirt cliù
Chionn a' phlanaid-s' a chùrsadh air n-ais;
Gum bi còisir air leth anns gach gèig,
An dasgaibh èibhinn air rèidh-shlios nan slat,
A' toirt lag-ìobairt le 'n ceileir d' an Triath
Air chaol chorraibh an sgiath anns gach glaic.

Cha bhi creutair fo chupan nan speur
'Sin nach tionndaidh ri spèirid 's ri 'n dreach,
'S gun toir Phoebus le buadhan a bhlàiths
Anam-fàis doibh is càileachdan ceart,
'S nì iad aiseirigh choitcheann á 'n uaigh
Far na mhiotaich am fuachd iad a-steach,
'S their iad guileag – *doro hidola hann*,
Dh'fhalbh an geamhradh 's tha 'n samhradh air teachd.

NOTES

The air 'Tweed side' appears with its text in the 1725 edition (Item 16) and in the 1733 edition (p.32) of William Thomson's *Orpheus Caledonius*.

833 *grian* Adv. MS 72.2.15 *sol*. The poet may have felt on reflection that *sol* in the sense of 'sun' was becoming obscure, or might be confused with the Biblical *Sòl*.

834 *Gu sign Chancer* Adv. MS 72.2.15 *Gus an chonsort. Cancer*, one of the signs of the zodiac, used perhaps loosely here as going with the month of June.

835 *A riaghlas co-throm* Adv. MS 72.2.15 *Ciall no comhthrom*
co-throm 1751 to 1802 *comhthrom*, 1839 ff *cothrom*. The sense is 'equally heavily' i.e. giving equal weight to (the twelve months of the year).

838 Adv. MS 72.2.15 reads *ch(uaidh?) an samhradh na Deaghlach a mfat*, with *na Deaghlach* substituted for the phrase *an tegh ghlair* which has been stroked out.

839–40 MS 72.2.15 reads
Sin thiunndaighar cursa gu seimh
so theas gréine thig an gemhrad go stad.
The 1751 version makes much better sense.
This first stanza of the poem has been used, in a short incisive article by Walter J. Mays (*Scottish Gaelic Studies* VIII (1955), 53-5) to date the composition of the poem to 1743. In that year the sun would have entered the sign of Cancer on Wednesday 1st June, and the summer solstice would have been on Saturday

11th June (according to the Julian Calendar; 22nd June in the Gregorian one). The only other possible years would be 1726 and 1737, but these are less likely, as the solstice in these was almost certainly on a Friday.

841–2 MS 72.2.15 reads
Ma dhimich thu noir uainn ar chuart
bi fuacht oirn ma n till thu ar thais,
with *noir* presumably meaning 'to the east'.

843 *gach là* This is the reading of MS 72.2.15. 1751 and the other early sources all read *gach aon la*, which disturbs the rhythm.
gu MS 72.2.15 *chum*

845 *Struidhidh* MS 72.2.15 *Struighar*, 1751 etc. *Struighidh*, 1809 *Struithidh*, 1874 ff. *Struthaidh. struidh* has the sense of 'decay, go to waste'.

846 'As living growth they virtually die'. The MS 72.2.15 reading is *aon èagidh aon bége iad ar fad*, with *bége* in non-Gaelic script. I am not able to suggest a convincing explanation of this reading. 1809 ff. read *crion-euguidh/eugaidh*, not presumably appreciating the sense of *ion-* 'almost'.

847 MS 72.2.15 *Terrnidh snodhac gu freimhiċibh chraobh*

848 'Wood-piths will suck in their life-giving juice'. MS 72.2.15 reads *S thig claonadh na saoidhecht as tech.* Does this mean 'the tangled remnants of hay come in'? The 1751 reading ties in much better with the previous line.

849 *geugan* 1924 substitutes *duilleach*
cùbhraidh MS 72.2.15 *úre*

850 *bha* MS 72.2.15 *bios*
trom-stràichte 1751 *trom-stráicht*, 1874 ff. *trom-stràcte*

851 *toirleum* MS 72.2.15 *tuirling*

852 MS 72.2.15 *is scriosfar a bhlath far gach slios*

854 *sproc* 1809 ff. *sprochd*. The 1751 reading is more appropriate, rhyming with *boc.*

855 MS 72.2.15 has *A caoi na mfuaran re mecainn gu gcluinn* crossed out and the following written above: *guth na(?) fuarain re mechainn do chuim.* It is curious that 1751 reverts closely to the original reading

856 *Deoch-thunta* This is included in the 1751 Glossary, glossed 'decanted drink'. The MS 72.2.15 reading is *Deoch cumpa.*

857 *Luighidh* MS 72.2.15 *Ruithidh*

858 *slèibhti* The 1751 reading has been kept. 1809 has *sleibhte*, 1839 ff. *slèibhtean.* MS 72.2.15 reads *Aon eagidh na sleiphtibh sna cnuic.*

859 *Grad-dhubhaidh* MS 72.2.15 has *dhubhaidh*, 1751 ff. *dubhaidh*

860 MS 72.2.15 *Failidh ruiscidh se faillainnach bocht*

861–2 The positions of *ghrinn* and *binn* are reversed in MS 72.2.15, which reads for 1. 862 *le n ceilaireadh grinn ambarr dois*

863 *ghlas-ghoib* So 1751 ff. 1839 ff. have *ghlas-ghuib.* MS 72.2.15 reads *Gu ndechaidh glas ghuib* – – –.

865 *bùirdeasaich* 1751 ff. *búirdeiseach*, 1809 ff. *bùirdeisich.* MS 72.2.15 reads *Togaidh buirdesaich* – – –, 1924 *Togaidh* – – –. The plural form is the appropriate one in the context.

866 *ceilearadh* 1751 ff. *ceileiridh*, 1809, 1839 *ceileiribh treis* MS 72.2.15 *ghreis*, 1839 ff. *greis*

867–8 MS 72.2.15 reads
S cho seinn iad a matins gu hárd
Na feispar sailm craibheach na mpres.
This earlier reading shows the Catholic terms *matin* and *vesper* less adjusted to Gaelic usage than in the 1751 readings. Mays (see 11. 839-40 *n*) makes the point that the poet converted to Catholicism not very long before the '45, and this reinforces the 1743 date for the poem.

870 *fasgaidh am* 1751 *fasgadh ann*, MS 72.2.15 *comhnidh a m*

871 MS 72.2.15 *Is iad aig caoi na ngabannuibh tla*

872 *o sgàileadh* So 1751 ff. MS 72.2.15 reads *fuigh sgáile*, 1839 *o sgàile*, and 1874 ff. *fo sgàile*. The sense 'under the shadow of your heat' is not convincing, but if we take *sgàileadh* as a variant of *sgaoileadh* (as in Older Gaelic), the sense of 'from the spreading of your heat' fits well.

873–4 MS 72.2.15 reads

Togidh dalltaibh srianbhuigh na nrós
barr mín chíach na nór ciabhan beg

875 MS 72.2.15 *S ionnann lilidh is gucaid na nrós*. The change from *S ionnann* 'the same' to *Sinean* 'teats, nipples' gives a lift to the imagery.

876 *Na flùran 's* MS 72.2.15 *S gach flóur is*

877 MS 72.2.15 *Le bechann cho deabhlar le bhruach*

878 *Cròdhaidh* MS 72.2.15 *Cráidh*

880 MS 72.2.15 originally had *na geal ur fas crann garruidh cho strep*, but deletes the first four words and inserts *teid aludh as crann* above. This does not seem to make complete sense.

881–8 This stanza is not included in MS 72.2.15.

882 *fèath-ghrùnnd* 1751 ff. *fiaghrunt*, 1874 ff. *fiath-ghrùnnd*. The sense is 'the calm bed' (of the lochs). The poet is thinking of sea-lochs here, as is clear from the reference to herring.

883 *dubh-dhonn* 1874 ff *dhubh-dhonn*. The final *n* of *aigeann* probably inhibited lenition of the *d* for the poet.

885 *tharr-ghealach* 1751 ff. *tharr-ai-ghealach*, 1809 *thar-ghealach*. The 1751 reading indicates the pronunciation of the svarabhakti vowel in mid-compound.

886 *meardha* 1751 to 1839 *mearradha*, again indicating the pronunciation. *usgraichean* The 1751 Glossary gives as one sense 'bells on liquor'.

887 *cairtealaibh* 1751 to 1809 *cairtealamh*, 1839 *tairtealan*

889–96 This stanza is not included in MS 72.2.15

891 *sìtheinean* 1751 ff. *síein'*

893 *maghannan* 1751 ff. *maodhunnan*, 1809 *monainnean*, 1839 *monunnan*

895 *sgreitich* – – – *dùldachd* 1874 ff. *sgreataich* – – – – *dùdlachd*

897 *meadair* 1751 ff. *meadoir*, 1809, 1839 *midear*, 1874 ff. *miodar/mìodar*. Presumably it is the plural form that is intended, matching *pàircean*.

897–904 This stanza is not in MS 72.2.15

899 *ìosal* – – – – *àrd* 1751 ff. *íosuil* – – – – *áird*. The traditional genitive plural is restored, as in 1839 ff. Perhaps this is taking undue liberties with the poet's usage, which seems to have fluctuated.
MS Gen 9 reads *torr* instead of *íosuil*.

901 *am musga* 1751, MS Gen 9 and 1802 *a musga*, Eigg *bha tattneach*, 1809 ff. *bha taitneach*. There can be no doubt that *a(m) musga* was the original reading. Perhaps it is to be related to 'musk', and this smell is often associated with certain plants/flowers e.g. musk rose or one type of mimulus. A more bizarre possibility is that this is a borrowing of 'music', going with the following reference to *fonn*.

902 *a maise* 1874 ff. *a mhaise*. The word *lompair*, however, to which the *a* may refer, is feminine.

903 *truagh* MS Gen 9 *truaigh*

905 *ùir MS 72.2.15, 1924 dhlù(th)*

906 'whose honey was as oil and powder'
D' am b' ola MS 72.2.15 Ga naileadh (i.e. *Gan fhàileadh*)

907 *bhalet* So 1751, MS Gen 9, 1802, 1839; Eigg, 1809 *thabhachd*; 1874 *thàbhachd*; 1924 *valet*

907–8 MS 72.2.15 reads

Gniomh laimh grian do phlainaid sgach uair
Bhith buscadh do ghruaige le sgil.

As usual, the 1751 reading introduces a livelier image, that of the valet, though it seems a pity to lose the more unusual word *busgadh* 'dressing': the succession of *g*'s in the new line may have been the attraction – i.e. adding a second initial *g*.

909 *iuchair* So MS 72.2.15. 1751 ff. *thiughair*, 1809 ff. *iuchair* (but 1839 *iughair*). *a ghnùis* So 1751 ff., 1874 ff. *a gnùis*, MS 72.2.15 *do ghnúis*. The poet here, as in other instances, thinks of the sun as masculine, no doubt with Phoebus in mind.

910 MS 72.2.15 *Ar modhanna driúchdanna dril*

911–12 MS 72.2.15 *Fior aoibhinn s gur cubhrig an smúid*
A geirigh barr cuirnean gach bil.
Seo dh' èireadh 1751 ff. *dh'eiridh*, 1809 ff. *dh'eireadh*

913 ff. The remaining stanzas are not included in MS 72.2.15.

914 'the fruit which made the branch/twig bend heavily, went away'.

915 *a' pheur* 1874 ff. *am peur*

916 'that would bend the branch like a bow immediately'.

919 *Taurus* a sign of the zodiac, linked loosely with the month of April.

921 *a' ghrian* Though *grian* is here feminine in form, it is referred to as a masculine later in the line.

922 *tropic Chapricorn* There is no attempt to accommodate the signs of the zodiac to Gaelic. Capricorn is linked with December.

923 *fearthainn* 1751 ff. *ferrin(n)*, 1809 *far-shion*. In origin this word is the verbal noun of Older Gaelic *feraid*, 'pours' etc. It comes to be used in the sense of 'rain' and 'rains'. Here it appears to be used as a plural, meaning 'showers'.

924 *sad* dust; thud, blow. Either sense is possible here.

926 *eighre* 1751 ff. *eireadh*, 1809 *èireoth*, 1874 ff. *éire*

927–8 The reference to frost and ice (*eighre*) in 1. 926 is continued here: 'water becomes hard pieces of glass, and smooth, tough cold-stone gray jewels'.

929 *Am mìos* 1751 *A mios*, 1874 ff. *A mhìos*. Consistently in this stanza and the following two, the poet uses *A mios* in the first line, and does not lenite the adjectives in that line, going on to lenite the following succession of adjectives. This curiosity has been retained, though the present editor is unable to offer a convincing explanation.

934 *ruith* 1751 ff. *rith*, showing that the poet's pronunciation gave perfect rhyme with *bith* and *cith* and *chrith*.

938 'that makes frequent calls on (eating) black gruel'.

940 *Bhrìsneach* 1839 *Bhriogsach*
thiugh goes with the garments mentioned (the breeches, stockings and breast-hoods, all made of *thick* cloth).

942 '(a month for) butter, bread, cheese, (but) lacking crowdie'. 1839 ff. *Imeach*

943 *Le 'm miann* Pre-1874 sources *Le miann*

944 'And does not despise any kind of stuff (for eating) provided it is warm'.

946–8 In these lines the series of adjectives is given in inflected form (*Ghionaich, Littich, Phoitich* etc.) in 1751 ff., as though the month were being addressed in the vocative case. Yet again this does not apply to the first line of the stanza. This can only be interpreted as an aberration on the poet's part, or on that of a Gaelic typesetter (which is unlikely).

947 *làghanach* 1874 ff. *làganach*

948 *Phòiteach* None of the sources have *ò*, but it would seem to fit the aural sequence better than *o*, as indeed *pòiteach* 'given to imbibing' fits better than *poiteach* 'with many pots'.

949–52 'and though we thatched our body outwardly against the piercing merciless wind, it is necessary to drink a dram to provide a lining for the chest that will kindle a bonfire in the breast'.

950 *-fhadas* 1874 *fhadai's*, 1924 *fhadaidh*

953 *greann dhubh* 1874 ff. *greann-dubh*. Dwelly notes that *greann* is feminine in various localities, including North Argyll.
956 *Ar – – – – ar* 1751 ff. *Air – – – – air*
959 *soillsein – – – coirein* 1751 *soilsen – – – coirein*. The standard forms of these nouns are *soillsean* and *coirean*, but there is a good deal of evidence for the *-ein* pronunciation.
960 *òr-pheall* 1751 ff. *oir-pheall*, 1809 ff. *or mheall*. *peall* can mean 'veil, covering', and this is the appropriate sense here.
961–6 The picture of the chorus of birds delicately singing their hymns on their perches in the wood is neatly developed. The perches are described as pulpits and desks, and the birds celebrate the movement of the planet and offer their praises to the Lord.
963 *hymns* 1839 *laoidh*
964 *air n-ais* 1809 ff. *air ais*
972 *Anam-fàis* 1751 ff. *Anam-fás*. But the 1751 Glossary gives '*Anam-fais* a vegetative soul'. 'Spirit of growth/potential to grow' seems to be the sense here.
975 *their* 1751 ff. *deir*.
975–6 The birds' chirping is presented in terms of pipe-music verbal notation followed by the exclamation 'Winter has gone and summer has come'.

ORAN NAM FINEACHAN GAIDHEALACH

Sources and Editions:

1751	51-9
MS Gen 9	36-42
1802	63-71
1806	6-11
1839	31-7
1874, 1892	29-35
1924	76-86
1984	72-84

Our text is based almost totally on the 1751 text. Readings in MS Gen 9 differ fairly minimally, and not persuasively in the case of this poem. It does not appear in Eigg, and this probably reduced the likelihood of its being included in later anthologies such as MacPhàrlain's of 1813. There is less editorial emendation than usual in the late editions, and usually the 1751 text can be preferred though it may seem eccentric to nineteenth/twentieth-century norms. One stanza (11. 1081-8) is not included in the early sources, and first appears in the 1874 edition, with no indication of its provenance. 1839 introduced a few variants, sometimes followed by 1874. J. L. Campbell's edition is also strongly based on the 1751 text, although a few significant differences of interpretation emerge in the current edition.

There can be no doubt that this poem is a pre-1745-campaign one, although it is possible that some touches were added later. The list of clans praised includes some that did not take part in the '45, or took the Hanoverian side, and it is worth underlining the poet's impartiality in retaining the stanza praising the Campbells in his 1751 collection. The editors of the 1924 edition show their own clerical restraint in the comment (p. 79) 'The Prince's camp was not augmented by the Campbells'. These editors have a less straight-laced comment on the Macphersons, who did join the campaign but missed Culloden: 'They tarried too long over their *brochan* on the way, and missed the battle'. Neither the MacLeods nor the Mackenzies came out as clans, though some individual groups did. We must therefore conclude that this poem was a recruiting one, allowed to stand in basically its pre-1745 form.

It belongs to a tradition of 'clan' poetry which goes back at least to Màiri Nighean Alasdair Ruaidh in vernacular Gaelic poetry, and has some roots in earlier classical Gaelic verse. Iain Dubh Mac Iain 'ic Ailein has a poem with the same title, which Mac Mhaighstir Alasdair would know well, and we can see that he decided, as was his wont, to build on these foundations but to change the architecture significantly. (John Macinnes, in 'The Panegyric Code in Gaelic Poetry and its Historical Background', TGSI L, 435-98, and specifically pp. 465-6, emphasises the traditional rather than the immediate motivation of many of these poems).

A clear plan can be seen in the present poem. The introductory section welcomes the Old and the Young Pretender, and sees Nature and the elements conspiring to ease their return to Britain from the Continent. The main body of the poem has fourteen stanzas addressed to individual clans, with a clear pecking order beginning with Stewarts, MacDonalds and Campbells. Each of these stanzas has complimentary references to its named clan, and also a vignette of the part they may play in the action. Sometimes this is described in more general terms: the MacDonalds are hounds unleashed on the enemy; the work of the Campbell sword-blades is described; the MacLeods will be like hawks claiming their prey; the Macintoshes will come with their pipes and satin banners; the Frasers' gun-flints will be red as embers with their constant bursts of fire. In all cases the description is enlivened by some imaginative figure, often based on natural observation. And the poem ends with gloating references to the carnage that will ensue, the plunder that will be available, and the final triumph that will be marked by the crowning of the Stuart king.

It is curious that it was Iain Dubh's clan poem that was included in the Eigg Collection (pp. 227-31) rather than the Editor's father's poem. Iain Dubh sometimes gives a full stanza to one clan, sometimes refers to two or three. Iain Dubh's poem can be seen as a starting-point for Mac Mhaighstir Alasdair's, but the later poet's construction is much more controlled, and his detail more arresting, though at the end of the day this must be seen as essentially a propagandist exercise, touched with the strength and elegance that are inseparable from his work.

Oran nam Fineachan Gaidhealach

A chomainn rìoghail rùnaich,
Sàr ùmhlachd thugaibh uaibh,
Biodh ur roisg gun smùirnein,
'S gach crìdh gun trèas gun lùb ann;
Deoch-slàinte Sheumais Stiùbhairt
Gu mùirneach cuir mun cuairt.
Ach ma ta gìomh air bith nur stamaig
A' chailis naomh na truaill.

Lìon deoch-slàinte Theàrlaich,
A mheàirlich, stràic a' chuach;
B'i siud an ìocshlaint àlainn
Thaith-bheothaicheadh mo chàileachd
Ged a bhiodh am bàs orm
Gun neart, gun àgh, gun tuar.
Rìgh nan dùl a chur do chàbhlaich
Oirnn thar sàl ri luas.

O tog do bhaideil àrda,
Chaol dhìonach shàr-gheal nuadh,
Ri d' chrainnghridh bìth-dhearg làidir
Gu taisdeal nan tonn gàireach;
Tha Aeolus ag ràitinn
Gu sèid e rap-ghaoth chruaidh
On àird-an-oir, 's tha Neptiun dìleas
Gu mìneachadh a' chuain.

Is bochd atà do chàirdean
Aig ro-mheud t' fhàrdail uainn,
Mar àlach maoth gun mhàthair
No beachainn bhreac a' ghàrraidh
Aig sionnach 'n dèis a fàsaich
Air fàillinn feadh nam bruach.
Aisig cabhagach le d' chàbhlach
'S leighis plàigh do shluaigh.

Tha na dèe ann an deagh rùn duit,
Greas ort le sùrd neamh-mharbh
Thar dhronnag nan tonn dùbhghorm,
Dhriom-robach bhàrr-chas shiùbhlach,
Ghleann-chladhach cheann-gheal shùgh-dhlùth
'Nam mothar cùl-ghlas garbh,
Na cuan-choirean greannach stuagh-thorrach
'S crom-bhileach molach falbh.

Tha muir is tìr co-rèidh dhuit
Mur dèan thu fèin a searg:
Dòirtidh iad 'nan ceudaibh
'Nan laomaibh tiugha treuna
A Briotainn is á Eirinn
Mu d' standard brèidgheal dearg:
A' ghaisridh sgaiteach ghuineach rìoghail,
Chreuchdach fhìor-luath gharg.

Thig do chinneadh fèin ort,
Na treun-fhir laomsgar gharbh
'Nam beathraichibh gu reubadh,
'Nan leòmhainnibh gu creuchdadh,
'Nan nathraichibh graid-leumnach
A lotas geur le 'n calg,
Le 'n gathaibh faobharach rinn-bheurra
Nì mòr euchd le 'n arm'.

'Nam brataichibh làn èidichte,
Le deileas geur gun chealg,
Thig Dòmhnallaich 'nan dèidh sin
Cho dìleas duit ri d' lèine;
Mar choin air fasdadh èille
Air chath-chrith geur gu sealg;
Is mairg nàimhde don nochd iad fraoch,
Long, leòmhann, craobh 's làmh-dhearg.

Gu neartaich iad do chàmpa
Na Caimbeulaich gu dearbh,
'N Diùc Earragh'alach mar cheann orr'
Gu mòralach mear prionnsail;
Ge be bheir air ionnsaigh
B'e siud an tionnsgnadh searbh,
Le lannaibh lotach dùbhghorm toirteil
Sgoltadh chorp gu 'm balg.

Gu tairbheartach glan caismeachdach,
Fìor thartarach 'nan rang,
Thig Cluainidh le chuid Pearsonach
Gu cuanna gleusda graid-bheairteach
Le 'spàinnichibh teann-bheairtichte
'S cruaidh fead ri sgailceadh cheann:
Bidh fuil da dòrtadh 's smùis da spealtadh
Le sgealpaireachd ur lann.

Druididh suas ri d' mheirghe,
Nach meirbh an àm an àir,
Clann Ghill Eòin nach meirgich
Airm ri uchd do sheirbheis,
Le 'm brataichean 's snuadh feirg orra
San leirg mar thairbh gun sgàth:
Am fòirne fearail nimheil arrail
'S builleach athlamh làmh.

Gun tig na fiùrain Leòdach ort
Mar sheobhgain 's eòin f'a spàig,
'Nan tùiribh lannghorm tinnisneach
Air chorr-ghleus streup gun tiomachas,
An rèiseamaid fìor innealta,
'S fàth gioraig dol 'na dàil,
'M bi iomad bòcan fuilteach foirmeil
Thèid le stoirm gu bàs.

Thig curaidhnean Chlann Chamshroin ort
Thèid meanmnach sìos nad spàirn,
An fhoireann ghuineach chaithreamach
'S neamh-fhiamhach an àm tarrainge
An lainn ghlas mar lasair dealanaich
Gu gearradh cheann is làmh,
'S mar luaths na dreige, 's cruas na creige
Chluinnte sgread nan cnàmh.

Thig mìlidhean Chlann Iain ort
Thèid fritheilteach gu d' chàmp,
Mar fhaloisg ris na sliabh-chnuic,
Is gaoth a' Mhàirt ga biathadh,
No marcaich air each srianach
A rachadh sìos gun chàird,
Cho ealamh ris an fhùdar ullamh,
An t-srad nuair bhuineadh dhà.

Gur cinnteach dhuibh dar coinneachadh
MacCoinnich mòr Cheann t-Sàil':
Fir làidir dhàna choinnealta
De'n fhìor-chruaidh air a foinneachadh,
Nach gabh fiamh no somaltachd
No sgreamh roimh theine bhlàr,
'S iad gu nàrach fuileach foinnidh
Air bhoil gu dol nad chàs.

Gur foirmeil pròiseil òrdail
Thig Tòiseachain 'nan rang,
Am màrsail stàtail còmhnard,
Gu pìobach bratach sròlbhuidh;
Tha rìoghalachd is mòrchuis
Gun sòradh anns an dream:
Daoine làidir neartmhor cròdha
'S iad gun ghò gun mheang.

Thig Granndaich gu ro thartarach
Neo-fhad-bheairteach do d'chàmp,
Air phriob-losgadh gu cruadal,
Gu snaigheadh cheann is chluas diu,
Choi'-nimheil ris na tìgearaibh
Le feachdraidh dìan-mhear dàn',
Chuireas iomad fear le sgreadail
Sa' bhreabadaich gu làr.

Thig a-rìs na Frisealaich
Gu sgibidh le neart garbh,
'Na seobhgaibh fìorghlan togarrach
Le fuathas bhlàr nach bogaichear,
An còmhlan feardha cosgarrach,
'S mairg neach do 'n nochd iad fearg
An spuir ghlas aig dlùths an dèirich
Bidh 'nan èibhlibh dearg.

'Nan gaisridh ghaisgeil lasgarra
Thig Lachannaich gun chàird,
'Na saighdibh dearga puinnseanta,
Gu claidheach sgiathach cuinnsearach,
Gu gunnach dagach ionnsaichte,
Gun chunntas ac' air àr,
Dol 'nan deannaibh 'n aodainn pheilear
Tiochd o theine chàich.

Gabhaidh pàirt de t' iorghail-s'
Clann Fhionghuin 's òirdheirc càil,
Mar thuinn ri tìr a' sìor-bhualadh,
No bile lasrach dìan-loisgeach,
'Nan treudaibh luatha sìor-chonfach
Thoirt grìosaich air an nàmh:
An dream chathach Mhuileach, Shrathach
'S maith gu sgathadh chnàmh.

Is mòr a bhios ri corp-rùsgadh
Nan closaichean sa' bhlàr,
Fithich anns an rocadaich
Ag itealaich 's a' cnocaireachd,
Cìocras air na cosgarraich
Ag òl 's ag ith an sàth:
Och, 's tùrsach fann a chluinntear mochthrath
Ochanaich nan àr.

Bidh fuil is gaorr da fhùidreadh ann
Le lùth-chleasan ur làmh,
Meangar cinn is dùirn diubh,
Gearrar uilt le smùisridh,
Cìosnaichear ur biùthaidh
D'an dùbhlosgadh 's d'an cnàmh,
Crùnar le poimp Teàrlach Stiùbhairt
'S Frederick Prionns f'a shàil.

NOTES

978 *uaibh* 1751 *uaimh*, MS Gen 9, 1802 *uaibh*, 1874 to 1924 *bhuaibh*
979 *roisg* 1874 to 1924 *ruisg*
980 *trèas* 1751, 1802 *tréas*. The use of accents in the 1751 text is not particularly consistent, but probably here it does indicate a long vowel in pronunciation. A borrowing from English 'treason', which takes the form *tréasan* in Irish. *lùb* 1874 ff. *lùib*
981 1751, in its usual fashion, has *S------ S------*. The reference is to James Stuart, the Old Pretender.
983 *gìomh* The more usual senses are 'defect, blemish', but the sense of 'fear' suits better here.
984 *A' chailis naomh* The chalice from which the toast to James Stuart is to be drunk is holy by virtue of his 'divine right' to rule.
985 *Theàrlaich* 1751 *T-----* Charles Stuart, the Young Pretender.
988 *Thaith-bheothaicheadh* 1751, MS Gen 9 *Thaithbheothaichidh*, 1839 *Dhath-*, 1874 ff. *Dh' ath*. The form with *taith-* rather than *ath-* is common in Irish.
991 'May the King of the elements send your fleet'. This line and 1. 1007 give clear evidence of composition before the launch of the '45 in July 1745.
994 *Chaol dhìonach caol* can be used to mean 'tightly-woven', and *dìonach* adds the sense of 'water-resistant'.
995 *chrainnghridh* 1751, MS Gen 9 *chrainnghri*, 1839 *crannaidh*, 1874 to 1924 *chrannaibh*. The High. Soc. Dict. gives the sense 'mast-rigging', quoting this line, but the qualifying adjective *bìth-dhearg* suggests that the reference is to the wooden parts of the mast-assembly.
997 *Aeolus* God of the Winds.
999 *àird-an-oir* 1839 – – *eir*, 1874 ff. – – *ear*. 'The east'. *Neptiun* Roman God of the Sea.
1005 *fàsaich* The 1751 and other early forms suggest that the poet used a nominative *fàsach* for 'laying waste', rather than the more usual *fàsachadh* which would give a reduced genitive *fàs'aidh*. 1839 *fāsachd'*, 1874 to 1924 amend to *fàs'chadh*, and 1984 to *fàsaichth'*.
1009 *dèe* The unusual plural form of the early versions is retained, in preference to *dè*, or the modern *diathan* which would be unacceptable rhythmically.

1012 *Dhriom-robach driom* is a variant of *druim.* In his 1741 *Vocabulary* the poet gives both *Druim* and *Drim* for 'back'.

1014 *mothar* The 1751 Glossary gives 'a prodigious high sea; also a loud report'.

1015 *stuagh-thorrach* 1874 to 1924 *stuadh-chor(r)ach.* The rhythm of this line is unusually clumsy, even with heavy emphasis on *cuan-* and *stuagh-*. The poet's eagerness to capture many aspects of the wild sea runs away with him.

1017 *co-rèidh* 1751 *choimh-re*, MS Gen 9 *coimh-re.* The sense may be 'equally at peace, equally well-disposed'.

1018 *a searg* Though this follows closely on the reference to land and sea, it refers more naturally to the Jacobite sympathisers: 'Sea and land are equally well-disposed to you, provided you do not let them wither away'.

1020 *laomaibh* MS Gen 9 *taōmadh.* There is only occasional disagreement between 1751 and MS Gen 9.

1021 *Briotainn* 1751 *Brittinn*, MS Gen 9 *Brittin*

1022 The description of the Prince's standard as 'red, of white cloth' may suggest a Lion Rampant in red on a white background. J. L. Campbell quotes Chambers on the standard as being 'a banner of red silk with a white space in the centre'.

1023 *sgaiteach* MS Gen 9 *sgainech*

1026–8 These lines evidently echo lines in the Harlaw Brosnachadh attributed to Lachlann MacMhuirich before the Battle of Harlaw in 1411. The relevant lines from that early poem are:

Gu laomsgar, gu làn-athlamh

- - - - - - - - -

A bheithrichean bunanta,
A leòmhannan làn-ghasta

It is possible that one of the MSS of the Harlaw Brosnachadh was in the possession of MacDonald of Dalness, Alasdair Mac Mhaighstir Alasdair's father-in-law (See Thomson, D. S. (1968), pp. 152, 156, and 148-9).

1029 *graid-leumnach* Later sources emend to the more usual *grad-l.*, but it is worth noting that the *graid-* form occurs in 1751 both here and in l. 1052 below.

1031 *gathaibh* The sense of *gath* lies ambiguously between 'sting', which goes with the serpents in l. 1031, and 'sharp weapon', which fits the reference to warriors.

1032 *arm'* This is the 1751 form, which may be short for dative pl. *armaibh.*

1034 *deileas* 1751, MS Gen 9 *delis. deileas* is a variant of *dealas*, 'eagerness, vehemence'.

1036 *Cho dìleas* 1751 *Choi'-dilis.* It would be equally appropriate to retain the form *choimh-dìleas.*

1040 A ship, a lion, a tree and a red hand are the four symbols in the MacDonald coat of arms.

1042 *Caimbeulaich* 1751 has the spelling *Caimpbeulaich*, which may be a conciliatory gesture on the poet's part to the Campbells (here praised in the hope that they may join the Jacobite side). There was a preference in that clan for a Norman origin of their name (*de Campo Bello*) rather than a Gaelic one which meant 'wry-mouthed'.

1043 *Earragh'alach* 1751 *Earraghaidhealach.* The rhyme requires syncope of this word.

1049 *tairbheartach* 1751 *tairbiartach*, MS Gen 9 *tairbiortach.* The most appropriate sense here is 'abundant, numerous'. The Macphersons are depicted marching, probably to pipe music.

1050 *rang* 1751 etc. *ranc.* The more sonorous Gaelic pronunciation is required, to assonate with *cheann* and *lann* later in the stanza.

1051 *Cluainidh* 'Cluny' Macpherson, chief of the Badenoch clan.

1052 *cuanna* 1839 *cuannda*, 1874 to 1924 *cuanta*

graid-bheairteach 1751 etc. *graid-*, later edd. *grad-*

1055 *spealtadh* 1751 *spealltadh*, MS Gen 9 *spalltadh*. The MS Gen 9 reading is probably an aberration, as *spealtadh* rhymes with *sgealpaireachd* in the next line.

1064 *athlamh* This adjective also appears in the Harlaw poem.

1066 *sheobhgain* 1751 etc. *sheochdain*. The context requires a plural form here. Is this an unconventional plural of *seobhag/seabhag*, 'falcon, hawk'? See also l. 1115.

1067 *tinnisneach tinnesnach* in Older Gaelic is used in the senses of 'urgent, violent, sudden'. It appears in the Black Book's MacDonald history: *ruathar --- roithinnisnech* (*Rel. Celt.* 11, 194).

1069 *fìor* So 1751 etc. 1874 ff. have *fhìor*, to reflect the feminine gender of *rèisimeid*. It may be argued that *fìor* here is not an adjective qualifying *rèisimeid* but an intensive adjective modifying *innealta*.

1071 *bòcan* 1751 etc. *bóchdan*

1073 *curaidhnean* 1751 etc. *cuirinnin*. 1874 and 1924 change to the more conventional plural *curaidhean*.

1075 *An fhoireann* The poet uses this word as a feminine noun, as in older Gaelic.

1081–8 This stanza is not in 1751 or MS Gen 9. It first appears in the 1874 ed., without any note as to its provenance. Despite the slight syntactical awkwardness of l. 1088 the style seems that of the poet.

1091 *coinnealta* Is this a variant of *coinnealach* 'supple, flexible'? The poet has '*coinniullach*, flexible, plyable' in his 1751 Glossary. Matheson (1951) takes this to be connected with *coinneal*, and glosses it 'shining, luminous'.

1092 'of the true steel, tempered'.

1096 *càs* The precise sense is difficult to pin down: the phrase *gu dol nad chàs* can be taken either as (a) to go to help you in your difficulty, or (b) to take part in your venture.

1098 *Tòiseachain* The 1751 form is followed. The poet would seem to have used *Tòiseachan* for 'a Macintosh'.

1099 *stàtail* 1751 *státoil*, MS Gen 9 *stãoil*

1108 *snaigheadh* 1751 *snaidh*. The rhythm requires two syllables here.

1110 *feachdraidh* High. Soc. Dict. gives 'armed infantry' for this.

1112 *Sa' bhreabadaich* 1751 etc. *'S a bhreabadaich*. The sense is 'in a state of kicking', i.e. with jerking limbs after wounding.

1115 *seobhgaibh* dat. plural of *seobhag*; a more conventional plural is suggested here than in l. 1066.

1117 *feardha* 1751 *fearradha*, MS Gen 9 *ferradh*, 1802, 1839 *fearradh*

1119–20 'Their grey gun-flints will be red embers because of the quick succession of loud gun-shots'. The poet glosses *dèireach* as 'an exquisite loud report; also a dull pain in the body'.

1121 *gaisridh* 1839 *gabraidh*

1132 *bile* High. Soc. Dict. gives as one sense 'a tree, cluster of trees'. This seems the sense here: 'like a flaming cluster of trees burning strongly'.

1133 *sìor-chonfach confach* is a contracted form of *confadhach*, 'furious, enraged'. The poet has the item '*confadh*, rage, madness, eagerness' in his Glossary.

1135 *Mhuileach, Shrathach* The Mackinnons were numerous in both Mull and Strath Swordale in Skye.

1145 *da fhùidreadh* 1751 etc. *d'a fhuidridh*, 1839 *shuidreadh*

1148 *smùisridh* 1751 etc. *smúisri*, 1839 *smuasrai*. A variant of *smuaisrich* 'smashing'?

1151–2 As usual the proper names are represented in 1751 only by their initials. Prince Frederick is presumably Frederick the Great of Prussia.

SMEORACH CHLANN RAGHNAILL

Sources and Editions:

McL MS 33	2-7
Eigg	246-50
1839	75-81
1841	121-3
1874, 1892	71-6
1924	180-88

The earliest MS source is McLagan MS 33, a small 8-page leaflet containing two poems. On its front page there is the date 1770, scored out but nevertheless suggesting a dating for the MS. The poem is, curiously, titled as follows: 'Oran Luadha, no Fucaidh, le Alasdair Mac Dhomhnuill'. This is the title associated with the song which begins 'A Mhòrag chiatach a' chùil dualaich' (and that title is used in the 1751 edition). Its use in McLagan 33 is presumably an aberration.

The poem does not appear in the 1751 *Ais-eiridh*, and its first appearance in print was in the Eigg Collection of 1776, where twenty-four stanzas are included. The next would seem to be in John Mackenzie's 1834-39 edition. Mackenzie's *Sàr Obair* text (1841) is very close to the 1839 text, but not identical.

Some special weight is given to the McLagan text, since it is so early, and has eleven stanzas more than the 1776 text. It is noticeable that the MacDonalds (1924) on several occasions have identical readings with McL, though they normally tend to agree with Mackenzie and Macpherson (1839 and 1874).

There is evidence in others of Mac Mhaighstir Alasdair's poems that stanzas or passages were added at dates later than that of the main composition. The references to certain chiefs or heirs in this poem suggest strongly that the poem was mainly composed before the start of the '45 and certainly before its conclusion. There is a toast to Alexander MacDonell of Keppoch who died at Culloden, and the toast to the young MacDonald of Sleat suggests that it was composed c. 1746, the year in which his father died. The final verse reads like a post-'45 comment.

The poem begins with four quatrains which pinpoint to some

extent the location and connections of the mavis which sings this song. The mavis is connected with the poet, but may not be totally identical with him. Connections are established with various Clanranald territories and leaders, including the mainland ones of Caisteal Tioram and Eilean Fhìonain and the Moidart line. The references in 11. 1165-6 have usually been taken to refer to Benbecula, but we need not take them as an assertion that the poet was brought up there. This seems unlikely. This section also includes fine detail about the bird's singing habits, and the poet reverts to more extended detail at various points in the poem.

The rest of the poem is concerned with description of the heroic Clanranald, and with toasts to members of the clan and to supporters from other clans. Several toasts to the Old and the Young Pretender are interspersed, some of these perhaps added after the failure of the '45, while there was still some expectation of a further rising.

Not unusually for this poet, the subject is explored showing a deep fascination with the language's lexical range and variety, which is exploited in the context of rhyme and alliteration.

SMEÒRACH CHLANN RAGHNAILL

Hoile bho hì riag hò roll il ò
Hoile bho hì riag hò ro ì
Hoile bho hì riag hò roll il ò
Smeòrach do Chlann Raghnaill mì.

Gura mise 'n smeòrach chreagach
An dèis leum bhàrr cuach mo nidein,
Sholar bìdh do m' eunaibh beaga:
Seinneam ceòl air bhàrr gach bidein.

Smeòrach mise do Chlann Dòmhnaill,
Dream a dhìthicheadh 's a leònadh,
'S chaidh mo chur an riochd na smeòraich
Gu bhith seinn 's a' cur ri ceòl daibh.

Sa' Chreig Ghuirm a thogadh mise
An sgìreachd Chaisteil Duibh nan cliar,
Tìr a tha daonnan cur thairis
Le tuil bhainne, mil is fìon.

Do shliochd nan eun on Chaisteal Thioram,
'S o Eilean Fhìonain nan gallan,
Moch is feasgar togbhar m' iolach,
Seinn gu bileach, milis, mealach.

Tha mi den ghur rìoghail, luachach,
'S math eun fhaotainn á nead uasal,
Ghineadh mi gun chol, gun truailleadh
Fo sgiathaibh Ailein Mhic Ruairidh.

Cinneadh glan, gun smùd, gun smodan,
Gun smal, gun luathrnadh, gun ghrodan,
'S iad gun ghìomh, gun fheall, gun sodan,
'S treun am buille 'n tiugh nan trodan.

Cinneadh rìoghail th' air am buaireadh
Mar mhire mheara na cruadhach,
'S daoimein iad gun spàrr, gun truailleadh,
Nach gabh stùr, gnè smal no ruadh-mheirg.

Cinneadh mòr gun bhòsd, gun spaglan,
Suairce, sìobhalta, gun rapal,
Coibhneil, cinneadail ri càirdibh,
Fuilteach, faobharach ri nàmhaid.

Raghnallaich nan òr-chrios tagach,
Nan lùireach, nan sgiath 's nan clogad,
Thèid a-sìos gu gunnach, dagach,
Na fir bhagant, shùnndach, chogach.

Siud na h-aon daoin' tha air m' aire,
Nach dèanadh air plùndrainn cromadh,
Dhèanadh anns an àraich gearradh,
Cinn gan sgaradh, cuirp gam pronnadh.

Ach mur tig mo Rìgh-sa dhachaigh
Triallfaidh mi do dh' uamhaidh shlocaich
'S bidh mi 'n sin a' caoidh 's a' basraich
Gus am faigh mi bàs le osnaich.

Ach ma thig mo Phrionnsa thairis
Cuirear mis' an cliabhan lurach,
Bidh mi canntaireachd gu baileach
'S ann 'na phailis nì mi fuireach.

Madainn Chèitein am bàrr badain
Sgaoileadh ciùil á gloic mo ghuibein
'S àlainn mo thururaich 's mo ghlagan,
Stailceadh mo dhà bhuinn air stuibein.

Gura mise cruit nan cnocan
Seinn mo leadain air gach bacan,
'S mo chearc fèin dam bheus air stocan,
'S glan ar glocan air gach stacan.

Crith-chiùil air m' ugan ga bogadh,
'S mo chompar uile làn beadraidh,
Tein-èibhinn am uchd air fadadh
'S mi air fad air dannsa 'leigeil.

Nuair chuirinn geoic air mo ghogan
'S a thogainn mo shailm air creagan
'S ann orm fèin a bhiodh an sogan,
Ceòl ga thogail, bròn ga leagail.

Eòin bhuchallach bhreac na coille
Le 'n òrganaibh òrdail mar ruinn,
'S feadag ghlan am beul gach coilich,
'S binn fead-choill air gheugaibh barraich.

'S mis' an t-eunan beag le m' fheadan,
Madainn dhriùchd am bàrr gach badain,
Sheinneadh na puirt ghrinn gun sgreadan,
'S ionmhainn m' fheadan feadh gach lagain.

Siud oirbh deoch-slàint' na h-armailt
Dh' èirich le Teàrlach on gharbhlach,
Na fir ghasda dhèanadh searra-bhuain
Air feòil 's air cnàmhan nan Dearg-chòt.

Olamaid fliuchadh ar slugain
'S cuirfeamaid mun cuairt làn nogain,
Slàinte Sheumais suas le suigeart,
Tosta Theàrlaich sìos le sogan.

Slàint' an teaghlaich rìoghail inbhich
Olamaid gu sùnndach geanail,
'S nigheamaid ar sgòrnan gionach
Le dràm milis, bruidhneach, glainneach.

Cuirfeamaid sìos feadh ar mionaich
Tosta nan curaidhnean clannach,
Nan colg sgaiteach, gasda, biorach,
'S ro-mhòr sgil air còmhrag lannach.

On tha mi tionndadh gu h-eirthir
Ullaichim m' acair gu cala:
Tosta Mhùideirt, ceann nan Seileach,
Slàinte eile, Triath nan Garrach.

Lìonaibh suas is òlaibh bras i,
Slàinte Raghnaill Oig o 's deas i,
Sguir da h-amharc, thugaibh ás i,
Siabaibh leibh i, ás a teas i.

Lìon a suas a' ghlainne cheudna,
Cuimhnichimid slàint' an t-Slèibhtich,
Ridir òg gasda nach euradh
Dol le sgairt a shracadh reubal.

Slàint' Iarl' Antrum, tosta prìseil,
'S na tha 'n Eirinn Chlannaibh Mìlidh;
Tha mo sheile 'bàthadh m' ìotaidh
Chionn gu bheil mo bheul làn mìslein.

Lìon a suas duinn glainn' an Deasaich,
Learganach nan gorm-lann claiseach,
Anns an ruaig nuair ghabhadh teas iad
Le lùth-chleasan bualadh Shasann.

Cò 'n nàmhaid sin riu a sheasadh
'S cruaidh rùisgte 'nan dùirn gu slaiseadh,
Laochraidh sgathadh cheann is leasraidh,
Na suinn sheasmhach, shùnndach, mhaiseach.

Greasam gu finid gu stopadh,
Ach cha mhiann leam a bhith bacach:
Puirt-chiùil na smeòraiche dosaich,
Tostam fìor sheabhag na Ceapaich.

Togamaid slàinte nan Gleannach
O Chomhann nam bradan earrach
Bheireadh air bòcanaibh pilleadh;
Cha b' ghioragach iad air bealach.

Dìolamaid an tosta seo bharrachd
Deoch-slàinte nam fiùran glana
Bho Chruachan Beann an trom-ghaillinn
'S bho Ghleann Nodha nan sonn fearail.

Dìolamaid gu foirmeil, frasach
Slàinte Bhaghasdail mun stad sinn,
Laoch treun a dh' èireadh sgairteil
Chur ratreut air bèistean Shasainn.

Cuimhnicheam Iain Ciar á Lathairn'
Aig nach robh an stoidhle cumhang;
Gheibh thu mùirn is onoir fhathast
Air sgàth do ghràis mar as cubhaidh.

Cuirfeamaid mun cuairt gu toileach
Slàinte Mhic Dhùghaill bhon Bharrach,
Cridhe rìoghail, reamhar, solais
Tha 'na bhrollach shìos am falach.

Ciod am fàth dhaibh bhith gar tagradh
'S nach urrainn iad chur ruinn cluigean;
Sguiribh d' ur bòilich 's d' ur spaglainn,
An rud a th' againn 's e Dia thug dhuinn.

Is ioma nàmhaid a tha bagr' oirnn,
Is luchd farmaid air am beag sinn,
Chan e mìorun bochd a lag sinn
Sinn bhith rag san chòir a leag sinn.

NOTES

1153–6 The chorus is set out as in McL, but with accents added.
1153–5 *hì riag* Eigg, 1839 *iriag*, 1874 *hìriag*
1156 *do Chlann* McL *Chlainn*, Eigg and later sources *le Clann*
1157 *chreagach* McL *Chreggich*
1158 *bhàrr cuach* McL *bhar*, Eigg *far*, 1839 *chuaich*, later sources *cuaich*
1159 *Sholar bìdh* There are eccentric spellings in the early sources, as *Beigh* in McL and *T'sholar bigh* in Eigg, but such will not be quoted except where they throw light on the reading.
1160 *bhàrr* Eigg *bàr*, 1839 *bhàrr*, later edd. *bàrr*
1162 *dhìthicheadh 's* Eigg *dhitigh*, later edd. *dhìtheadh a's/is*. The McL and 1839 reading, with the verb *dìthich* 'destroy' is better as to sense and metre. The verb in the later sources is *dìth* 'die, perish'.
1163 *mo chur chur* omitted (accidentally?) in McL. 1839 has *'S chuireadh mis'*.
1164 *daibh* McL, 1839 *doibh*, Eigg *Dhoibh*, later edd. *dhaibh*
1165 *Chreig Ghuirm* 1839 *chreig ghuirm* (no caps.) A locality in Benbecula? The *smeòrach* here may not be the poet himself, but the clan songster, though he gives it connections that are closely associated with his own: Benbecula (if this is the reference in 11. 1165-6), Moidart and Loch Sheil.
1166 *Chaisteil Duibh* So also 1839 and 1874. Eigg has *chaisteal bhuiribh*, and 1924 has *Chaisteil Bhuirgh* with footnote 'Borve Castle, in Benbecula'.
1168 *mil is fion* Eigg *meala 's fion*, 1839 *meal', a's fion*. Later edd. *mheala 's fhìon(a)*. In the McL reading we can take *tuil* as qualifying only *bhainne*.
1169 All sources apart from McL start the line with *Sliochd*.
on Chaisteal Thioram Eigg *fo'n chaisteal tioram*
1169–70 *Caisteal Tioram* Caisteal Tioram in Moidart is said to have been the principal seat of Clanranald until 1715, when it was burned down and deserted (*Clan Donald*, 291, caption), according to Moidart tradition, on the chief's (Alan's) orders (*Ibid.*, 319).
1171 *togbhar* 1839 ff. *togar* The more archaic form is characteristic of the poet.
1172 *bileach* Eigg *bilich*
1173 *luachach* McL *luachaich*
1176 *sgiathaibh* So 1839, later edd. *sgiathan*
Ailean Mac Ruairidh Alan, 4th Chief of Clanranald (d. 1505), the direct progenitor of the line that was to produce the Moidart succession.
1177 *smùd* All other sources *smùr*. *smùd* 'dust, mote etc.' fits equally well, and gives the additional bonus of a consonantal agreement with the *smod* of *smodan*.
1178 *luathrnadh* Eigg *lua rua*, 1839 ff. *luaith ruaidh*. McL's form seems quite credible, as a 'verbal noun' formed from the same root as *luath* 'ash', and meaning 'covering with ash'.
ghrodan McL *Roddan*, 1839 *no ghrodan*
1180 *buille 'n* McL, Eigg *buil an*, 1839 *buill 'an*
1181 *buaireadh* McL *Buaidhreadh*, Eigg *buantachd*, 1839 ff. *buaineadh*. It is difficult to decide between these readings, taken in conjunction with the different readings for 1. 1182. Retaining McL's reading, the sense might be 'A royal kindred in turmoil like the bubbling movements of steel'.
1182 *Mar mhire mheara* Eigg *A mire mhearagh*, 1839 *A meribh meara*, later edd. *A mìr de mhearadh*. McL and Eigg, and probably 1839, are in basic agreement,

but the later sources try to avoid the implications of *mire* by changing the reading to *mìr* 'a small portion', which hardly suits the heroic context. If we take *mire* as a plural form of *mir* rather than of *mire*, the adjectival plural *meara* is more easily acceptable.

1183 *spàrr* 1839 *spar*. The sense seems to be 'an intrusive wedge' i.e. a blemish in the diamond.

1185 *spaglan* Eigg *spàran*, 1839 *sparan*, later edd. *spàrran*. *spaglan* 'ostentation' fits well, and rhymes with *rapal* (1. 1186) 'nonsensical talk'. The form *ràpal* 'noise' would fit better with the long *à* reading of Eigg etc.

1186 *rapal* McL's *Rossal* is unsuitable metrically. 1839 and later edd. have *ràpal*.

1187 *Coibhneil* 1839 *Caomhail*
cinneadail Eigg *aithnideil*, 1839 *cineadail* Though Eigg's reading, 'ready to give recognition', makes sense, *cinneadail* fits more neatly into the alliterative context.

1189 *tagach* 'nailed, studded' 1841 *taghach*

1191 *Thèid a sìos* 1839 ff. *A théid sìos*

1193 *daoin' tha* Other sources *daoine th' air*

1194 *plùndrainn* 'plundering'. 1839, 1841 apparently disapproved of this borrowing, reading *spùileadh*.

1197–1204 These two stanzas not in Eigg. They may be post-1746, in view of the references to the Prince coming (again?). See too 11. 1229-30.

1198 *Triallfaidh* Other sources *Triallaidh*
uamhaidh McL *umhaidh*, other sources *uamhaig*. We may perhaps take *uamhaidh* as a dative of *uamh(a)*.

1199 *a' – – – a'* Other sources *ri – – – ri*

1203 *baileach* 1839 *builleach*, 1841, 1874 *buileach*, 1924 *bailceach*. Perhaps what we have here is an adj. based on *baile*, so 'feeling at home'.

1204 *'na phailis* 1839 *an aroìs*, 1841 *'san àrois*, later edd. *'na àros*. The McL reading preserves internal rhyme with *baileach*.

1205 *am bàrr badain* McL *bachdain*, Eigg *m bàr gach badain*, 1839, 1874 *(a)m bàrr gach badain*, 1924 *'m bàrr gach bacain*.

1206 *á gloic* Eigg *a ghloic*, 1839 *o ghlaic*. Armstrong lists a feminine noun *gloc*, with the sense, among others, of 'throat'.

1207 *thururaich* Eigg *thruitrach*, 1839 *thruitreach*, 1841 *chruiteach*. The later sources agree with McL here.

1208 *bhuinn air stuibein* 1924 *bhonn air stoban*

1210 *bacan* Eigg *bachdan*

1211 *dam bheus* Eigg *'na bheus*, 1924 *'na beus*, 1839 and 1874 *gam bheus*, variously apostrophied.

1213 The singing of the male thrush 'softens' the female (?).
ugan McL *Inntin*
ga bogadh The reference is apparently to a female or a feminine noun, suggesting that it may refer back to *cearc* in 1. 1211.

1214 *chompar* McL *Chomtur*, Eigg *chom-tur*, other sources *chom tur*. The close agreement of the two earliest sources, and the slightly strained solution of later editors, suggest that we have a rare but genuine form here. Can it be a misreading or mis-recording of *chompar*? *compar* is not uncommon in earlier Irish texts, apparently in the sense of 'body' or 'midst' (for citations see RIA Dict.).

1215 *uchd* Eigg *uch*

1216 It is difficult to be sure of how to take this line. Our reading here is McL's. Eigg has – – – *gu dannsa air leagail*, and 1839 follows this. The later sources do likewise but substitute *leigeil* for *leigail*. The sense seems clear enough: 'and I am completely given over to dancing'; the problem is whether to accept one of the idioms or both.

1217 *Nuair* McL, Eigg *Nar*, 1839 *'Nuir chuirean.* It is difficult here again to give a confident interpretation: 'When I let my cackling take a different course' or 'When I twisted my cackling throat'.
1218 *creagan* 1839 *chreagan*
1219 *sogan* Eigg, 1839m 1874 *frogan.* 1924 here agrees with McL's *sogan.*
1220 *thogail* McL *thogbhail* This line is reminiscent of folktale style, e.g. *'Thog iad ceòl 's leag iad bròn'* in 'Gaisgeach na Sgèithe Deirge' (cf. Watson, 1915, 1929, p. 89).
1222 *mar ruinn* McL *Maireann*
1244 *fead-choill* McL *Fead Choill*, Eigg *feid ghoill*, 1839, 1841 *fead-ghuil*, later sources *feadail.* The early forms are peculiar, as *coille* is a feminine noun.
1226 *badain* Eigg *baidan*
1227 *na puirt* McL *a Puirt*
sgreadan 1841 *spreadan*
1228 *m' fheadan* 1839, 1874 *m' fheadag*
1229–40 These lines are not in Eigg. See 11. 1197-1204 *n.*
1229 *Siud oirbh* 1839, 1874 *Togamaid*
1230 *Teàrlach* McL *T---*, which is the style favoured by Mac Mhaighstir in *Ais-eiridh* when there are references to the Old and the Young Pretender.
1231 *searra-bhuain* McL *shearbh-bhuain* The form with *searra* (cf. *seàrr*, 'cut, reap') is more vivid.
1234 *cuirfeamaid* McL *cuirfemid*, other sources *cuireamaid.*
1235–6 McL has *Sh----* and *Th----* for the royal references.
1238 *geanail* McL *anois.* 1841, 1874 and 1924 agree on *geanail*, which fits the rhyming pattern.
1239 *sgòrnan gionach* The other sources have *sgòrnain ghiona(i)ch* which is perhaps more logical though not obligatory.
1240 *bruidhneach* 1839 *suileach*, later sources *srùlach.*
1241 *Cuirfeamaid* Other sources *Cuireamaid.* Eigg's orthography is odd, as often: *Cuir a miad sìos feasgar.*
1243 *sgaiteach, gasda* 1839 *gasda sgaiteach*
1244 *'S ro-mhòr* 1839 *Tro mhor*
còmhrag lannach The three earliest sources do not use the dative here; 1874 and 1924 amend to *còmhraig lannaich.* Is this a genuine instance of non-insistence on the dative in an indefinite statement?
1245 *tionndadh* All other sources *teannadh.* Either reading makes good sense.
h-eirthir 1839 *oir-thir*
1246 McL *Ullmhaichim – – – – h ealamh*
1247 *Mùideart* used here of Ranald MacDonald of Clanranald, Chief from 1730 to 1766, but here addressed as leader of the men of Moidart and Sheil.
1248 Eigg has *'S an slainte eil' ud triach nan garrach* and this is the formulation used by all sources except McL.
Triath nan Garrach John MacDonald of Glengarry, Chief from 1721 to 1754.
1249–52 This stanza is not in Eigg, 1874 or 1924, but 1839 and 1841 have it.
1250 Raghnall Og was out in the '45, and succeeded his father Ranald as chief in 1766.
deas 1839 *deis*
1251 *Sguir da h-amharc* 1839 *Sguiribh dh' amharc*
1252 McL *Shiabaibh i, as a Teas i* is a syllable short, and the 1841 reading is chosen instead. *ás a teas i* 'take it out of its heat (literally), be done with it!'
1253 *Lìon a suas* 1839, 1841 *Stràc suas*, 1874 *Lìon suas*, 1924 *Lìonaibh suas*
1254 *an t-Slèibhtich* Sir James MacDonald of Sleat, who was to succeed to the chiefship, as a minor, in 1746. The fact that a toast to the young Sleat is included may suggest a dating for this stanza soon after his father's death in 1746.

1255 *nach euradh* McL *nach Earragh*, Eigg – – – *eirigh*, 1839 *na eireadh*, 1924 *'na éirigh*. The sense is 'who would not refuse'.
1256 *reubal* Eigg *bheastan*, later sources *bhèistean*
1257 *Iarl' Antrum* All the sources give the form *Antram*, although *Aondruim* is generally the preferred form. Alexander 5th Earl of Antrim is the person referred to.
1258 *Chlannaibh Mìlidh* Clanna Mìlidh or the Sons of Mìl are regarded as the original Scottic settlers in Ireland.
1259 *sheile* Eigg *sheilligh*, 1839, *shileadh*, 1841 *shile*. The word *seile* means 'saliva'. The rush of saliva induced by the sweetness (the rich drink and the thoughts that go with the toasts?) is drowning his thirst.
1260 *mìslein* 1874 to 1924 *mìlsein*
1261–4 This stanza is not in Eigg.
1261 *an Deasaich* 1839, 1874 *do'n Deasach*, 1924 *nan Deasach*
1262 *Learganach* The other sources have the plural *Learganaich*, which accords better with the reference in 11. 1263-4. The change from singular *Deasach* to the plural referring to his clansmen may well reflect the original.
The *Learganach* is John MacDonald of Largie in Kintyre. He took part in the '45.
1263–4 In 1839 and the later sources these two lines come at the end of the next stanza, and its final lines are joined to our 11. 1261-2 here.
1263 *bualadh Shasann* 1924 *Shasuinn*. 1839, 1841 and 1874 have italicised *shaisean*, implying a loanword (*sashes*?)
1266 *cruaidh rùisgte* 'bared steel'
dùirn McL *dorn*
slaiseadh Eigg *slais rich*, 1924 *slaisrich*
1267 McL has only *Laochraidh* followed by a blank for this line. Eigg reads *Laoich a scathaidh cheann is leasrach*. 1841 and later sources as in our text.
1268 *sheasmhach* Eigg *sheasrach*, 1839 *sheasach*
1269 *stopadh* Eigg *stoppa*
1271 *na smeòraiche dosaich* McL *nan smeoraiche dossach*
1272 *seabhag na Ceapaich* 'the hawk of Keppoch' i.e. Alexander MacDonell of Keppoch, who was killed at Culloden in 1746.
1273–4 The reference is to the MacDonalds of Glencoe.
1275 *bòcanaibh* McL *Bocan a*. The sense of the line is 'who would make spectres turn back'.
1277–80 This stanza is not in 1839, 1841.
1279 *Bho* McL, Eigg *Fo*
an trom-ghaillinn 1874 to 1924 *na trom-ghaillin(n)*. The reading *an* here can be interpreted as the preposition rather than the definite article.
1280 *Ghleann Nodha* McL *ghleannan Nuadh*, Eigg *ghleann nothadh*. The reference is to the Macintyres of Glen Noe.
1281–4 This stanza is not in McL or Eigg. In other sources it comes just after the Earl of Antrim stanza.
1282 *Baghasdal* Alexander MacDonald of Boisdale, South Uist.
1285–1300 These stanzas are not in Eigg.
1285 *Cuimhnicheam Iain Ciar á* McL *Cuimhneachan churaidhean*, 1839, 1841, 1874 *Chuimhnicheam* – – –, 1924 *Cuimhnicheam curaidhean Lathurn*. The specific reference to Iain Ciar, John MacDougall of Lorn, is retained (from 1839 etc.), as it seems to be reinforced by 11. 1287-8, especially in McL, which reads *thu* and *do*.
1287 *thu* 1839, 1841 *e*, 1924 *iad*
fhathast McL *fasd*, 1839, 1841 *fhathach*
1288 1839 *A's caitheadh drais mar as cubhaidh*, with *drais* in italics. Is this the borrowing of 'drawers', perhaps used here of stylish trousers?

1290 *Mhic Dhùghaill* The MacDonald editors explain this as a reference to MacDonald of Morar, 'patronymically called Macdougall'. Both Alan of Morar and his son John were 'out' in the '45 (1924 ed., 187).
1291 *solais* McL *soluisht.* Perhaps we should read *so-laist*', 'warm, easily fired'.
1292 *bhrollach* Other sources *bhroilleach*
1293 *bhith gar tagradh* McL *a bhi Fair' oirn* (which is less satisfactory as to rhyme).
1294 *urrainn iad* 1839 *urr' iad*, other sources *urrainn daibh*
cluigean McL *Cluiggein*, glossed 'affront'. The word means 'pendant; little bell' etc. Is this an oblique reference to cursing (bell, book and candle)?
1295 *d'ur* McL *d'ar*, other sources *de'r*
1296 1841 *'N rud tha againn, 's Dia thug dhuinne*
1297–1300 This stanza is not in 1839, 1841.
1297 McL *'S iomad Namhad a ta bagr' oirn*
1298 McL *farmad*
1300 *san* 1874 to 1924 *'s a'*
The final stanza reads as if it was composed after the failure of the '45.

ORAN A RINNEADH A' BHLIADHNA 1746

Sources and Editions:

1751	116-23
1802	128-35
1839	111-16
1874, 1892	103-8
1924	118-24
1984	94-104
1993	52-8

The 1751 text is the basic one, with in the main only minor editorial adaptations imposed by the 1839, 1874 and 1924 editions. Most of these are discarded here. There are no closely contemporary manuscript sources known to me of this poem.

In spite of some internal evidence that the poem, or part of it, was composed during the '45 Rising and its immediate aftermath (see especially the opening two stanzas, and the references in the last five stanzas to Hanoverian oppression, reflecting the Cumberland ravages), this is a careful, logical exposition of the poet's point of view. The opening stanzas probably date from after the battle of Culloden. In spite of these pressures he develops the theme of royal Stuart legitimacy, and Hanoverian illegitimacy, in a controlled way, emphasising the genealogical expertise that his people had developed over the centuries, making clear political judgements on the Act of 1701 and its later consequences, and unleashing his satiric powers on the Hanoverian dynasty in a long succession of comparisons to pigs, boars, piglings and ravens. His argument alternates between emotional and intellectual approaches, with the intention of enlisting support from a wide range of listeners, and it is still underpinned by an optimism that had survived many years of political frustration. Some of the visual imagery is exceptionally vivid, and this must rank as one of the poet's most arresting and skilful political poems (for further general comment see Thomson, D. S., 'Alasdair Mac Mhaighstir Alasdair: his political poetry', TGSI, Vol. 56, 185-213).

It may be useful to set out, briefly, the thematic development of the poem:

(a) ll. 1301-20: the cold dreich weather is described, but it will change, for good weather will arrive with the rightful king, as will supplies of French wine etc.

(b) ll. 1321-30: The Gaelic historians are urged to record the events of the year.

(c) ll. 1331-40: He urges the clansmen to fight for their rights.

(d) ll. 1341-70: The legitimacy of the Hanoverian claim is repudiated, as is the 1701 Act.

(e) ll. 1371-80: The opposition to the Stuart dynasty now on religious grounds is questioned.

(f) ll. 1381-1400: Hanoverian supporters are likened to users of prostitutes. The legitimacy of the Hanoverians is again questioned.

(g) ll. 1401-20: The Hanoverians are satirised as boars, pigs etc., and their savage indifference to their 'subjects' is underscored, in telling images of deprived children, ravenous ravens etc. There is a reference here to the internecine conflict between the Highlanders also.

(h) ll. 1421-40: King James and Prince Charles are addressed, exalted and welcomed.

(i) ll. 1441-50: A final disparaging reference is made to the pig-snouted Hanoverians, and a prayer is made for the Stuart return to Whitehall.

The poet uses a ten-line stanza, with a fluid rhyming pattern which begins regularly with *a b a a*, but thereafter varies almost from verse to verse, producing such line-ending sequences as *a b a a a c a d e d*; *a b a a c d c c d c*; *a b a a c d c e f e*. There may be a trace of influence from such poets as Gavin Douglas, who uses in 'The Palice of Honour' a nine-line stanza, with such rhyme-schemes as *a a b a a b b a b* and *a a b a a b b c c*.

ORAN A RINNEADH A' BHLIADHNA 1746

'S fuar fearthainneach gach lò,
Gach oidhche dorcha doineannach,
'S tùrsach donn gach lò,
Murtaidh trom le ceò:
Ach mosglaibh suas, a shlòigh,
'S ur n-airtneal trusaibh chum ur cairteal',
'S cairtibh uaibh ur bròn;
Tha lèig ri muir 's ri speur
Ri bhith aig Aeolus 's aig Neptiun.
'S thig gach tlachd 'na dèidh.

Thig soineann leis an R[ìgh],
Teichidh sneachd is èighre uainn;
Fògrar dòrainn shìon,
Thig sòlas, falbhaidh pìan;
Gach seòrsa de gach fìon
Thig o'n Fhr[aing] 'na thunnachaibh,
'S gun caisg sinn uile ar n-ìot;
Gheibh sinn tuil d'ar mìann,
'S m' ar nàimhde dh' fhàg sinn uireasach
'S dlùth chuireas sinn ar lìon.

O sheanchaidhnibh nan clann,
Suas dèanaibh eachdraidh èifeachdach,
O sheanchaidhnibh san àm
Glacaibh dubh is peann!
Seo a' bhliadhna chòrr
An tilg a' ghrian le meadh-bhlàths biadhchar
Gathain chiatach òirnn;
Bidh driùchd air bhàrr an fheòir,
Bainne 's mil gun luach gun mhargadh,
Airgead agus òr.

Na gabhaibh sìth o Dh[eòr]s';
Le 'r dòchas neartor fìrinneach
Creidibh dìan sa' chòir,
Gun tig relìobh nas leòr;
Na biodh ur dòchas fann:
Gur h-ann air rèir mar chuireas sibh
A bhios ur buinnig ann;
O, fuirichibh, a Chlann,
'S chì sibh ur n-uil' uireasan
Da bhuinnig le cruas lann.

Ciod e do cheart-s' air crùn,
Ach adhaircean bhith sparradh ort?
'S co-sean ri d' chòir o thùs
Brìos òir-cheard bha Renfriù.
Ach bha ion-faileis ann
Do thrustar do dh' act Pàrlamaid
A dh'fhoil an crùn ma d' cheann.
Ach tog seo leat nad sgèith:
An t-Uilleam rinn an t-act-s' dhuit
Gum b'eucoireach e fèin.

Dèan aithridh thùrsach gheur
'S grad thoir air n-ais na th'agad uat;
Dèan aithridh ghuineach 's gèill,
'S le br[aoim]-bh[rui]c toilich t'fheum;
Cùm agad do chuid fèin
Is leig uat còir an atharraich
Gun chlaidheamh, gun dad streup;
Dia, daoine 's nàdur treun
Bidh ann a lèig m'an oighr'
Thoirt dhachaigh, choibhreas ceart a threud.

Craobh-sheanchais teaghlaich rìgh,
Na h-ìochdarain bidh eòlach uimp';
Craobh-sheanchais teaghlaich rìgh,
Bidh map dhi 'n iomad tìr;
'S ma chuirear car 'm bi foinn
San t-snàithean dhìreach oighreachdail
Gun toir fa-near an fhoill;
Ach gairmidh Dia le sgoinn
Chum an ionaid dhleasdannaich
Ceart oighre deas an loidhn.

Chan eil an leisgeul ann
Ach saobhadh fann mì-dhiongmhalta;
'S i 'n eucoir shoilleir th'ann
Do neach a bheirte dall;
Mas creideamh an aon chùis,
Chionn nach d' fhuair e oideachd
Anns an teagasg a rinn Lùth,
O! nam b'e sin an càs
Cuim' na chuir sibh 'shinn-seanair
Gu mìorunach gu bàs?

Chan eil ur gaol d'ur Rìgh
Ach mar air an t-siùrsaich choitcheanta;
'S cuglach staid ur Rìgh,
Cuairt thoirt da 's bhith sgìth;
Gun d'fhògair sibh a-rìs
Le 'r n-iomluas sliochd a' mhairteoir sin
Le ascaoineachd ur crìdh;
'S 'na dhèidh sin ged thug uaibh
Do dh'Anna crùn a sinnsireachd,
Gun phuinnseanaich sibh luath.

O 's caol an teud, a Dh[eòr]s'
Air na sheinn thu gu trì rìoghachdaibh;
Gur meallta 'n t-act le 'n chleòc
Iad thusa nad R[ìgh] òirnn;
Tha lethcheud pearsa 's còrr
As faigse fuil is tagraichean
Na thusa san Roinn Eòrp';
Bu leathoireach lag càm
'M meur boireann o na bhuineadh thu,
B' fhìor iumallach sa' chrann.

O! 'n cullach sin R[ìgh] D[eòr]s',
Mac na cr[ài]n[e] Gearmailtich!
'S e 'chàirdeas ruinn 's a dhàimh
Gaol fithich air a' chnàimh;
Gun d' fheann e sinn o'r bèin;
Ghlac is chreach an cealgaire
'S gun mharbh e sinn gu lèir;
Na daoine cha leis fèin,
'S ann uime sin gur coma leis
Ged phronnamaid a chèil'.

An leanabh nach leis fèin,
Ged dhèanta dà leth chothrom dheth
Cha tiomaichd' e le a phèin;
A chrìdh gun tlus gun deur;
Is amhail sin mar tha
Ged chuirt' a h-uile Breatainneach
Gun mhèin gun chead gu bàs;
O nach leis fèin am pàist
Cha ghluaist' an neach nach b'athair dha
Gu fabhar no gu bàigh.

Greas ort, a Sh[eumai]s chaoimh,
'S tu 's R[ìgh] 's as athair talmhaidh dhuinn
F'an athair nèamha naomh;
Gabh tlus ri d' chlainn 's bi caoin;
'S os leat fèin a' Chlann,
Cuir casg air croich 's air geuragaibh
Tha reubadh dhinn nan ceann;
Is cuir do threud fo lann,
'S na leig a bhith dar geur-leanmhainn
Feadh garbhlaich, slèibh is bheann.

Mo chion-sa S[eur]l[a]s ruadh,
Ceart oighr' an fhìor R[ìgh] dhleasdannaich;
Cha toir sinn duibhse fuath
Gun cuirear sinn san uaigh;
Cha dèan croich no tuagh,
Glacaireachd no creachannan,
Gu bràth ar sracadh uat;
Tha 'n diog ud ceangailt shìos
An caigeann ris gach anam dhinn
Cho daingeann ri Beinn Shìont.

Och, a Rìgh nan dùl,
Na leig-sa neart a ghnàth thar cheart;
Ochòin, aon Dia ta 'd thriùir,
'S ann duit as lèir gach cùis:
Tog dhinn a' mh[u]c 's a cuing,
'S a h-àl breac brothach oirceanach
Le 'n cuid chrom-shoc thar tuinn;
Is cairt gu glan Whitehall
Air chionn an teaghlaich rìoghail sin
Bha 'sinnsreadh ann an tàmh.

NOTES

The 1751 edition gives the air/model: 'Air fonn, Let history record &c'.

1301 *fearthainneach* 1751, 1802 *fearrannach* See 1. 923*n*.

1302 *doineannach* 1751 etc. *doinshíonach* The 1751 form may suggest that the poet was connecting the word with *sìon* 'weather'. See *Celt. Rev*. X, 143.22

1306 *chum ur cairteal'* 1751 *chum air chairteal'*, 1984 *uaibh air chairteal'*. The 1751 reading is awkward, but if we regard the lenition in *chairteal'* as an aberration it is easier to make sense of it: 'draw in your depression to your quarters' i.e. dispose of your depression. Another possible emendation is *chum a chairteal'* 'to its quarters'.

1307 *uaibh* 1874 *bhuaidh*, 1924 *bhuaibh*

1308 *lèig* 1751 *léig* This is a borrowing of English 'league'. Aeolus, god of the winds, and Neptune, god of the sea, are to be in league with sea and sky, and produce good weather. The poet gives *lèig* the feminine gender. Matheson's

(1951) suggestion that the sense is possibly 'A. and N. are to lay siege to sea and sky' seems less convincing.

1311 *soineann* 1751 *soin-shion*. Here the poet again defines his etymology of the word. See 1. 1302*n*.
Rìgh As often with personal or place-names, 1751 has simply *R*---. See also 1. 1316 etc.

1312 *èighre* 1751 *éiridh èighre* 'frost, ice' is included in MacEachen's Dictionary, probably reflecting West Inverness-shire usage.

1313–15 The grouping of rhymes *Rìgh, shìon, pìan* and *fìon* suggests an *ì* pronunciation for the four at this point, though it may be an *ia* pronunciation that is used in the instances of *ìot* and *lìon* in 11. 1317 and 1320 (as there is often a different rhyme sequence in the latter parts of stanzas).

1316 *thunnachaibh* 1751 *thunnachabh* Later editors change to *thunnaichean/thunnaichibh*.

1318 'we will get what we desire in flood (in full measure)'.

1319 *nàimhde* So 1751. This may have been the poet's normal plural form of *nàmhaid*, rather than *nàimhdean*.

1321 *sheanchaidhnibh* 1751 *sheanachainnibh*

1322 *Suas dèanaibh* – – – 1751 *Suas deanamh* 1874 ff. have *Suas, deanaibh*, and 1984 interprets this as 'arise, write – – –'. It may well be, however, that the poet is using a calque of English 'make up', and that the sense is 'compile an effectual chronicle'.

1326 *meadh-bhlàths* 1751 *meubhlás*, 1874, 1924 *maoth-bhlàs*

1327 *Gathain chiatach* 1751 *Gaithain chiatoch* It is the plural of the diminutive *gathan* we have here, with appropriate lenition of the following adjective. 1874 ff. *Gaithean/Gathan ciatach*.

1328 *bhàrr* 1874, 1924 *bàrr*

1336 *air rèir* So 1751. 1874 ff. *a réir*. 1751 reading may either represent the poet's usage or it may be a slack notation. The sense is 'according to'.

1338 *fuirichibh, a Chlann* This can be interpreted literally 'wait, clansmen' i.e. it may be addressed to the clansmen as they dispersed after Culloden. On the other hand, we can consider the interpretation 'just wait – – – and see, all your needs will be supplied – – –'.

1339 *uireasan* 1874, 1924 *uireasbhuidh*. The singular form may be supported by *Da bhuinnig* in the following line, but a plural *uireasan* seems to fit the sense better.

1341–50 Here the poet addresses King George II directly, discusses what he sees as his dubious right to the throne, referring apparently to his German ancestors who may have had horned helmets (unless he is suggesting also that he is a devil with horns). The reference to *Brìos* in 1. 1344 is quite specific: 'Bryce a goldsmith who lived in Renfrew'. Brice Semphill, a goldsmith in Renfrew, was thought to have a claim to the kingship.
He then goes on to refer to the Act of Settlement (1701) which resulted eventually in the crown coming improperly to George. The Act of Settlement is referred to as a reprobate Act of Parliament. Finally he refers to the Dutch King William, 'who made this Act for you', calling him a guilty person.

1345 *ion-faileis* 'equivalent of a shadow'. John Lorne Campbell (1984) translated this as 'pretence', which seems to hit the mark.

1347 *dh' fhoil* The High. Soc. Dict. gives as one sense of *foileadh* 'acting imperfectly or in a hurry', and this fits our context well.

1348 Literally 'lift this with you in your wing'. A more modern idiom would be 'put this in your pipe and smoke it'.

1349 *t-act-s'* 1751 *t acts'*, 1874, 1924 *t-Achd*, 1984 *t-achd-sa*

1351 *aithridh* 1751 *aithri*, 1874, 1924 *aithre*. The 1874 and 1924 editors make this masculine, reading *tùrsach, geur*.

1352 *air n-ais* 1874, 1924 *air ais*
1354 *le br(aoim) bh(rui)c* 1751 *Br--- bh---c*, 1839 *bròim bruic*, 1874, 1924 *br---m-bruic.* John L. Campbell comments 'I have not felt called upon to restore a line that MacDonald with unusual delicacy expurgated himself'. With only a hint of diffidence the full text is restored here. The sense is 'Give relief to your need with a badger's fart'.
1356 *an atharraich* 'the other person'. This usage seems to be quite well attested. See exx. in Dwelly.
1360 This line can be interpreted in two ways: (1) who will rightly comfort his flock, (2) who will support his flock's right.
1361 *craobh-sheanchais* genealogical tree, pedigree. In Older Gaelic the forms *cráeb choibneasa* and *cráeb geinelaig/craobh geinealaigh* are used in a similar sense.
1364 *iomad* 1874, 1924 *ioma*
1365 *foinn* Is this word related to Older Gaelic *foindel*, 'wandering'? The sense of 'twist, twisting' seems to be required.
1366 *snàithean* 1751 *snaithen* Diminutive of *snàth* 'a thread'.
1367 *Gun toir* This refers back to *Na h-ìochdarain* 'the underlings will notice – – –'.
1370 *loidhn* 1751 *loin.* A borrowing of English *line.*
1372 *saobhadh* The sense is evidently 'dissembling, prevarication'.
1377 *Lùth* A short form of *Luther*, perhaps dictated by the metre?
1378 *nam* 1751 *ma'm*
1379 *'shinn-seanair* The great-grandfather of Prince Charles was Charles I, who although a Protestant was put to death in 1649, while now, says the poet, the position is that a Catholic must not succeed to the throne.
1381–4 The poet uses the image of the prostitute, used for a short while and then rejected, to discredit the treatment of the rightful Stuart line.
1383 *cuglach* 1874, 1924 *cioglach*
1386 *iomluas* 1751 *iumalas* no doubt reflects the poet's pronunciation.
a' mhairteoir The martyr here refers to Charles I.
1388 *ged thug* 1751 *go d' thug*
1389 *Anna* Queen Anne
1390 *phuinnseanaich* 1751 *phoinseonaich* The sense here is 'became poisoned'.
1391–1400 This stanza emphasises insistently the relative remoteness of the Hanoverian claim to the throne, claiming that there are more than fifty people in Europe with stronger claims, especially through male lines. The Act of 1701 is again castigated.
1396 *faigse* 1874 ff. *faisge* The poet's form is well attested; it is the comparative form of *fagas/fagus* 'close'.
1399 *a na* 1874, 1924 *as 'n a*
1400 *iumallach* 1874 ff. *iomallach* The *-u-* form underlines the internal rhyme that is required here.
1401 King George is referred to as a boar, the son of a German sow. In 1751 the word for 'sow' is given as *cr---n.* This reticence or caution is surprising.
1403 The poet uses one of his sharp Nature images: King George's friendship and love is that of the raven for the bone of a dead carcase. A similar image comes in 1. 1405, where George skins the Highlanders ('he flayed us from our pelt').
1411–13 'Though two equally heavy halves were made of the child that does not belong to him, he would not be softened by its pain'. The image of the child is continued in 11. 1418-9.
tiomaichd' So 1751. 1874 ff. *tiomaich.* The sense is 'he would not be softened' rather than 'he does not soften'.
1416 *Breatainneach* 1751 *briottainneach* The internal rhyme requires *ea* rather than *io.*
1417 *mhèin* 1751 *mhein. 1984 has bhinn. binn* and *cead*, 'sentence' and

'permission', go well together, but *mèin* 'clemency, mercy' makes equally good sense.

1420 *fabhar* Matheson (1951) suggests that a pronunciation with short *a* (rather than *fàbhar*) is indicated here.

1421 *Greas ort* 1751 *Greos-ort*
Seumas i.e. King James III, the Old Pretender, who died in 1766.

1423 *nèamha* 1751 *neamha*, 1874 ff. *nèamhaidh* It is possible to take the sense as 'father of heaven' rather than 'heavenly father', though this makes little or no difference to the sense.

1425 *a' Chlann* The capital *C* is used in 1751. The image of the fatherless child in the previous stanza is picked up here, but the single child becomes the 'clan' i.e. the Highlanders. Later, in l. 1428, the clan becomes a 'flock'.

1426 *geuragaibh* J. L. Campbell (1984, p. 103) translated 'axe', which fits well, along with *croich*, as to sense. Literally 'little sharp-pointed ones'.

1430 *slèibh is* 1874, 1924 *shléibhtean 's*

1433 *duibhse* 1751 *duibhs'*, 1839 ff. *dutsa/duitse*. It is surely the honorific plural that was intended.

1438 *diog* The sense seems to be 'breath, life', or possibly 'being, purpose of life'.

1440 *Beinn Shìont* An Ardnamurchan mountain, part of the poet's landscape.

1442 *leig-sa* 1751 *leigs'*

1445 *mhuc* 1751 *mh-c*. See ll. 1401-2*n*.

1446 *oirceanach* 1751 *oirceneach*, 1839 *uirceanach*, 1874 ff. *uirceineach*. The form with *o* has an ancient pedigree (see Old Gaelic *orc, oircnín*), and fits the internal rhyme scheme better.

1448 *cairt* 1751 ff. *cart*

1448–50 Notice the rhyme between *-hall*, pronounced in a Highland way, and *tàmh*.

1450 *sinnsreadh* 1874, 1924 *sìnnsrean*

BIRLINN CHLANN RAGHNAILL

Sources and Editions:

McD	92-4 (for Section 4 only)
Eigg	146-66
McL 15	1-8
R.I.A.	1-21
P. Campbell (Argyll and Bute District Archives, DRI/67/17)	
1809	160-80
1813	1-21
1839	156-76
1841	136-42
1874, 1892	166-85
1910	221-55
1924	370-400
1933	37-59
1961	46-64

Some of the above editions do not have truly separate authority, and some impose editorial choices that can not be justified. The Eigg version is the earliest printed one, but the version represented by McLagan 15, R.I.A. MS E ii 1, and P. Campbell may be contemporary or earlier. Subsequent editions are based on the Eigg version, until J. L. Campbell's 1961 edition. Dr Campbell was not aware of the McLagan MS 15 and P. Campbell texts, which are closely related to the R.I.A. one, nor of the MacDiarmid fragment.

The most detailed edition of the poem is that of Angus MacLeod in *Sàr Orain.* MacLeod gives a great deal of detail on galley construction, and a valuable textual commentary, and the present edition owes much to his sterling work.

It is not proposed to provide a detailed textual apparatus for this edition, but to concentrate on the earlier sources, showing in some detail the relationship between the Eigg, McLagan, R.I.A. and P. Campbell texts, and referring to persuasive editorial interpretations in later editions. Textual variants will not be given exhaustively even for the early sources, as the Eigg version in particular has many readings that are merely eccentric orthographically or are misprints. More detail is given of significant McL, R.I.A. and P. Campbell readings, especially since the McL and P. Campbell versions are unpublished.

The McL 15 and R.I.A. texts are extremely similar, though not identical, and one must conclude that they are both copies of the same original, or just possibly that one is a copy of the other. The differences between the two versions are practically all minute orthographical variations (*sheolaigh/sheolaidh, airmseach/ airmseadh, airstil/airsteal*); a handful may be more significant (*re/ag, fiadh-ghair/fadh-ghair*). They provide, however, a good crop of readings that differ from those of Eigg, though there is a strong relationship with the Eigg text, especially when that text is shorn of its misprints. A Uist rather than a Mainland pronunciation surfaces especially in part of the Eigg text, but also in the McL and R.I.A. versions. It is difficult to be certain that this is to be traced back solely to the poet. The differences between Eigg on the one hand and McL and R.I.A. on the other are often orthographical (e.g. *fon/fuidh'n, Gad dhatadh/Ge do attagh, traladh/troladh*). A fair number are more significant (with such contrasts as *an comh-dhia/a choimh-Dhia, taoidibh/teudaidh, dugharra/durragha, thuairefudh/thuairipidh, maom/màm*), and a number give distinct readings (*Irchiulich/Ireghiullach, Bigh/Beo, gruamach/guamach, Dhorann/Orduigh ann, fuaim/garbh, cathadh/ dall-cheò*). These are discussed in the Notes. Importantly, McL and R.I.A. have a few lines not in Eigg but clearly belonging to the poem (see 11. 1664-5, 1693, 1929).

P. Campbell refers to an incomplete version of the 'Birlinn' in the papers of the Rev. Patrick Campbell, who was minister of Kilninver and Kilmelford from 1757 to 1797, and whose father was John Campbell, tacksman of Stronmilchan near Dalmally. These papers were deposited in the Argyll and Bute District Archives by Mrs Catherine Graham Taylor, of Kings Bridge, Devon. I am indebted to Rev. Roderick MacLeod, Manse of Cumlodden, for bringing this MS to my attention, and sending me a photo-copy of it. This version begins at Section 9 (1. 1708 of the present edition), the previous pages of the MS having gone missing. Some of the introductions to sections are shortened, and in a few cases a short sequence of lines is missed out. This version is closely related to the McL 15 and R.I.A. versions, but has a fair number of variants, which are noted below.

There can be no doubt that the combined evidence of McL, R.I.A. and P. Campbell allows us to make more confident decisions on the minutiae of the text.

The text of Eigg was re-published by Patrick Turner in 1809, under the orthographically revised title *Comh-chruinneachadh Orain Ghaidhealach, le Raonull MacDhomhnuill.* The title-page has the addition 'Ath-leasaichte Le Paruig Tuairneir'. Turner's editorial work on the 'Birlinn' text is mainly confined to some orthographical tidying and correction of misprints. There is no evidence of his having had access to another text. Many of the corrections are obvious and sensible, but some are misjudged. It did not seem necessary to include variant readings from the 1809 edition.

Subsequent editions of the 'Birlinn' are largely based on the Eigg text, but introduce a wide range of editorial emendations which go well beyond orthographical normalisation. MacPharlain's edition of 1813 introduces various changes in word-endings (e.g. *-an* for *-aibh* in some instances; nominative rather than genitive), and also word substitutions (e.g. *tearuinte* for *trèanont, tonn* for *sonn*), and many of his emendations were adopted by John Mackenzie, and became standard, especially after the publication of his *Sàr Obair* in 1841. Many of these are confirmed in Donald C. MacPherson's edition of 1874, and it in turn was frequently followed by the editors of the 1924 edition. MacPherson introduced further 'normalisations', and some readings which seem to have been his own.

Angus MacLeod's edition of 1933 is the first scholarly one of the 'Birlinn'. He refers, in specific instances, to the readings of earlier editors, but does not provide an extensive textual apparatus. His aim is clearly to produce a text which is as close as possible to the Eigg one, allowing for its eccentricities. He did not have the benefit of the McL, R.I.A. and P. Campbell texts to interpret or reinforce or supplement the Eigg one.

Given the somewhat haphazard history of editions of this poem, it seemed excessive to produce exhaustive variant readings. Instead, variants are given in cases where they can help to reach conclusions about the original text, and are largely ignored where they concern only printers' errors and unconventional spellings. But it is hoped that a sufficient range of variants has been given to show something of the different profiles of editions and their inter-relationships.

Turning to the poem itself, it may be of interest to speculate as to how it came to be composed, and to analyse its structure and style and effect. The tradition in the island of Canna was that it was composed there, and that the poet lay under an upturned boat by the shore while he was composing. The South Uist tradition is that it was composed in South Uist. For a poem of this length, it may well be that parts of it were composed in the two locations. Mac Mhaighstir Alasdair would know of the practices of earlier bards, of composing in a darkened room or with a heavy stone on the poet's chest, and he may have adopted the Canna pose as an appropriate variant for a galley poem.

What is of greater significance is the evidence in the poem of his acquaintance with earlier Gaelic verse and story which touch on similar themes. Several of these points of contact have been noted by earlier editors, and are briefly commented on here. It is likely that the poet was familiar with the 'Beannachadh Luinge' (Ship's Blessing) which is included in Carswell's writings (see *Foirm nan n-Urrnuidheadh*, ed. R. L. Thomson, 110-11), where there are successive blessings from God the Father, his son Jesus, and the Holy Spirit. This formula is also used by Eachann Bacach in his mid-seventeenth-century poem 'A' Chnò Shamhna', which ends:

Cuir ga caitheamh an Triùir seo:
Cuir an t-Athair air thùs ann,
Biodh am Mac 'na fhear iùil oirr',
An Spiorad Naomha ga stiùireadh gu nòs.
(Ó Baoill, 1979, 24)

Alexander Carmichael collected some examples of similar blessings in the second half of the nineteenth century, such as the 'Urnaigh Mhara' (*Carmina Gadelica*, I, 332-4) and the 'Beannachadh Cuain' (*ibid*., 324-6), which invokes various saints as well, and names Là Fhèill Brìde, the 1st of February, as the choice day for a sea voyage. The same collection (Vol. 3, 171ff.) has several examples of prayers made before beginning a journey.

At several points in the course of the 'Birlinn' poem, parallels exist in earlier Gaelic literature. Some of these are very close, others more general. One of the closest is to be found in the description of the launching of 'An Iùbhrach Bhallach' (The Speckled Ship(?)) in the tale variously entitled 'Ridire na Sgiatha Deirge' and 'Gaisgeach na Sgèithe Deirge'. J. F. Campbell published a version of this in his *Popular Tales of the West Highlands*, Vol. 2 (1860), 455ff. This was noted from a Colonsay and an Islay reciter. The Colonsay man's father had come from Mull, and he had learnt the story from him. This brings it close to the area of Mac Mhaighstir Alasdair's experience as a resident in Morvern. The launching of the *iùbhrach* on a stormy day is described:

Chuir ad a mach i, 's thug ad a toiseach do mhuir, 's a deireadh do thìr.
Thog ad na siuil bhreaca, bhaidealacha, bhàrr-rùisgte,
An aodann nan crann fada, fulannach, fiùghaidh.

Bha soirbheas beag, laghach aca mar a thaghadh ad fhé'
\- - - - - - - - -
An fhairge 'fulpanaich 's a' falpanaich; - -
An lear dearg 's an lear uaine 'lachannaich,
'S a' bualadh thall 's a bhos ma bòrdaibh.
An fhaochag chrom chiar a bha shìos an grunnd an aigein,
Bheireadh i snag air a beul-mòr agus snag air a h-urlar.

(This passage appears in identical form in Kenneth MacLeod's version of the story: MacLeod, K., 1988, 153). Echoes of this passage occur in the 'Birlinn', e.g. 11. 1842-3, 1916-7. Such passages, sometimes referred to as 'runs', are of a formulaic nature, and are standard features of heroic folktales, often using pairs of synonymous words, and also alliteration. A short example can be quoted from a story collected by Seán Ó hEochaidh in Co. Donegal in the 1920s:

> *Thog siad a gcuid seolta go bucóideach go bacóideach go barr na gcrann díreach, le croidhe córacha, sa chruth 's nach rabh dadaidh le móchtáil aca acht caoineadh rónta, plé péisti móra, scairteach na n-easconn, feadalach na bhfaoileann - - - -*
> (They raised their sails, bulging and billowing, to the top of the straight masts, with a fair wind, so that they could hear nothing but the wailing of seals, the converse of great beasts, the calling of eels, the crying of gulls - - - -).

Discussing this passage in his paper 'The Functioning of Long Formulae in Irish Heroic Folktales' (*The Heroic Process*, ed. Bo Almqvist et al., 471 ff.) Kevin O'Nolan refers to parallels in the *Odyssey* and the *Iliad*. It is clearly an ancient and widely disseminated feature of story-telling. Mac Mhaighstir Alasdair was certainly acquainted with it in the Gaelic context, and may have encountered it in his reading of classical literature also. Angus MacLeod refers also to the description of a storm at sea in the Irish translation of the *Aeneid*, and to passages from Irish tales such as *Acallam na Senórach* (where a salmon touches the curach's side) and *Cath Ruis na Ríg* (where seals and walruses rise out of the stormy seas on which the ships have embarked). It may be significant also that Gavin Douglas, in his *Aeneados*, Book 1, Chap. 3, 1. 49, describes as one of the effects of the storm induced by Aeolus the splitting of "roves and syde semmys" (i.e. the metal plates to which rivets are attached and the seams of the boat).

Closer parallels occur with passages in *Cath Finntrágha*, and these are particularly relevant since Mac Mhaighstir Alasdair is identified as the scribe of a MS copy of this tale (Adv. MS 72.2.11

in the National Library of Scotland). Angus MacLeod (1933, 120-21, 124-5) notes some of the parallels.

It is generally accepted that the poem 'Iorram Cuain', a 90-line poem in couplets ascribed to Mac Mhaighstir Alasdair, was an earlier exploration of the theme that he was to expand so memorably in the 'Birlinn'. There are many echoes of the 'Iorram' in the 'Birlinn'. The voyage is a January/February one, with wild seas, stout oars and oarsmen, foam and phosphorescence, a rowing song sung by a named member of the crew, gaining harbour and the consolations of food, drink and sleep. Naturally there are identities in vocabulary and description. But it is clear that the 'Birlinn' is a much more ambitious and considered work, backed up by 'research' of various kinds, and with a carefully designed plot or structure. It probably dates from very close to the year 1750, after the poet's recovery from the trauma of the '45 and the subsequent uneasy years. The Clanranald loyalty is still apparent, and the poem may be in part a celebration of the warrior qualities of that clan, though it is not involved with the recent military activities.

There is no question of the poem describing an actual voyage or an existing galley, though a few named crew members are apparently actual characters. No doubt one or more perilous sea-trips lie beneath the descriptions, including Prince Charlie's tempestuous crossing to Uist in late April 1746, referred to in the poet's Journal (*The Lyon in Mourning*, II, 323). But such trips had become merely part of a much more elaborate construct. Much earlier armour and weaponry take their place in this construct, and perhaps an earlier kind of galley also. Some earlier editors have devoted great industry to assessing the nature of the galley, and have sometimes been puzzled by, or critical of the poet's nautical accuracy. At the end of the day we must accept this as a poet's rather than a sailor's work, driven by lively observation and intense linguistic involvement, and repeatedly fuelled by an imagination which is sometimes inspired by earlier literary precedents.

The construction of the poem's plot is careful and deliberate, beginning with the ship's blessing which is a well-judged elaboration of the more formulaic traditional blessings, and moving to a blessing of the arms and armour, which include Spanish swords, breastplates of mail, gauntlets, shields, bows and arrows, as well as dirks and pistols. Here the sea is pictured as the warrior to be duelled with, so that the weaponry described is symbolic of the crew's heroism. The lengthy Section 3 is an 'Incitement to rowing to the point of departure', and describes in great detail the oars, the strong oarsmen and the motion and effect of the oars. In

Section 4, with the sixteen oarsmen in place, their leader Calum Garbh sings a rowing-song which directs the men's efforts, describes their movements and also the sea they traverse. In the short Section 5 the Clanranald chief instructs his nobles to appoint a skipper. In Section 6 the steersman is described in great detail, both physical and mental, and in Sections 7 to 15 so are various members of the crew, who have particular functions (relating to handling the sail and tackle, to acting as look-out, baler etc.). There is a good deal of technical detail in these sections, together with physical description and character-drawing. The man whose job it is to warn the crew of heavy billows, for example, must not be too laid-back, though he must not be cowardly either. He must react quickly, and give authoritative instructions, and he must have complete control of this function, as cross-chat on such matters can lead to confusion. In Section 15, to take one of many vivid references in this poem, members of the crew must be able to climb the rigging as swiftly as May squirrels.

Section 16, running to over 180 lines, describes the main voyage, and the horrific storm encountered, the eventual subsidence of that storm, and the final smooth rowing to Carrickfergus. We can understand that the main storm was encountered on the crossing from the Outer Isles to Islay, and that the final crossing to Ireland was relatively calm.

The account of the storm has often been criticised in the past, as being too fantastic, especially in the description of the creatures of the deep which are washed to the surface. Angus MacLeod comments "lack of restraint may easily result in bathos, and the appeal of the monsters of the Minch, for instance, may not unfairly be so described". But MacLeod is less critical of other aspects of the storm description: "Here hyperbole, if somewhat overwhelming in its intensity, is effective". The hyperbole, and intensity, of the poem are in fact central to it, and if one draws back and observes it as a whole, a reasonable conclusion is that the build-up to the enormous climax of the storm, and the subsequent calm, are very deliberately handled: they are all part of the plot.

The wealth of vocabulary in this poem is quite extraordinary, and this wealth is skilfully integrated with the metrical patterns, giving an urgent but tightly-controlled movement to the verse. On the technical and linguistic levels at least, this must rank very high in the poet's surviving output.

BIRLINN CHLANN RAGHNAILL

1. *Beannachadh Luinge*

Gum beannaicheadh Dia long Chlann Raghnaill
A' cheud là do chuaidh air sàile,
E fèin 's a thrèin-fhir da caitheamh
Trèin a chuaidh thar maitheas chàich,
Gum beannaich an Coimh-dhia naomh
An iùnnrais, anail nan speur,
Gun sguabte garbhlach na mara,
G'ar tarraing gu cala rèidh.
Athair, a chruthaich an fhairge,
'S gach gaoth a shèideas ás gach àird,
Beannaich ar caol-bhàirc 's ar gaisgich
'S cùm i fèin 's a gasraidh slàn.
A Mhic, beannaich fèin ar n-acair,
Ar siùil, ar beairtean, 's ar stiùir,
'S gach droineap tha crochte ri 'r crannaibh,
'S thoir gu cala sinn le d' iùl.
Beannaich ar racain 's ar slata,
Ar crainn 's ar teudaibh gu lèir,
Ar stagh 's ar tarraing cùm fallain
'S na leig-s' ann ar cara beud.
An Spiorad Naomh biodh air stiùir,
Seòlaidh e 'n t-iùl a bhios ceart,
'S eòl da gach longphort fon ghrèin,
Tilgeamaid sinn fèin fo 'bheachd.

2. *Beannachadh nan Arm*

Gum beannaicheadh Dia ar claidhean
'S ar lannan Spàinnteach geur, glas,
Ar lùirichean troma, màilleach
Nach geàrrte le faobhar tais,
Ar làmhannan cruadhach 's ar gòrsaid
'S ar sgiathan eun-dealbhach, dualach;
Beannaich gach armachd gu h-iomlan
Th' air ar n-iomchar 's ar crios-guaille:
Ar boghannan foinealach iubhair
Ghabhadh luthadh ri uchd tuasaid,
'S na saighdean beithe nach spealgadh
Ann am balgan a' bhruic ghruamaich;
Beannaich ar biodag 's ar daga

'S ar n-èile gasd' ann an cuaichean
'S gach treallaich catha is còmhraig
Tha 'm bàirc MhicDhòmhnaill san uair seo.
Na biodh simpleachd oirbh, no taise,
Gu dol air ghaisge le cruadal,
Fhad 's a mhaireas ceithir bùird dhith
No bhios càraid shùdh dhith fuaighte,
Fhad 's a shnàmhas i fo ur casaibh
No dh'fhuir'eas cnag dhith an uachdar,
Dh' aindeoin aon fhuathais gam faic sibh
Na meataicheadh gart a' chuain sibh.
Ma nì sibh cothachadh ceart
'S nach mothaich an fhairg' sibh dìblidh
Gun ìslich a h-àrdan 's a beachd
'S d' ur cosnadh sgairteil gun strìochd i.
Do chèile-còmhraig air tìr,
Mur faic e thu cinntinn tais,
'S dòich' e bhogachadh san strì
Na chinntinn idir nas brais'.
Is amhail sin ata 'mhuir mhòr:
Coisinn i le colg 's le sùrd
'S gun ùmhlaich i dhuit fa-dheòidh
Mar a dh' òrdaich Rìgh nan Dùl.

3. *Brosnachadh iomraidh gu ionad seòlaidh*

Gun cuirt an iùbhrach dhubh dhealbhach
An àite seòlaidh;
Sàthaibh a-mach cleathan rìghne,
Liagh-lom, còmhnard,
Ràmhan mìn-lunnacha, dealbhach,
Socair, aotrom
A nì 'n t-iomradh toirteil, calma,
Bos-luath, caoir-gheal,
Chuireas an fhairge 'na sradaibh
Suas sna speuraibh,
'Na teine-sionnachain a' lasadh
Mar fhras èibhlean,
Le buillean gailleacha tarbhach
Nan cleath troma
A bheir air bhòc-thuinn thonn-anfaich
Lot le 'n cromadh;
Le sginean nan ràmh geal tana
Bualadh cholainn

Air mhullach nan gorm-chnoc gleannach,
Gharbhlach, thomach.
O, sìnibh, tàirnibh is lùbaibh
Anns na bacaibh
Na gallain bhas-leathann ghiùthsaich
Le lùths ghlac-gheal:
Na fuirbidhnean troma treuna
A' luigh suas orr'
Le 'n gàirdeanan dòideach, fèitheach,
Gaoisneach, cnuacach,
Thogas 's a leagas le chèile,
Fo aon ghluasad,
An gathan liagh-leabhar rèidhe
Fo bhàrr stuaghan;
Iorghaileach, garbh an tùs clèithe
Ag èigheach shuas orr'
Iorram a dhùisgeas an spèirid
Anns na guaillean,
Sparras a' bhirlinn le sèitrich
Roimh gach fuar-ghleann,
Sgoltadh na bòc-thuinne beucaich
Le saidh chruaidh chruim,
Dh' iomaineas beanntainean bèisteil
Roimh 'dà ghualainn.
Hùgan le cuan, nuallan gàireach,
Heig air chnagaibh,
Faram le bras-ghaoir na bàirlinn
Ris na maidibh,
Ràimh gam pianadh 's bolgain fhal' air
Bois gach fuirbidh,
Na suinn làidir, gharbha, thoirteil
'S coip-gheal iomradh,
Chreathnaicheas gach bòrd dhe 'darach,
Bìth is iarunn,
'S lannan dan tilgeil le staplainn
Chnap r'a sliasaid.
Fòirne fearail a bheir tulgadh
Durrgha, dàicheil,
Sparras a' chaol-bhàirc le giùthsaich
An aodann àibheis;
Nach pillear le frìth nan tonn dubhghorm
Le lùths ghàirdean;
Siud an sgioba neartmhor, sùrdail
Air chùl àlaich,
Phronnas na cuartagan cùl-ghlas

Le rinn ràmhachd,
Gun sgìos, gun airtneal gan lùbadh
Ri uchd gàbhaidh.

4. *Iorram*

Ann sin, an dèidh do na sia feara deuga suidh air na ràmhaibh, chum a h-iomradh fon ghaoith gu ionad seòlaidh, do ghlaodh Calum Garbh mac Raghnaill nan Cuan iorram oirre, 's e air ràmh-bràghad, agus is i seo i:

A-nis, on rinneadh bhur taghadh,
'S gur coltach dhuibh bhith nur roghainn,
Thugaibh tulgadh neo-chladharra dàicheil.

Thugaibh tulgadh neo-chearbach,
Gun airtneal, gun dearmad,
Gu freasdal na gailbhinne sàil-ghlais.

Tulgadh danarra treun-ghlac
A righeas cnàmhan is fèithean,
Dh' fhàgas soilleir o cheumannan àlaich.

Sgobadh fonnmhor gun èislein
Ri garbh-phrosnachadh 'chèile
'S iorram ghleusd' ann am beul fir a bràghad.

Cogall ràmh air na bacaibh,
Leòis is rùsgadh air bhasaibh,
'S ràimh da snìomh ann an achlaisean àrd-thonn.

Biodh bhur gruaidhean air lasadh
'S biodh bhur bois gun leòb chraicinn
Fallas mala bras-chnapadh gu làr dhìbh.

Sìnibh, tàirnibh is luthaibh
Na gallain liagh-leabhar ghiuthais
'S dèanaibh uidhe roimh shruthaibh an t-sàile.

Cliath ràmh air gach taobh dhith
Masgadh fairge le saothair
Dol 'na still ann an aodann na bàirlinn.

Iomradh comh-luath, glan, gleusda
Sgoltadh bòc-thuinne beucaich,
Obair shùnntach, gun èislein, gun fhàrdal.

Buailibh cothromach, treun i,
Sealltainn tric air a chèile,
'S dùisgibh spiorad nur fèithean 's nur gàird'nibh.

Biodh a darach a' collainn
Ris na fiadh-ghleannaibh bronnach
'S a dà shliasaid a' pronnadh gach bàirlinn.

Biodh an fhairge ghlas thonnach
Ag at 'na garbh-mhothar lonnach,
'S na h-àrd uisgeachan bronnach a' bàirich.

A' ghlas-fhairge sìor chopadh
Steach mu dà ghualainn thoisich,
Sruth ag osnaich o shloistreadh a h-eàrrlainn.

Sìnibh, tàirnibh is lùbaibh
Na gathain mhìn-lunnach chùl-dearg
Le iomarcaidh smùis air garbh-ghàirdean.

Cuiribh fuidhibh an rubh' ud
Le fallas-mhail'ean a' sruthadh
'S togaibh seòl rith' o Uibhist nan cràdh-ghèadh.

5. *Dh' iomair iad an sin i gu ionad-seòlaidh*

'S an sin nuair thàrr iad an t-seòlaid
Gu fìor ghasda
Shaor iad na sia ràimh dheuga
Steach roimh 'm bacaibh;
Sgathadh grad iad shìos r'a sliasaid
Sheachnadh bhac-bhrèid;
Dh' òrdaich Clann Raghnaill d'a uaislean
Sàr sgiobaire-cuain bhith aca
Nach gabhadh eagal roimh fhuathas
No gnè thuarapaidh a thachradh.

6. *Dh' òrdaicheadh, an dèidh an taghadh, a h-uile duine a dhol ann an seilbh a ghrama àraidh fèin, 's 'na cho-lorg sin, ghlaodhadh ris an stiùireamach suidhe air stiùir anns na briathraibh seo:*

Suidheadh air stiùir trom-laoch leathann,
Neartmhor, fuasgailt
Nach tilg bun no bàrr na sumaid
Fairge uaithe:
Clàranach taiceil, làn spionnaidh,
Plocach, màsach,
Mìn-bheumanach, faicleach, furachail,
Làn nàistinn,
Bùnnsaidh, cudthromach, garbh, socair,
Solta, lùthmhor,
Eirmseach, foighidneach, gun ghriobhag
Ri uchd tùilinn;
Nuair a chluinn e an fhairge ghiobach
Teachd le bùirein
Chumas a ceann caol gu sgibidh
Ris na sùghaibh,
Chumas gu socair a gabhail
Gun dad luasgain,
Sgòd is cluas ga rian le amharc,
Sùil air fuaradh;
Nach caill aon òirleach na h-òrdaig
D'a cheart chùrsa
Dh' aindeoin bàrr sumaidean mara
Teachd le sùrdaig;
Thèid air fuaradh leath' cho daingeann,
Masa h-èiginn,
Nach biodh lann no reang d'a darach
Nach toir eubh asd';
Nach taisich 's nach tèid 'na bhreislich
Dh' aindeoin fuathais,
Ged a dh' atadh a' mhuir cheann-ghlas
Suas gu chluasaibh,
'S ged a bhristeadh e 'na dheannaibh
Steach mu ghuaillibh;
Nach b' urrainn am fuirbidh chriothnachadh
No ghluasad
O ionad a shuidhe, 's e treunant,
'S ailm 'na asgaill,
Gu freasdal na seana-mhara ceanna-ghlais
'S gleanna-gharbh ascaoin;

Nach criothnaich le fuaradh cluaise
An taod-aoire,
Leigeas leatha ruith is gabhail
'S làn 'na h-aodach,
Cheanglas a gabhail cho daingeann
'M bàrr gach tuinne,
Falbh dìreach 'na still gu cala
'M bàrr gach buinne.

7. *Dh' òrdaicheadh a-mach fear-beairte*

Suidheadh toirteal-laoch garbh-dhòideach
An gloic beairte,
A bhios staideil, làn de chùram,
Graimpidh, glac-mhor,
Leigeas cudthrom air ceann slaite
Ri h-àm cruadhaich,
Dh' fhaothaicheas air crann 's air acfhainn,
Bheir dhaibh fuasgladh,
Thuigeas a' ghaoth mar a thig i
A-rèir seòlaidh,
Fhreagras mìn, le fearas-bheairte,
Beum an sgòid-fhir,
Sìor chuideachadh leis an acfhainn
Mar a dh' fhaodas,
Mura fàillnich buille-bheairte
Reamhar ghaoisid.

8. *Chuireadh air leth fear-sgòid*

Suidheadh fear-sgòid air an tobhtainn,
Gàirdean làidir
Nan ruigheannan gaoisneach, fèitheach,
Reamhar, cnàmhach;
Cràgan tiugha, leathann, cliathnach,
Meur-gharbh, cròcach,
Mach 's a-steach an sgòid a leigeas
Le garbh-sgròbadh;
An àm cruadhaich a bheir chuig' e,
Gaoth ma shèideas,
'S nuair a nì an oiteag lagadh
Leigeas beum leis.

9. *Dh' òrdaicheadh air leth fear-cluaise*

Suidheadh fear cnaparra, taiceil,
Gasda, cuanda
Làimhsicheas a' chluas neo-lapach
Air a fuaradh,
Bheir imrich a-sìos 's a-suas di
Chum gach urracaig
A-rèir 's mar a thig an soirbheas
No bàrr urchoid,
'S ma chì e an aonrais ag èirigh
Teachd le osnaich
Lomadh e gu gramail, treunmhor
Sìos gu stoc i.

10. *Dh' òrdaicheadh don toiseach fear-eòlais*

Eireadh màirnealach 'na sheasamh
Suas don toiseach
'S dèanadh e dhuinn eòlas seasmhach
Cala a choisneas,
Sealladh e an ceithir àirdean
Cian an adhair,
'S innseadh e do dh' fhear na stiùireadh
'S math a gabhail,
Glacadh e comharra-tìre
Le sàr shùil-bheachd,
On 's esan as dia gach sìde
Is reul-iùil duinn.

11. *Chuireadh air leth fear air calpa na tàirne*

Suidheadh air calpa na tàirne
Fear gun soistinn,
Snaomanach fuasgailteach, sgairteil,
Foinnidh, solta,
Duine cùramach gun ghriobhag,
Ealamh, guamach,
A bheir uaipe 's dhi mar dh' fheumas,
Gleusda, luaineach,
Laigheas le spadhannan troma,
Treun air tarraing,
Air cudthrom a dhòid a' cromadh

Dh' ionnsaigh daraich;
Nach ceangail le sparraig mun urracaig
An ròp frithir
Ach gabhail uime daingeann, seòlta
Le lùb-ruithe,
Air eagal, nuair sgairtear an t-abhsadh,
I chur stad air,
Los i ruith 'na still le crònan
Bhàrr na cnaige.

12. *Chuireadh air leth fear-innse-nan-uisgeachan agus an fhairge air cinntinn tuilleadh is molach, 's thuirt an Stiùireamaich ris:*

Suidheadh fear-innse gach uisge
Làimh ri m' chluais-sa
Is cumadh e shùil gu biorach
An crìdh an fhuaraidh.
Tagham an duine leth-eaglach,
Fiamhach, sicir,
'S cha mhath leam e bhith air fad
'Na ghealtair riochdail.
Biodh e furachair nuair chì e
Fuaradh froise,
Cia dhiùbh bhios an soirbheas 'na deireadh
No 'na toiseach;
Gun cuireadh e mise am fhaicill,
Suas dam mhosgladh,
Ma nì e gnè chunnairt fhaicinn
Nach bi tosdach;
'S ma chì e coltas muir-bhàite
Teachd le nuallan
Sgairteas cruaidh ceann-caol a fiodha
Chumail luath ris;
Biodh e àrd-labhara, cèillidh,
'G èigheach bàirlinn,
'S na ceileadh e air fear na stiùireadh
Ma chì gàbhadh.
Na biodh fear-innse-nan-uisgean
Ann ach esan:
Cuiridh griobhag, briot is gusgal
Neach 'na bhreislich.

13. *Dh' òrdaicheadh a-mach fear-taomaidh, 's an fhairge a' bàrcadh air am muin, rompa 's 'nan dèidh*

Freasdladh air leaba na taoma
Garbh laoch fuasgailt
Nach fannaich gu bràth 's nach tiomaich
Le gàir chuaintean,
Nach lapaich 's nach meataich fuachd sàile
Na clach-mheallain
Laomadh mu bhroilleach 's mu mhuineal
'Nam fuar-steallaibh,
Le crumpa mòr cruinn garbh fiodha
'Na chiar dhòidibh,
Sìor-thilgeadh a-mach na fairge
Steach a dhòirteas;
Nach dìrich a chaoidh a dhruim lùthmhor
Le rag-eàrlaid
Gus nach fàg e siola an grùnnd
No 'n làr a h-eàrrlainn,
'S ged chinneadh a bùird cho tolltach
Ris an ruidil
Chumas cho tioram gach cnag dhith
Ri clàr buideil.

14. *Dh' òrdaicheadh dithis làidir ghramail gu draghadh nam ball chùl-aodaich, 's coltas oirre gun tugte na siùil uatha le roghairbhid na sìde*

Cuiribh càraid làidir, chnàmh-reamhar,
Ghairbhneach, ghaoisneach,
Gu freasdladh iad tàirneant, treunant
Buill chùl-aodaich,
Le smùis agus le meud lùiths an
Ruighean treuna
'N àm cruadhaich a bheir orra steach
No leigeas beum leis,
Chumas gu sgiobalta a-staigh e
'Na teis-meadhan,
Ordaich ann Donncha MacCarmaig
'S Iain mac Iain,
Dithis starbhanach theòma, ladarn
Dh' fhearaibh Chanaigh.

15. *Thaghadh seisear gu fearas-ùrlair, an earalas gu fàilnicheadh aon fhear de na thuirt mi, no gu sgrìobadh anfadh na fairge mach thar bòrd e, 's gu suidheadh fear dhiubh seo 'na àite*

Eireadh seisear ealamh, ghleusda
Làmhach, bheòtha
Shiùbhlas 's a dh' fhalbhas 's a leumas
Feadh gach bòrd dhith
Mar gheàrr-fhiadh am mullach slèibhe
'S coin da còpadh;
Streapas ri cruaidh-bhallaibh rèidhe
Den chaol-chòrcaich
Co-ghrad ri feòragan Cèitein
Ri crann rò-choill;
Bhios ullamh, ealamh, treubhach,
Falbhach, eòlach
Gu toirt dhi 's gu toirt an abhsadh
'S clabhsail òrdan;
Chaitheas gun airtneal, gun èislein
Long Mhic Dhòmhnaill.

16. *Do bha h-uile goireas a bhuineadh do sheòladh nis air a chur ann an deagh riaghailt, agus theann a h-uile laoch tapaidh, gun taise, gun fhiamh, gun sgàthachas, thun a' cheart ionaid an d' òrdaicheadh dha dol, is thog iad na siùil ann an èirigh na grèine Là Fhèill Brìghde, a' trogbhail a-mach bho bhun Loch Aoineart an Uibhist a' Chinn a Deas*

'Ghrian a' faoisgneadh gu h-òr-bhuidh
As a mogal,
Chinn an speur gu dùldaidh, dòite,
Làn de dh' oglachd,
Dh' fhàs i tonn-ghorm, tiugh, tàrr-lachdann,
Odhar, iargalt,
Chinn gach dath bhiodh ann am breacan
Air an iarmailt:
Fadadh-cruaidh san àird-an-iar oirr',
Stoirm 'na coltas,
'S neòil shiùbhlach aig gaoith gan riasladh,
Fuaradh-frois' oirr'.
Thog iad na siùil bhreaca, bhaideal-
acha, dhìonach,
Shìn iad na coilpeinean raga,
Teanna, rìghne

Ri fiodhannan àrda, fada
Nan colg bìth-dhearg;
Cheangladh iad gu gramail, snaompach,
Gu neo-chearbach
Roimh shùilean nan cromag iaruinn
'S nan cruinn fhailbheag;
Cheartaich iad gach ball den acfhainn
Ealamh, dòigheil,
'S shuidh gach fear gu freasdal tapaidh
'Bhuill bu chòir dha.
'Sin dh' fhosgail uinneagan an aeir
Ballach, liath-ghorm
Gu sèideadh na gaoithe greannaich
'S bannail, iargalt;
Tharraing an cuan a bhrat dùbhghlas
Air gu h-uile,
Mhantal garbh, caiteanach, ciar-dhubh,
'S sgreataidh buinne;
Dh' at e 'na bheanntaibh 's 'na ghleanntaibh,
Molach, robach,
Gun do bhòc an fhairge cheigeach
Suas 'na cnocaibh,
Dh' fhosgail a' mhuir ghorm 'na craosaibh
Farsaing, cràcach,
An glaicibh a chèile ri taosgadh,
'S caonnag bhàsmhor;
Gum b' fhear-ghnìomh bhith 'g amharc an aodann
Nam màm toinnte,
Lasraichean sradanach sionnachain
Air gach beinn diubh,
Na beulanaich àrda, liath-ghorm
Ri searbh bheucail,
Na cùlanaich 's an cladh dùldaidh
Ri garbh gheumnaich;
Nuair a dh' èireamaid gu h-allail
'M bàrr nan sonn sin
B' èiginn an t-abhsadh a bhearradh
Gu grad-phongail;
Nuair theàrnamaid le ion-slugaidh
Sìos sna gleanntaibh
Bheirte gach seòl a bhiodh aice
'M bàrr nan crann dith;
Na ciasanaich àrda chroma
Teachd sa' bhàirich,
Mus tigeadh iad idir nar gaire

Chluinnt an gàirich,
Iad ri sguabadh nan tonn beaga
Lom, dan sgiùrsadh,
Chinneadh i 'na h-aon mhuir bhàsmhor,
'S càs a stiùireadh;
Nuair a thuiteamaid fo bhàrr
Nan àrd-thonn giobach
Gur beag nach dochainneadh a sàil
An t-aigeal sligneach.
An fhairge ga maistreadh 's ga sluistneadh
Roimh a chèile,
Gun robh ròin is mialan-mòra
'M barrachd èiginn;
Anfadh is confadh na mara
'S falbh na luinge
Sradadh an eanchainnean geala
Feadh gach tuinne,
Iad ri nuallanaich àrd, uaimhinn-
each, searbh-thùrsach,
'G èigheach gur ìochdarain sinne
Dragh chum bùird sinn.
Gach mion-iasg a bha san fhairge
Tàrr-gheal, tionndaidht',
Le gluasad confadh na gailbhinn
Marbh gun chùnntas;
Clachan is maorach an aigeil
Teachd an uachdar,
Air am buain a-nìos le slacraich
A' chuain uaibhrich;
An fhairg' uile 's i 'na brochan
Strioplach, ruaimleach
Le fuil 's le gaorr nam biast lorcach
'S droch dhath ruadh oirr',
Na biastan adharcach, iongnach,
Pliutach, lorcach,
Làn cheann 's iad 'nam beòil gu 'n giallaibh,
'S an craos fosgailt.
An àibheis uile làn bhòcan
Air an cràgradh,
Le spògan 's le earbaill mhòr-bhiast
Air a màgradh.
Bu sgreamhail an ròmhan sgriachaidh
Bhith da èisdeachd,
Thogbhadh iad air caogad mìlidh
Aotrom cèille:

Chaill an sgioba càil gan claisneachd
Ri bhith 'g èisdeachd
Ceileireadh sgreadach nan deomhan
'S mothar bhèistean.
Foghar na fairge 's a slacraich
Gleac r'a darach,
Fosghaoir a toisich a' bocsaich
Mhuca-mara;
'Ghaoth ag ùrachadh a fuaraidh
As an iar-àird,
Bha sinn leis gach seòrsa buairidh
Air ar pianadh,
Sinn daillte le dall-cheò fairge
Sìor dhol tharainn,
Tàirneanach àibhseach rè oidhche
'S teine-dealain,
Peileirean beithrich a' losgadh
Ar cuid acfhainn,
Fàileadh is deathach na riofa
Gar glan thachdadh.
Na dùilean uachdrach is ìochdrach
Ruinn a' cogadh,
Talamh, teine 's uisge 's sian-ghaoth
Rinn air togail.
Ach nuair dh' fhairtlich air an fhairge
Toirt oirnn strìochdadh
Ghabh i truas, le faite-gàire
Rinn i sìth ruinn.
Ged rinn, cha robh crann gun lùbadh,
Seòl gun reubadh,
Slat gun sgaradh, rac gun fhàillinn,
Ràmh gun èisl' air,
Cha robh stagh ann gun stuagh-lèimneadh,
Beairt gun ghaiseadh,
Tarraing no cupladh gun bhristeadh,
Fise, faise!
Cha robh tobhta no beul-mòr ann
Nach tug aidmheach,
Bha h-uile crannghail is goireas
Air an lagadh;
Cha robh achlaisean no aisne
Dhith gun fhuasgladh,
A slat-bheòil 's a sguitichean-asgaill
Air an tuairgneadh;
Cha robh falmadair gun sgoltadh,

Stiùir gun chreuchdadh,
Cnead is dìosgan aig gach maide
'S iad air dèasgadh;
Cha robh crann-tarrann gun tarraing,
Bòrd gun obadh,
H-uile lann bha air am barradh
Ghabh iad togail;
Cha robh tarrann ann gun trochladh,
Cha robh calpa ann gun lùbadh,
Cha robh aon bhall bhuineadh dhì-se
Nach robh nas miosa na thùbhradh.
Ghairm an fhairge sìoth-shàimh ruinne
Air crois Chaol Ile,
'S gun d' fhuair a' gharbh-ghaoth shearbh-ghlòireach
Ordan sìnidh.
Thog i uainne do dh' ionadaibh
Uachdrach an aeir,
'S chinn i dhuinn 'na clàr rèidh mìn-gheal
An dèidh a tabhainn.
'S thug sinn buidheachas don Ard-rìgh
Chum na dùilean
Deagh Chlann Raghnaill a bhith sàbhailt
O bhàs brùideil.
'S an sin bheum sinn a siùil thana,
Bhallach, thùilinn
'S leag sinn a crainn mhìn-dearg, ghasda
Fad a h-ùrlair,
'S chuir sinn a-mach ràimh chaol bhasgant
Dhaite, mhìne
Den ghiuthas a bhuain MacBharrais
An Eilean Fhìonain,
'S rinn sinn an t-iomradh rèidh tulgan-
ach gun dearmad,
'S ghabh sinn deagh longphort aig barraibh
Charraig Fhearghais.
Thilg sinn acraichean gu socair
Anns an ròd sin,
Ghabh sinn biadh is deoch gun airceas
'S rinn sinn còmhnaidh.

NOTES

The title 'Birlinn Chlann Raghnaill' does not seem to come into use until the 1874 edition. McL's title reads 'Beannachadh Luinge, maile re Prosnachadh Fairge, Rinneadh Do Sgiob & do Bhirlinn le Tighearna Chlann-Raonuill', and this is virtually identical with R.I.A. (which reads *maille*) and with Eigg, which omits the '&'.

The early versions do not give a separate sub-title to the first section.

1451 *beannaicheadh* McL and R.I.A. *Beannuigheadh*, Eigg, 1841 *beannuiche*, 1924 1933 (*metri causa*) *beannaich*

1452 *chuaidh* So McL. R.I.A. *chuidh*
sàile Later edd. have *sàil/sàl*; the monosyllable fits the metre better.

1454 *chuaidh* So McL. R.I.A. uses this form here.

1455 *an Coimh-dhia McL, R.I.A. a Choimh-Dhia*, Eigg *an comh-dhia*, 1813, 1839 *an co-dhia*, 1933 *an Coimhdhe*. It is difficult to make a confident decision here. Clearly the word in question is that which appears as *Coimhdhe*, *coimdiu* etc. in earlier sources (see R.I.A. Dict sub *coimdiu*), and it is used of 'lord, master', but particularly of 'the Lord'. It is a masculine noun in early usage. Our early sources give it an etymology connected with *dia*, and Eigg gives it as a masculine noun. It is possible that McL and R.I.A. are using the preceding *a* as the possessive, meaning 'may his holy Lord bless the storm---'.

1456 *iùnnrais* The early sources all give *iunrais*. The High. Soc. Dict. has *iunnrais* in the senses of 'stormy sky, tempest'.

1457 *Gun McL, R.I.A. Gu*, Eigg *ga*

1458 *G'ar* So McL. R.I.A. *'Gar*, Eigg *Gar*. The reading *gu ar tarraing* 'in order to draw us' is more convincing than *gar t.* (=*aig ar*) 'drawing us'.

1460 *a* Only in McL, R.I.A. and 1813.

1461 *caol-bhàirc* Post-Eigg versions have *bhàrc*. As not infrequently with feminine nouns the dative may here have taken the place of the nominative.

1462 *'S* Omitted in post-Eigg sources, apart from 1813, 1841.

1463 *acair* McL, R.I.A., Eigg, 1813, 1841 *achdair* (a Uist pronunciation, which may have been used by the poet here).

1464 *ar* Eigg *air*
beairtean McL, R.I.A. *Beirtin*

1465 *droineap* Eigg *droinip*
crochte McL, R.I.A. *Crochta*, Eigg *croichte*

1467 *racain* McL, R.I.A. *Rachdain*, Eigg *rachdan*. See 1463*n*.
slata McL, R.I.A. *slat*, Eigg *slatt*, 1924 *slata*, 1933 *slatan*. A plural form might be expected here, as with the other nouns in 11. 1467-8, and also for metrical reasons.

1468 *teudaibh* McL *teudaidh*, R.I.A. *Teudan*, Eigg *taoidibh*, 1813 *taoduibh*, 1841, 1933 *taodaibh*

1469 *cùm* McL, R.I.A. *Cunn*

1470 *ann ar cara* McL, R.I.A. *ann ar gara*, Eigg *ann rar caraibh*. Later edd. choose the modern usage *nar caraibh*. The sense is 'in our vicinity, near us'.

1471 *biodh air stiùir* Eigg *bidh – – –*, 1813 and later *air an stiùir*

1472 *Seòlaidh* McL *Sheolaigh*, R.I.A. *Sheolaidh*, 1874 *Seoladh*

1473 *da* McL, R.I.A. *do*
fon Eigg, McL *fuidh 'n*, R.I.A. *faoi 'n*

1475 *claidhean* A variant plural of *claidheamh* 'sword'.

1476 *Spàinnteach* McL, R.I.A. *Spaineach* Swords with Spanish blades were much prized.

1477 *troma* McL, R.I.A. *tromadh*
màilleach Eigg, 1874, 1933 *màillich*. The reading adopted is the adjectival one; *màillich* is the genitive of a noun.

1479 *làmhannan* Eigg *labhannan*, 1813, 1839 *lannan*, 1874 ff. *làmhainnean*

1480 *eun-dealbhach* 1813, 1839 *an-dealbhach*, 1874 ff. *ion-dealbhach*. The original sense of 'bird-decorated, bird-shaped' seems preferable.

1481 *gach armachd* 1874 ff. *ar n-armachd*

1483 *boghannan* McL, R.I.A. *Bodhanan*, Eigg *Boghanan*, 1874 ff. *boghachan*. Some of the detail in this description of weapons would be more appropriate for a time earlier than c. 1750. This ties in with the idea of a traditional galley expedition rather than a contemporary one.

1488 *ar n-èile* 1874, 1924 *ar fèileadh*

1489 *catha is* McL, R.I.A. *Catha &*, Eigg *Cath, agus*

1490 *bàirc* 1841 ff. *bàrc*. See 1461*n*.

1491–2 *simpleachd* McL, R.I.A. *siomplachd*, Eigg *simplichd*
gu dol McL, R.I.A., Eigg *gun dol*, 1841 *Gu'n dol*, 1874 ff. *Gu dol*
It is difficult to make sense of the *gun* reading. The lines probably mean 'Do not show meekness or weakness in enjoying heroism with firm resolve'.

1494 *shùdh* This word is glossed 'seam' in both McL and R.I.A.

1495 *fo ur* McL, R.I.A. *fuidh ar*, Eigg *fuidh'r*
casaibh 1813, 1841, 1874 *casan*

1496 *dh' fhuir'eas* This is the McL reading, suggesting a svarabhakti roll in the middle of the verbal form. R.I.A. has *dh' fhuireas*, Eigg *d' fhuireas*, 1839 *dh' aireas*, 1841 *dh' fhaineas*. 1874 and 1924 *dh' fhuirgheas* suggests the same effect.

1497 *fhuathais* This is apparently in the genitive after *dh' aindeoin*. 1813, 1841 and 1933 change to *fhuathas*.
gam faic Eigg *ga'm faic*, McL, R.I.A. *gu faic*

1499 *cothachadh* McL, R.I.A., Eigg *cothacha*

1501 *ìslich* McL, R.I.A. *Ioslaich*

1502 *cosnadh* McL, R.I.A. *Coisneadh*, Eigg *cosnadh*, 1813, 1839 *gar cothacha*

1503 *cèile-còmhraig* 'fellow combatant'. The scenario here might be that of a galley-full of warriors approaching land where their enemies await them. More probably, the fight with the sea is compared to single combat on land.

1505 *dòich'* Eigg *doiche*, McL, R.I.A. *doch'/doch*, 1841 *dàch'*. The sense required is of the comparative: 'he is more likely to soften in the struggle'.

1507 *sin ata* Eigg *shin ud tà*

1508 *Coisinn i* 1841 *Coisinnidh*

1509 *gun ùmhlaich i* Eigg *umhlaich i*, 1924, 1933 *ùmhlaichidh i*

1511 *dhealbhach* Angus MacLeod suggested that it might be desirable to emend this to *dhìonach*, since *dhealbhach* recurs in l. 1515. He quotes a similar passage from 'An Duanag Ullamh', a sixteenth-century poem no doubt known to Mac Mhaighstir Alasdair:

Loingis leathann làidir luchdmhor
Dealbhach dìonach.

1513 *Sàthaibh --- cleathan* McL, R.I.A. *Sathaimid --- Cliathan*. Eigg's *Sathibh --- cleathan* is the better reading (a) since a later command in this section (*sìnibh, tàirnibh is lùbaibh* in l. 1531) takes the same form, and (b) since *cleath* in the sense of 'post, pole etc.' seems more appropriate than *cliath*, with its specific sense of 'hurdle, wattle'. The poet is referring here to large oars.

1515 *Ràmhan mìn-lunnacha* 1874 *Ràimh mhìn-lunnach* This editorial change is quite unjustified; it has the additional defect of reducing the syllable count from eight to six in a section set consistently in the *Sneadhbhairdne* metre.

1518 *Bos-luath* 1874 ff. *Bas-luath*

1523 *gailleacha* So Eigg. McL, R.I.A. have *gaileacha*, 1813 ff. *gailbheacha*

1524 *cleath* Eigg *clèath*, McL, R.I.A. *Cliath*

1525 Eigg *A bheir air bhoch-thinn thonn-an-faich*
McL, R.I.A. *Bheir air Bhōc-thuinn thonn-anfaich*
1813, 1839 *A bheir air bochd-thuinn thonnaich*
1874 *Bheir air na bòchd-thonnan anfhach*
1924 *Bheir air na bòcthonnan anfhach*
1933 *Bheir air na bòcthonnan onfhach*
Our reading stays close to the earliest ones. *anfach* is an uncommon word, quoted by High. Soc. Dict. in the sense of 'overflowing'. Lines 1525-6

translate 'that (referring to the oars) in their descent will wound the swelling waves that have a torrential overflow'.

1529 *mhullach* Eigg *mhullaich*, 1813 ff. *mullach*

1530 *Gharbhlach, thomach* This is the reading of Eigg, McL, R.I.A., 1813 and 1839. 1874 omits the lenition, and 1924 and 1933 retain it only in *thomach*. 1841 also reads *ghleannach* in 1. 1529. MacLeod (1933) takes *garbhlach* to be the noun meaning 'rugged hummocky region'.

1531 The reading of McL and R.I.A. is followed. Eigg's line has a syllable too many: *O' sinibh 's tarnibh agus lùbabh.*

1532 *bacaibh* Eigg *bachdabh*, 1874 *bachdan*. R.I.A. glosses this word 'where the Oar rests on the gunnel' and McL glosses 'where the oar Rests'.

1533 *bhas-leathann bas* can be used of the spoke of a wheel, and here evidently of the blade of an oar.
ghiùthsaich giùthsach means a pine forest; so here 'of the pine forest'.

1534 *ghlac-gheal* McL and R.I.A. *ghlac gheal*, Eigg *ghlaic-gheal*, 1874, 1924 *ghlac geal*, 1933 *glac-gheal*. The fists presumably are white through hard gripping of the oars.

1535 *fuirbidhnean* So 1874 ff. The early sources have *fuirbin(n)in troma* McL *tromadh*

1536 *A' luigh* Eigg, McL, R.I.A. *a luidh*, 1841 ff. *(A') laighe*

1537 *gàirdeanan* Eigg *gaoirdenin*, 1813, 1839 *gaoirdeanaibh* represent probably a Uist pronunciation.

1538 *Gaoisneach* R.I.A. *gaisneach*
cnuacach Eigg, 1813, 1841 *cruachdach*

1540 *Fo aon* McL, R.I.A. *fuidh aona*, Eigg *Fudh aona*. These early readings give a five syllable line, but represent a normal pronunciation.

1541 *An gathan liagh-leabhar* Eigg *Agaithean lia-leabhar*, 1813 *A gaithean liath-reamhar*, 1841 *A gathan liath-reamhar*. The *An* of early sources presumably refers to *their* oars. *gath*, which can mean 'spoke', here refers to the oars, whose blade (*liagh*) is in each case long (*leabhar*).

1543 *Iorghaileach* Eigg *Irchiulich*, McL, R.I.A. *Ireghiullach*, 1813 *Iurchuilich*, 1839 *Iurghuilich*, 1874 ff. *Iorcallach*. The word in the early sources means 'loudly shouting', and goes naturally with *Ag èigheach* in the next line. *Iorcallach* 'a champion' (<Hercules) is hardly justified.

1544 *orr'* McL, R.I.A. *orra* This presumably refers to 'them', the other rowers. 1839 reads *suas orr*, and 1924 has *"Suas orr'!"*, as though this were a command. 1874, 1933 have *shuas oirr(e)*, presumably meaning 'to the upper end (stem) of the boat'. The rowing-song is led by the front oarsman.

1545 *spèirid* Eigg, 1813, 1839, 1933 *speurad*, McL *spīrid*, R.I.A. *spèrid*

1547 *sèitrich* Eigg *shei-èrich*

1548 *Roimh* Eigg *Roibh*, McL, R.I.A. *throimh*. These early readings suggest the dialectal variant *roimh* for *troimh*. The couplet 11. 1547-8 seems to refer quite specifically to the *iorram* of 1. 1545. That rowing-song blowingly/pantingly drives on the galley through the glens/troughs of the sea.

1549 *bòc-thuinne beucaich* Eigg *boch-thuinn a beachdich*, McL *Bōc-thuinn a' beuchdaich*, R.I.A. *Bòc-thuinn ag beucaich*. The 1874 interpretation is followed here, as it was in the 1933 ed.

1550 'with a hard bent (*crom*) prow'. *Saidh* is glossed 'The Bow' in McL and R.I.A.

1551 *beanntainean* All the early sources support this reading, changed to *beanntaichean* in 1874 and 1933.
The use of *bèisteil* no doubt describes the horrific/beastly aspect of the waves, but may contain a premonition of the strange sea-creatures that appear later in the poem.

1553 *gàireach* Eigg *gàirich*, 1874 *ghàirich*

1553–4 *Hùgan* suggests a rolling movement, *heig* a sharp retort. These are onomatopoetic symbols.

1557 *bolgain fhal'* McL, R.I.A. *Bolgain fhala*, Eigg – *fhol*, 1813 – *fhola*, 1874 *balgain-fhal'*, 1933 *balgain fhola.*

1560 *coip-gheal* So McL and R.I.A. Eigg *Scop gheal*, other edd. *cop-gheal.* The form *coip-gheal* is probably intended as a superlative.

1562 *Bìth* Eigg *Bigh*, McL, R.I.A. *Beo*. The reading *beo* is an aberration. The reference is to the tar or caulking, here bracketed with the oak and iron that go into the galley's frame.

1563–4 Angus MacLeod translates 'Roves (i.e. washers) are thrown off by the crashing of the seas (*staplainn chnap*) on her quarter (*sliasaid*)'.

1566 *Durrgha* McL, R.I.A. *durragha*, Eigg and later *Dugharra, Dùgharr'*. The form *durrgha* resonates with *tulgadh* in the previous line.
dàicheil The commoner meanings are 'handsome, elegant', but the word has other senses, 'hard, severe' going better here with *durrgha* 'grim'.

1567 *a' chaol-bhàirc* See 1461*n*
giùthsaich oars (made of pine).

1569 *frìth* Eigg *frith*, McL, R.I.A. *Frioth*, 1813 *frigh*, 1839 ff. *friogh*. Both *frìth* and *friogh* can mean 'anger, rage'.

1570 *ghàirdean* McL, R.I.A. *gairden*

1574 *rinn* So Eigg, McL and R.I.A. 1813, 1841 and 1924 have *roinn*, 1874 *rogha*, 1933 *roghainn*. Disyllabic forms do not fit the metre. *rinn* 'point' can also be used in the sense of 'sharpness'. The line may be translated 'with precision of oarsmanship'.

1575 *gan lùbadh* Eigg *gun lubadh*, McL, R.I.A. *ga'n*. All subsequent edd. favour *gun*, but the distinction in McL and R.I.A. between *gun – – – gun* in the earlier part of the line and *ga'n* in the later is very deliberate. If we accept this reading the reference is to the oars, 'bending them', whereas *gun lùbadh* would mean 'without bending', i.e. the oarsmen are unbending in the face of danger. As to sense, either reading is possible.

4. *Iorram* This heading is supplied.
In the explanatory introduction to this section, the older forms of Eigg, McL and R.I.A. are mainly retained e.g. *Ann sin, sia feara deuga* (here Eigg has *fearabh deug*, McL, R.I.A. *se feara deuga*), *do ghlaodh* (rather than modern *ghlaodh*).
There is an additional source for this section: MacDiarmid's MS collection of c. 1770, pp. 92-4.

1578 *nur roghainn* McL, R.I.A. *bhar Raghuinn*

1579–80 *tulgadh* McL *Tulgaidh*

1581 *airtneal* Eigg *airstil*, McL, R.I.A. *Airsteal*,
McD *airsneul*, 1813 *airsneal.*

1582 'to take precautions against (to cope with) the storm and its foam-spotted seas'.

1583 *danarra* Eigg *dannara*, McL, R.I.A. *Danfheara*
treun-ghlac Eigg, McD *-ghlachd.*

1585 *o cheumannan* Eigg *o cèimanan*, McL *o Ceiminin*, R.I.A. *o (a) Ceiminin*, Henderson, McD *a ceumanan.*
Angus MacLeod (1933) explains *soilleir* as a noun meaning 'clear, smooth water immediately astern of a boat; the size of this space is an indication of the speed of the boat'. Taking *ceum* in the sense of 'pace, speed' makes clearer sense: 'that will leave a clear water-space due to the speed of the oars'.

1586 *èislein* 1924, 1933 *éislean*

1587 *phrosnachadh 'chèile* McD, Eigg, 1813 *phrosnach a chèile*, 1841, 1874, 1933 *bhrosnach' a chéile*. Either reading makes the same sense.

1588 *am beul* 1813 *o bheul*, 1841, 1924 *bho bheul*

fir a 1839 *fir ramh*

1589 *Cogall* Glossed in McL 'wearing of the Edge by the oars', R.I.A. 'The Edge worn by the Oars'. *cogall* has the general sense of 'friction, rubbing'. Mac Mhaighstir Alasdair's Vocabulary (1741) gives '*cogul* saw-dust'.

1593 *bois* 1874 ff. *bas.* The dative of this feminine noun frequently is used as a nominative.

1594 'sweat from the (eye)brows rapidly pittering on the floor (of the boat) off you'.

1597 *roimh* 'through'. See 1548*n*.
'make your way through the ocean's currents'.

1598 *dhith* McD *dhibh*

1601 *comh-luath* Eigg *coibh-luadh*, McL, R.I.A. *comh-luadh*, 1813, 1839 *cò'-lath*, McD, 1874 ff. *còmhla.* The earlier readings suggest the sense of 'equally fast' (rowing).

1602 *Sgoltadh* Eigg *Scoilte*, 1933 *Sgoilteadh*

1604 *cothromach McL, R.I.A. Co-thromach.* The scribe here has the specific sense of 'equal weight' in mind.

1605 McD *fèithibh, 's 'nar gairdein*, 1839 *féithean gu laidir*

1607 *collainn* Eigg, McD *colluin* The High. Soc. Dict. gives '*collainnich* strike, thresh, thump', and it seems that the shorter form was used by the poet.

1610 *thonnach* Eigg *thoinnach*, McD *thomach*

1612 *a' gàirich* Eigg *sa garraich*, Henderson *'s a' gàirich*, 1813, 1841, 1874, 1924 *'sa ghàraich/'s a' ghàirich.*

1615 *o shloistreadh a h-eàrrlainn* Eigg *o sloistradh a hearr-linn*, 1813, 1839, 1924 *a' sloistreadh a h-earr-linn.* Three of the earliest sources have interesting variants: McL, R.I.A. *a' pocsadh a h Earr-iar'n* and McD *a' bogsadh a h earr-luing.* The idea of the sea boxing with the ship is intriguing, but the more sober interpretation is reluctantly followed here.

1617 *gathain* McD *gathan*, 1874 ff. *gaithean/gathan*
cùl-dearg red-backed. The precise sense of *cùl* is not clear. The *dearg* refers to the red pine of which the oars were made and *cùl* is often used of hair: is a fanciful connection being made here?

1618 *iomarcaidh* Eigg *ui-maircidh*, 1813, 1839 *iumaircidh*, 1874 ff. *iomairceadh*

1619 *fuidhibh* McD *foidhibh*, 1813 ff. *fothaibh*
cuiribh fuidhibh 'pass (that headland)'.

1620 *fallas-mhail'ean* Eigg *faltas mhailain*, McL, R.I.A. *Fallas/Fallus mhailin*, McD *mhaildhean*, 1933 *mhailghean*

1621 *seòl* 1813 *seoil*, 1841 ff. *siùil*

1622 *t-seòlaid* Eigg *t sheol-shiodh*, McL, R.I.A. *t sheol-shìd*, 1813 *an seoil shioda*, 1839 *an seoil shithe*, 1841 *na seoil shìthe*, 1924 *na siùil-shìthe*, 1874 *a seòladh*, 1933 *do 'n t-seòlaid.* The sense is 'when they won their way to the haven'.

1624–5 McL and R.I.A. read – – – *dheuga steach* – – –. The metrical division of the lines requires at least one extra syllable in 1. 1624 (strictly there should be two) and only four syllables in 1. 1625.
roimh 'm bacaibh Eigg *roibh bacabh*, 1841 *tro' bacaibh*, Henderson, 1874 *romh 'm bachdan*, 1924 *troimh 'm bacan*, 1933 *troimh bhacaibh*

1624–7 'They released the sixteen oars, taking them in through their rests; they were quickly dropped down against her (the boat's) side, to avoid (the) belaying pins'. The use of *sgath* in the sense of 'drop' is unusual, the more common sense being 'cut'.

1628 *Clann Raghnaill* Apparently used here, as in English, of Clanranald, the chief. So too in 1. 2002.

1629 *sgiobaire-cuain* Eigg *sgiob-fhearabh* – – –, *McL sgipfheara* – – –, 1813 *sgipirean*, 1841 ff. *sgiobairean* – – –.

1631 *thuarapaidh* Eigg *thuairefudh*, McL, R.I.A. *thuairipidh*, 1813, 1839 *thuaireadh*, 1841 *thuairgneadh*, 1874 ff. *thuairgnidh*. The older sources suggest *tuarapadh/tuaireapadh* 'mishap, accident' rather than *tuairgneadh* 'confusion', though either of these senses fits.

Section 6 Introduction
ann an seilbh a ghrama àraidh fèin 'in charge of his own particular task'. *grama* is the genitive of *grèim* 'grip', here extended to the sense of 'task' (most of which involved gripping oar, rope, tiller etc.)
'na cho-lorg sin 1874 ff. *an co-lorg sin*
stiùireamach 1841 *ri fear na stiùrach*, 1933 *stiùradair*

1634–5 'Whom neither base nor crest of the sea billow will throw away from it (*uaithe*)', i.e. away from the tiller.

1636–7 *taiceil* Eigg *taichdail*
plocach Eigg *plochdach*. As often, the Eigg version shows S. Uist influence in its spelling of such words.

1638 This line's final syllable, strictly, goes with l. 1639. Eigg to 1924 place *furachail* in l. 1639.

1639 *nàistinn* McL, R.I.A. *Naisinn*, glossed 'Care', 1874 *màistinn*

1642 *Eirmseach* Eigg *Airm-sheach*, McL *Airmseach*, R.I.A. *Airmseadh*
ghriobhag McL, R.I.A. *ghriofag*, 1813, 1839 *ghriomhag*, 1874 ff. *ghriobhaig*

1643 *tùiling* A variant of *tùirling* 'descending etc.', here of seas falling on to a ship.

1644 *chluinn* 1813, 1839 *chi*, 1874 *chì* (with footnote indicating that *chluinn* is the Eigg reading), 1933 *chì*

1645 *bùirein* 1924, 1933 *bùirean*

1646 *chumas* McL, R.I.A. *chunbhas*

1648 *socair* Eigg *sochdrach*, 1813, 1841, 1933 *socrach*

1650 *ga rian* McL *gu rian* with gloss 'regularly'.

1652 *òirleach na h-òrdaig* 'inch of the thumb'. The breadth of the thumb was a traditional way of measuring an inch.

1654 *bàrr sumaidean* Eigg , McL, R.I.A. *bhar/Bharr sumaidin*

1658 *biodh – – – d'a* Eigg *be – – – na*, 1813 ff. *bi – – – 'na*
reang 1933 *crann*

1662 *Ged a dh' atadh* Eigg *Gad dhatadh*, McL, R.I.A. *Ge do attagh*, 1813, 1839 *Ge do dh-atadh*, 1874 ff. *Ged dh' atadh*.

1664–5 These two lines appear only in McL and R.I.A.

1666 *chriothnachadh* Eigg, 1841 ff. *chreanachadh*. The final syllable goes metrically with l. 1667.

1668 *treunant* Eigg *trèanont*, McL, R.I.A. *treanont*, 1813, 1839 *tearuinte*, 1841 *tearainnte*. The 1841 reading is followed in all subsequent edd., but Angus MacLeod in 1933 suggests that the Eigg reading may be a variant of *treubhant*.

1670 This line has more syllables than the norm, even if we exclude the two svarabhakti ones in sean*a*-mhara and cean*na*-ghlais.

1671 *gleanna-gharbh* 1813, 1839 *gleann-ghaoir*

1672 *criothnaich* Eigg *crithmich*, 1813, 1839 *critheanaich*, 1841 ff. *crithnich*

1673 *taod-aoire* Glossed 'Bolt rope' in McL and R.I.A.

1674 In explanation of this line Angus MacLeod (1933) says: 'To avoid luffing, he 'veers' slightly, so that the boat will take the wind (*gabhail*) and that the boat will not lose 'way' (*ruith*)'.

1675 *'na h-aodach* 1813 to 1924 *a h-aodaich*

1676 *cho daingeann* 1874 to 1924 *gu daingean*

1678 *still* McL, R.I.A. *stioll*

1679 *bàrr* Eigg, 1813 ff. *àird*. Perhaps the Eigg reading is to be preferred, rather than repeating *bàrr*, but the alliteration between *bàrr* and *buinne* is also a desideratum.

Section 7. In McL, this section was omitted at first, and added at the end of the MS, with an indication that it should be placed at this point. The fact that Sections 7 and 8 both begin with *Suigheadh* probably explains the oversight.

1680 *toirteal-laoch* Eigg *toitear-laohc*, McL, R.I.A. *Taitfhearlaoch*, 1813 *toirt-laoch*, 1839 *toirtearlach*, 1841 ff. *toirtealach*. The evidence for *taitfhear-laoch* is somewhat persuasive, but it is easier to make sense of *toirteal-laoch* 'bulky hero'.

1681 'in charge of the apparatus, in control'.
gloic So Eigg, McL, R.I.A. 1813 ff. *glaic*. The *o* form is probably a dialectal variant.

1682 *staideil* Eigg *staidil*, McL, R.I.A., 1813, 1841, 1924 *staideil*, 1874, 1933 *stàideil*. The form with short *a* has perhaps the sense of 'steady'.

1683 *graimpidh* 1841 *graimear*. Angus MacLeod (1933) relates this to *grèim* 'grip' and suggests the senses of 'unyielding, resolute'.

1689 *A-rèir* 1813, 1839 *Do reir*, McL, R.I.A. *air Eir*, 1874 ff. *a réir*

1693 This line appears only in McL and R.I.A. Angus MacLeod (1933) speculates that a line has been missed.

1694 *buille-bheairte* McL, R.I.A. *Buille-bheirste*, Eigg ff. *buill bhea(i)rte*. The sense is clearly 'ropes of the tackle' i.e. *buill-*, but the metrical norm of eight syllables gives some support to *buille*, perhaps as a variant form of the plural of *ball*.

1696 *tobhtainn* Eigg *tottaidh*, McL *Tautuinn*, R.I.A. *toutainn*, 1813 *toutaidh*, 1839 *tota*, Henderson *tobhtaidh*, 1874 ff. *tobhta*. The latter is the common form, but the early sources suggest a variant or variants.

1699 *cnàmhach* Eigg *chnabhach*, McL, R.I.A. *chramhach*. One of several instances of lenition of a final adjective in a sequence qualifying a noun, especially in the genitive plural.

1700 *cliathnach* Eigg, McL, R.I.A. *chlia(')nach*. Note lenition here of a final adjective qualifying a nominative plural. Angus MacLeod suggests the senses 'of wide span' or 'with strong sides'.

1701 *Cròcach* This adjective is also lenited in the three earliest sources.

1703 *garbh-sgròbadh* Eigg *nèart scrobagh*, 1813 ff. *neart sgròbaidh*

1704 'in time of hardship/difficulty who will haul it (the sheet) in'

1705 'will let it (the sail) furl'(?)

1709 *cuanda* Eigg, McL, R.I.A., P. Campbell *cuainte*. Perhaps this should be retained as a variant of *cuanda*.

1712 This reading combines elements of the early readings to restore the strict syllabic length of the lines.
P. Campbell, McL, R.I.A. *(a) Sios 's a suas a chum gach Urracaig*, Eigg *sios sa suas i,/A chum-gach urracaig*, 1924, 1933 – – – *di*. It may well be that the Campbell, McL, R.I.A. reading should stand, and that the added *di* is not necessary to the sense of moving the tack (*cluas*) up and down to each thole-pin (*urracag*).

1716 *aonrais* So Eigg, McL, R.I.A.; 1813, 1839 have *ionrais*, P. Campbell *iunrais*. All later edd. have *iùn(n)rais*.

1718 *treunmhor* McL *treun-mhear*

1718–19 'He would bare/reduce it with a strong powerful grip down to the gunwale'.

1720 *màirnealach* Eigg *mar-nialach*, McL *Mair-nealach*, R.I.A. *Mair-nialach*, P. Campbell *mairneallach*. The sense is 'mariner, sailor'. The R.I.A. Dict. compares Med. Latin *marinellus*, and the early sources here seem to recognise a connection with *muir/mara* 'sea'.

1723 *Cala a* McL, R.I.A., P. Campbell *Cala*. This is another instance of syntactic displacement: the normal order would be *a choisneas cala*, 'that will win harbour/take us to harbour'.

1724 *an* Eigg *ne*, McL, R.I.A., P. Campbell *na*, 1839, 1874, 1924 *'n*

1726 *na stiùireadh* Eigg *na stiuradh*, McL, R.I.A. *'ga stiuradh*. The usual form is *stiuire*, but *stiuireadh* occurs also in 1. 1774.

1730 *'s esan* Eigg, McL, P. Campbell, 1813 to 1924 *'se sin*, R.I.A., 1933 *is e sin*. The reference seems to be specifically to the look-out man. He is their Lord of the weather and guiding-star.

Section 11 Title: *calpa na tàirne* is explained by MacLeod (1933) as the lower section ('down-haul') of the halyard.

1732 *calpa* McL, R.I.A. *chalpa*, P. Campbell *cholpa*

1733 *Fear gun soistinn* Angus MacLeod (1933) interprets *soistinn* as deriving from *so-fhoistinn* 'tranquillity, – – – unconcern'. He adds "Thus *fear gun soistinn* would be a responsible person, full of concern for his task".
McL and R.I.A. have a completely different reading for this line: *Tuirr gharbh thoirteil*, and P. Campbell reads *Tuir-gharbh thoirtil*. It is difficult to make satisfactory sense of this. If we accept the lenition in *gharbh*, it may be advisable to read *tur-gharbh*, 'extremely large-bodied'; or we might read *tùr* 'tower'. It is more comfortable to stay with the Eigg reading.

1735 *solta* Eigg *soilta*, McL, R.I.A. *socair*, P. Campbell *sochdair*

1737 *guamach* So McL, R.I.A.; P. Campbell *cuanda*, Eigg ff. *gruamach*. The sense of *gruamach* 'surly' does not accord as well as that of *guamach*, which can mean 'careful, exact' as well as 'pleasant'. The senses 'careful, exact' are quoted as 'Common Speech' in the High. Soc. Dict.

1740–41*troma,/Treun* McL, R.I.A., P. Campbell *treuna trom*

1745 *ròp frithir* Eigg *taoid frithir*. McL glosses *frithir* 'Ticklish'. All later edd. have *taod*.

1746 *uime* McL, R.I.A. *uimpe*, P. Campbell *impe*. This feminine form does not go with either *ròp* or *taod*.

1748 *sgairtear* McL, R.I.A., P. Campbell *Sgairtir*, Eigg *Scairta*, 1813, 1839, 1933 *sgairte*, 1874 to 1924 *sgarar*. There is a choice to be made here between *sgar* 'sever, stop' and *sgairt* 'shout'. MacLeod (1933) prefers the latter.

1751 Eigg, McL, R.I.A. *Far na craige*, P. Campbell *bhār na cnaige*, 1813, 1839 *Far na cragaibh*, 1841 ff. *Bhàrr na cnaige*

1748–51 In McL, R.I.A., P. Campbell 11. 1751-2 come before 11. 1748-9.

1753 *Làimh* 1813, 1841, 1874, 1933 *Làmh*

1756 *Tagham* Eigg *Taothabh*, 1813 ff. *Taghaibh*, P. Campbell *Taghamh*

1759 *ghealtair* McL, R.I.A. *gheilt-fhear*

1762 *Cia dhiubh* So McL, R.I.A., 1874, 1924; Eigg *Co dhui*, 1813, 1839, 1933 *co dhiubh*. The sense is 'which of them, whether'.

1767 *bi* McL, R.I.A., P. Campbell *biogh*

1768 *coltas* P. Campbell *cosmalachd*

1772 *àrd-labhara* 1813 ff. *àrd-labhrach*

1774 *na ceileadh e air fear* P. Campbell *innseadh do Dh fhear*

1778 *griobhag* Eigg, P. Campbell *giabhag*, McL, R.I.A. *giobhag*, 1841 *giamhag*, 1839, 1874 ff *griobhag*. *giobhag* is used of a giddy female. Presumably it has arisen in this context from a mis-reading or mix-up between the two words.

Section 13: Sheriff Nicolson pointed out (*An Gaidheal* VI, 59) that in this introduction 'the imagination of the poet goes ahead, the galley being not yet under sail'.

1780 *taoma* 1839 ff. *taoime*

1781 *Garbh laoch* 1813 ff. *Laoch (a) bhios*

1782 *gu bràth* P. Campbell *a chaoidh*

1787 *'Nam* Eigg ff. *Na/'Na*

1788 *garbh* Eigg *tuìgh*, 1813 ff. *tiugh*

1790 – – – *thilgeadh* – – – *fairge* McL, R.I.A. *th(e)ilgeil* – – – *taoma*, P. Campbell – – – *taomadh*

1793 *-eàrlaid* McL, R.I.A. *Earrlaid.* 11. 1792-3 translate 'who, with obstinate confidence will not ever straighten his agile back (until – –)'.
1794 *siola* P. Campbell *sil*, Eigg ff. *sile*
1798 *chumas* P. Campbell *chumadh*
Section 14. Introduction: *laidir ghreamail* follows *dithis* in McL, R.I.A. P. Campbell *ghreimil*
1800 *làidir* not in P. Campbell
1802 *tàirneant, treunant* Eigg *tairnent treinn i cert*, 1813, 1839 *tearuinnt treun ceart i*, 1874 to 1924 *tèarainnte, tréun, ceart*, 1933 *tèaruinnt' treuncheart*
1804 P. Campbell *Le mead neart is lùis an*
1808 *sgiobalta* McL, R.I.A. *Sgibilte*, Eigg *sgiobiolte*, 1813, 1839, 1874 *sgibidh*
1810 *Ordaich ann* McL, R.I.A. *orduigh ann*, Eigg *Dhorann*, 1839 *Dh' ordaichein*, 1841 *Dh-ordaicheadh*, 1874 *Dh' òrdaichinn*, 1924 *Dhòrainn*, 1933 *Dh' fhóghnadh*
1812 *ladarn* McL, R.I.A. *ladrona*, Eigg, 1839 *ladorn*
Section 15. Introduction: *sgrìobadh* Eigg *spìonadh*
1819 *còpadh* P. Campbell *chòpadh.* Campbell has a gloss *sharachadh* above the word.
1822 *Co-ghrad* So Eigg, McL, R.I.A.; 1813 ff. *cho grad*
1826 *abhsadh* Eigg, McL, R.I.A., 1813, 1839 *ausadh*, 1874 ff. *abhsaidh*
1827 *clabhsail* glossed 'loud' in McL and R.I.A. High. Soc. Dict. gives 'quiet, methodical' as the meaning. Angus MacLeod (1933) reports that *clabhsail* can mean 'open, draughty' (of a house or room).
òrdan 1839 *òrdail*, 1874, 1933 *òrdugh*
1828 *airtneal* McL, P. Campbell *airstil*, R.I.A. *airsteal*, Eigg *arsteal*
Section 16 Introduction: The early sources begin *Do bha*, which seems a confusion of older *Do bhì* and later *Bha.* The final part of the Introduction (*a' trogbhail ---- Deas*) is not in McL, R.I.A. or P. Campbell. The form *trogbhail* seems eccentric, though *togbhail* is a common earlier form of *togail.*
1830 *'Ghrian* So McL, R.I.A.; Eigg *Gre'an*, 1874 *A' Ghrian*, other sources *grian*
1832 *dùldaidh* So McL, P. Campbell; R.I.A. *dùlaidh*, Eigg *dubuidh*, 1813 *dùbhui*, 1839 *dùbhuidh*, others *dubhaidh. dùldaidh* is a variant of *dùdlaidh* 'gloomy, dark'.
1838 *oirr'* The early sources have *orr(a)*, apart from P. Campbell's *uirre.* 1874 ff. *oirr'*. Either is possible, *orra* referring to the crew, *oirre* to the sky. There is a similar division between sources in 1. 1841, but *oirr'*, referring to the sky, is more likely there.
1840 *aig gaoith* So McL; Eigg has *gaodh*, R.I.A. *aig a ghaoith*
1842–3 For metrical purposes, two syllables of *bhaidealacha* go in 1. 1842, and two in 1. 1843.
1844 *coilpeinean* Eigg *coilepenan*, McL, R.I.A., P. Campbell *Co(i)lpinin.* Mac Mhaighstir Alasdair in his Vocabulary gives *coilpen* as one of the words for 'rope' or 'tow'.
1847 Angus MacLeod (1933) translates 'of the resin-red tapering points', i.e. the points of the shafts to which the ropes are attached.
1851 *fhailbheag* So McL, R.I.A.; P. Campbell *ailbhig*, Eigg, 1813, 1839 *ailbheag.*
1854 *tapaidh* Here 'active, quick', or perhaps used as an adverb, 'actively, quickly'.
1856 *uinneagan an aeir* McL, R.I.A. *Fuineagan an Aeïr*, P. Campbell *fuinneagun an aithir*, Eigg ff. *uinneagan an athair.* The form *aeir* is perhaps used as a monosyllable, keeping the syllable count to eight.
1859 *bannail* So Eigg; McL, R.I.A., P. Campbell *b' Anail.* Angus MacLeod (1933) connects this word with M. Irish *band, bann* 'effort, deed, feat', suggesting 'vigorous, fierce' as the sense.
1863 *'S* Not indicated separately in early sources, apart from P. Campbell.
1864 *bheanntaibh --- ghleanntaibh* Eigg *bheannabh --- ghleannabh*

1866 *bhòc* Eigg *bhochd*, McL, R.I.A. *Phochd*, P. Campbell *bhòchd*
1872–5 Not in P. Campbell
1873 *màm toinnte* So McL; Eigg *maom teinnti*, R.I.A. *Màm teinnti.* Eigg's reading is followed by all later sources, but *màm* 'a large round hill' is more convincing than *maom* 'ourburst etc.', and is reinforced by the reference in l. 1864.
1876 *liath-ghorm* So McL, R.I.A. Eigg ff. *lia(th)-cheann*
1878 *cladh* can be taken in either of its senses (1) ditch (2) rampart.
dùldaidh McL *duldaidh*, R.I.A. *dudlaith*, Eigg *dudaid*, 1839 ff. *dùdaidh*. See l. 1832*n*.
1879 *garbh* So McL, R.I.A.; Eigg ff. *fuaim*
1881 *sonn* So McL, R.I.A., P. Campbell, Eigg; 1813 ff. *tonn*. The later reading is satisfactory in a literal way, but the early reading *sonn*, apparently referring to the waves or hills of ocean as 'heroes', has its attractions.
1884 *theàrnamaid* This follows the McL and R.I.A. and P. Campbell readings. Eigg *thuttagh mid* is followed by later sources (*thuiteamaid*).
ion-slugaidh 1813 *h-aon slugadh* MacLeod (1933) draws attention to the older usage of *ion* + genitive of the verbal noun.
1888 *ciasanaich* So McL, R.I.A., P. Campbell; Eigg has *ceosanaich*, 1813 ff. *ceòsanaich*. The form in McL is glossed (in a later hand) 'broad-bottomed', and *ceòs* and *cias* are both used of 'buttock'. I have heard *ciaslaichean* used in a similar sense in Lewis (c. 1940). Here the reference is to 'broad-bottomed waves'.
1890 *gaire* McL, R.I.A. *gairre*, Eigg *gairrabh*, P. Campbell *garabh*, 1813, 1839 *caramh*, 1874 ff. *caraibh*
1892 *ri* McL, P. Campbell *re*, R.I.A. *ag*, Eigg *n* (misprint for *a* or *ri*?)
1894 P. Campbell *Gu'n cinneadh na h aon-mhuire*
h-aon McL, R.I.A. *h aona*
1896–9 Not in P. Campbell
1898 *sàil* here means the 'heel' or 'keel' of the galley.
1899 *t-aigeal* Eigg *taigeal*, McL, R.I.A. *t Aigin*. The two forms *aigeal* and *aigeann* are partly interchangeable, but in some usages *aigeal* refers to the sea-bed, *aigeann* to the ocean.
1900 *sluistneadh* Eigg *sluistnedh*, McL, R.I.A. *sluaisnidh*, P. Campbell *sluaisneadh*, 1813, 1839, 1924 *sluistreadh*, 1874, 1933 *sloistreadh*. The forms in *ui*/*oi* go better with the short *ai* of *maistreadh*, but perhaps the *n* form should be retained.
1901 *Roimh* P. Campbell *trid*
1902 *robh* Eigg, McL, R.I.A. *raibh*
1904 *confadh* So McL, R.I.A.; Eigg *tonfadh*, 1813, 1839 *tonnan*, Henderson *tonnadh*, 1874, 1924 *confhadh*
1908–11 Not in P. Campbell
1908–9 *àrd, uaimhinneach* So McL, R.I.A.; Eigg *uabhainneach*, 1813, 1874 ff. *àrd-uamhannaich*. The final syllable goes metrically with l. 1909.
1910 *gur* So the early sources. 1874 ff. present the direct speech of the animals "Is – – – –", which seems logical enough.
1913 The tiny fish are pictured as lying with their white bellies up.
1914 *confadh* So McL, R.I.A., P. Campbell; Eigg ff. *confach*/*confhach*
1916 *aigeil* McL, R.I.A. *aigein*, P. Campbell *aigen*. See 1899 above.
1918 *a-nìos* McL, R.I.A. *a nios*, P. Campbell, Eigg *a nuas*. The form *a-nìos* 'upwards, from below' is historically more accurate.
1921 *strioplach* McL, R.I.A., P. Campbell *stroipleach*
1923 *oirr'* Early sources *orr'*, but no doubt the reference is to the sea.
1926 *'s iad 'nam* So McL, R.I.A., P. Campbell. Eigg reads *sianam*. Later sources all feature *sian* e.g. 1813 *sian nam*, 1839 *cheann-sian*, 1874, 1924 *cheann – sian am*, 1933 *cheann, sian am*. The line seems best taken in the sense of 'With

many heads, consisting of mouthes down to their gills'.

1929 *a* Only in McL, R.I.A., P. Campbell. The line translates 'pawed', i.e. the sea is being pawed by all these odd creatures.

1932 *ròmhan sgriachaidh* McL, R.I.A. *Romhain-scriachaidh*, P. Campbell *ròmhain sgriachaidh*, Eigg *robhain scriachdach*, 1874 ff. *sgriachadh.*

1936–7 These two lines are not in McL and R.I.A., but the rhyme-scheme requires them. P. Campbell has these lines.
gan claisneachd Eigg *gan claosneachd.* 'The crew lost their pleasure of hearing in listening (to the screeching music of the demons)'

1938 *Ceileireadh* R.I.A., P. Campbell *ceilirin*

1940 *Foghar* McL *Fiadh-ghair*, R.I.A. *Fadh-ghair*, P. Campbell *Fadhar*, Eigg *Fadhghair.* These forms seem to be suggesting etymologies of the word, based on *gàir*; *foghur* is a long-attested word.

1942 *Fosghaoir* So McL, R.I.A. Eigg has *Fosghair.* The sense is 'loud shouting/noise'.
bocsaich McL, R.I.A. *pocsadh*, P. Campbell *cnotadh*, Eigg ff. *sloistreadh*

1946 *seòrsa* McL, R.I.A., P. Campbell, 1813 *seorta/seòrta*

1947 *pianadh* McL *grianadh*

1948 *daillte* So McL, R.I.A.; P. Campbell, Eigg *dallta*
dall-cheò So McL, R.I.A.; P. Campbell *dalla-cheo*, Eigg ff. *cathadh*

1950 *àibhseach* So McL, R.I.A., P. Campbell; Eigg ff. *aibheasach/aibheiseach*

1952–3 These lines are missed out (presumably by accident) in 1874. *peileirean-beithrich* MacLeod (1933) glosses 'fire-balls'. *beithir* is a 'thunder-bolt'.

1954 *deathach na riofa* P. Campbell *deatach.* MacLeod (1933) credibly interprets this as 'the smoke of sulphur'. In the form *ruibh* it is better attested in Irish.

1957–8 Missed by mistake from 1839 version.

1962 *faite-gàire* McL, R.I.A. *feata gaire*

1962–3 McL, R.I.A. have a comma after *truas*, and do not begin 1. 1963 with *'S* (nor does Eigg).

1967 *èisl' air* McL, R.I.A. *Eisl air*, P. Campbell *èis*, Eigg *èislair*, 1813, 1839 *èisleir*, 1841 ff. *éislein/éislean.* The form *èisl'* is presumably a contracted form of *èislean.*

1969 Eigg *Beairt ghaisidh*

1970 *Tarraing no cupladh* MacLeod (1933) argues that *tarraing* refers to the halyard, rather than to nails (e.g. Eigg *Tarrun*), which are listed later. He would prefer *cupaill*, 'shrouds' to *cupladh* 'coupling', but the three earliest sources have *cupladh.*

1973 *aidmheach* So McL, R.I.A. Eigg has *aidnniach*, where *nn* is probably a misprint for *mh.* The sense is 'testimony'.

1976 *achlaisean* McL, R.I.A., 1813 *Achlaisin.* The form *achlasan* is preferred in later sources.
aisne So McL, R.I.A., 1813. This is strictly the genitive.

1978 *slat-bheòil* MacLeod (1933) explains as 'wale', the external rounded strip running from stem to stern along the edge of the top strake.
sguitichean-asgaill glossed 'Seats fore (and) aft' in McL, R.I.A.

1979 *tuairgneadh Glossed 'disturbed' in McL, R.I.A.*

1981 *chreuchdadh* McL, R.I.A. *chreuchdnadh*, Eigg *chreachdadh*

1983 *dèasgadh* McL, R.I.A. *deisgeadh*, P. Campbell *dèisgneadh*

1984 *crann-tarrann* McL, R.I.A. *Crann-tarruinn* MacLeod (1933) glosses 'tree-nail; wooden pegs used in boat-building'.

1986 *barradh* McL, R.I.A. *Barraibh*, P. Campbell *baradh*

1988 *trochladh* McL, R.I.A., P. Campbell *troladh* (Campbell adds an alternative reading, *chamadh*), Eigg *traladh*, 1874 ff. *tràladh.* This word is better attested in Irish, as *trochlugad/trochloghadh*, in the sense of 'decaying, damaging'. The forms in our early sources may indicate the poet's pronunciation.

1989 *calpa* Glossed in McL 'blunt nail' and in R.I.A. 'A kind of nail'. MacLeod (1933) glosses 'rivet, bolt'.

1988–91 The metre changes for this quatrain to $2(8^2 + 8^2)^{2+4}$

1992 *sìoth-shàimh* P. Campbell *sìochaidh*, Eigg *sìchaibh*, 1813, 1839, Henderson *siochaint*

1993 *crois Chaol Ile* P. Campbell – – – *chaoil-ìlidh.* 1924 changes this to *còrs' Chaol-Ile*, and MacLeod (1933) tends to agree, both because no 'cross' is known at the Sound of Islay, and because the use of *air* would be unusual with *crois*. Perhaps *crois* here refers to some kind of crossing or navigational marking in the Sound of Islay.

1995 *Ordan* McL, R.I.A., P. Campbell, Eigg *Ordon*

1997 *aèir* air, sky. See l. 1856*n*. A monosyllable is required here.

1998 *mìn-gheal* McL, R.I.A., Eigg *mìngeal/mingeal*

1999 *tabhainn* McL, P. Campbell, Eigg *tauthuinn*, R.I.A. *Taubhuinn*, 1813, 1839 *taghunn*

2000 *buidheachas* P. Campbell *buicheadas*

2001 'who shaped the elements'

2005 *tùilinn* 'twilled linen' (Eng. *twilling*). P. Campbell's reading here is *dhlùtha.*

2007 Eigg *Air fad hùrlair*, 1813 ff. *air fad a h-ùrlair*

2008 *bhasgant* So McL; Eigg *bhaistgant*, 1874 ff. *bhaisgeant'*

2010 *MacBharrais* I have not been able to identify the holder of this unusual name.

2012–3 P. Campbell *'S rinn sinn an rèth iumradh, gun mheang gun iumrall gun dearrmad*

2015 *Carraig Fhearghais* Carrick Fergus or Knock Fergus in Antrim. This place had many associations for MacDonalds. Iain Mòr of Islay had married Marjory Bisset, of the Glens of Antrim, early in the fifteenth century, and later MacDonalds extended the Antrim estates further, and Scottish (Southern) MacDonalds were frequently involved in Irish matters in the fifteenth and sixteenth centuries.

IMRICH ALASDAIR MHICDHOMHNAILL AS EIGNEIG DO DH'INBHIR-AOIDH

Sources and Editions:

Eigg	143-6
McL 120	Item 9
Colin Campbell	Collection MS C, 3-6
1809	157-60
1839	88-91
1874, 1892	81-4
1924	270-74

There are two early texts of this poem, very similar to each other: (1) in Ranald MacDonald's Eigg Collection of 1776, and (2) in McLagan MS 120. The relationship of these two texts is very close, suggesting that they are versions of the same original, showing various editorial preferences, and one change of stanza order. McLagan MS 120 is a sixteen-leaf medium-size MS, with the title 'Orain ghaoidhealach', and including poems by Màiri Nighean Alasdair Ruaidh, Am Bàrd Mathanach and others. This is the only poem by Mac Mhaighstir Alasdair in the MS. The McLagan version of the poem has a more detailed heading: 'Imrich Alastair Mhic Dhonmhnuill as Eagnaig do dh' Inbhir Aoidh, nar chuir Herison as cainil air'. This is a reference to the priest William Harrison who was in charge at Morar and Arisaig during the '45 and for some years after that (see C. MacDonald (1889, 1989), 136). The implication of the McLagan title is that the priest excommunicated the poet, the title using the form *as cainil* i.e. *ás-coinneal* 'candle-outing' rather than the better-attested *coinneal-bhàthadh*.

MS C in the Colin Campbell Collection (presently housed in Edinburgh University Library) is in the hand of Donald MacNicol (see a description in Ó Baoill, 1983). In the Campbell MS our poem is headed 'Imrich Ala.^{r} mhic Mh.^{r} Ala.^{r} a Eigneig do dh' Innir-aoigh – no on tSagairt gus an tEispig'. This sub-title is apparently picked up in a note written into my copy of the 1809 edition: 'An allegory between a severe capricious priest and a mild humane Bishop – the Poets complaint of the Priest to the Bishop'. Whether this comment implies a tradition that Mac Mhaighstir Alasdair made a formal complaint to the Bishop, or is simply glossing by later copyists, is not clear. In other respects the Campbell MS text (or the MacNicol text as we should probably think of it) is extremely close to that of McLagan 120.

The later editions make the usual editorial emendations, often obscuring the individual usages that are most probably represented by the early sources. Many of these are restored in this edition.

The initial *e* of *Eigneig* is long, according to the evidence of 11.2076-7, which end-rhyme on a long *e*.

The poet's twin gifts of natural observation and vivid satire are entertainingly brought into play here, as he contrasts the harsh environment of Eigneig and the genial one of Inbhir-aoidh. The contrast is greatly exaggerated in the linkage of the hated priest and factor with Eigneig.

IMRICH ALASDAIR MHICDHOMHNAILL AS EIGNEIG DO DH'INBHIR-AOIDH

Dh' fhalbh mi á nathrachan creagach,
Làn conaisg 's de phreasaibh sgrogach,
Bioran droighinn ann dam bhriogadh
Roimh 'm chliabh gu neimhneach dam bhrodadh.

Fonn crainntidh, tioram, nach lagach,
Gun mhìn-fheur, gun lòn, gun bhoglach,
Cho tioram ri spuing gu sradadh,
Ghabhas fadadh 's lasadh tograch.

Gun nòinin, gun sòbhrach, gun siumrag,
Air dul 'na theine le tiumarachd,
Siud am fearann nach eil iumlan,
Fo speuran nan sìontaidh iumluath.

Liath-reothadh gun deisear grèine
Feadh srath a ghlinne 's a shlèibhtean,
Cranna-shneachda 'spìonadh a speuran,
Froiseadh mu m' chluasan 's mu m' eudann.

Am fonn sgrainngeil, grìomach, tomach,
Chinn de gach nì solta lomach,
Baile caol gun sult, nach bronnach,
Loma-làn de bhratagan croma.

Gart an Fhaoillich gach aon ial air,
'S e daonnan an caithreim fiabhrais,
Gun Iuchar, gun Chèitein grianach
Ach fadadh-cruaidh san àirde 'n iar air.

'S e buain froise de chloich-mheallain
Dhèanadh ar cluasan a sgioladh;
Cha dèanadh ar barail ar mealladh:
Sin an fhras as doirbhe sileadh.

Am maor thug dhòmhs' a' bhàirlinn spreigeil,
An crom-shrònach 's a smig ga spagadh,
Ghairm e rium mar ghlaistig sgreadaidh
M' iumraich a thogbhail an gradaig.

Ghabh mi còmhnaidh an Inbhir-aoidhe,
Bail' ion-mholta, solta, gaolach,
'S e gu solach, torrach, maoineach,
Mùirneach, sò-ghradh'ch, forach, faoilidh.

Baile gun ghlaistig, gun bhòcan,
'S caisrigte gach crann 's gach fòid dheth,
Gun deanntag, gun charran, gun fhòtas,
Loma-làn chluaran, lili 's ròsan.

A mhaghan a' bòrcadh de nòinein,
Stràchta de dheagh mhiosan òirdheirc,
Cha chinn lus bhios searbh am fòid dheth,
Barrach, bainneach, mealach, sò-ghradh'ch.

Fiamh a' ghàir air srath 's air mòr-bheinn,
Am madainn Mhàigh is grian gan òradh,
'Cur anam-fàis le blàths 'nam pòraibh,
H-uile là toirt bàrr air bòidhcheid.

Baile blàth, 's maith fàs gach seòrs' ann,
Dealt an àigh air bàrr gach feòirnein,
Beò-chluig-chiùil an dos gach mòr-chrainn,
Tilgeil cheileir-gràidh o'n sgòrnain.

B' oirfeid èibhinn geum na còisridh
Am bàrr nan geug a' seinn an òran,
Leadain theud-bhinn, ainglidh, ghlòrmhor,
'S laoidhean grèidhte, ceud-fath'ch, ceòlmhor.

'S fortan leam gun d' fhàg mi Eigneig,
Ionad cruaidh nan dris bu ghèire,
Am fonn sporach, sgorach, beura,
Dh' fheannadh m' fheòil mar thoirc dhroch rèasair.

Fàilt ort fèin, a Phàrthais fhaoilidh,
Inbhir-aoidh am baile tlachdmhor;
Bidh m' anam 's mo chorp gu naomha
O fhuair mi sgaoilte ás na glasaibh.

Chuibhtich mi taghadh na piocaid,
Am fear a bha riochdail 'na chaisein,
Dhèanadh ascaoin-eaglais chruaidh orm
Mun cluinneadh a chluas trì chasaid.

Chuibhtich mi ascart is teine
'S gach nì bhiodh 'na bhoile gu lasadh,
Chuibhtich mi seangan nan crioman
'S gach nì biorach bhiodh gam speachadh.

Chuibhtich mi spuir a' chait fhiadhaich
'S dòbhran iargalta na braclainn,
An neach sin a chàineadh gu daor mi
'S a bheum gun adhbhar a chlag rium.

Gun do theich mi on fhraoch-sgriachain
Loisgeadh m' fhiasag dhìom le shradaibh,
'Cur bhramannan dearga tein' ás,
'S gun tholl e gun deireas mo chraiceann.

Gun chuibhtich mi rìgh nan searbhag,
Domblas, eanghlas, 's tombaca,
'S gach biastag a bha dam itheadh:
Coinnspeach, criothlagan is beachan.

Ach o thàinig mi dh' Inbhir-aoidh
Thionndaidh riumsa caoin gach ascaoin,
Is gach rud bha 'cur orm trioblaid
Rinn Dia gu sgiobalt' an casg dhiom.

NOTES

2020 *nathrachan* McL *Nárachan* This may be the poet's own coinage, based on *nathair* 'snake, adder', so 'the place frequented by adders'.
2021 *conaisg* Eigg *coinisg*
de McL, Eigg *do.* Omitted in Colin Campbell MS
sgrogach McL *sgrógach* The very occasional accents in the McL text seem to mark stress rather than length of vowel.
2022 *bioran* Here the plural of *bior* 'thorn etc.', not the diminutive.
droighinn McL *draothan*, Eigg *dreathun*
dam Colin Campbell MS and later edd. have *ga m/'g am*
2023 *Roimh 'm* McL *Throimh*
2024 *crainntidh* C. Campbell *cranntui'*
lagach 1839 *ladhach* This is presumably an emendation to the sense of 'lovely' (*laghach*), which fits well as to sense. For the poet, *lagach* may have implied 'with attractive dells/hollows'.
2025 *bhoglach* Later edd. *bhoglaich* Here used to contrast soft, marshy ground with dry, rocky ground.
2026 *spuing* Eigg *spuinac* The old sense of 'tinder' is the appropriate one here.
sradadh Eigg *sradach* The internal rhyme with *fadadh* in l. 2027 favours the *-adh* reading.
2027 *lasadh* McL *lásas*
2028 *nòinin* Later edd. substitute the later forms *neòinein, neòinean*
siumrag McL *siomrag*, C. Campbell and later edd. *seamraig*. The *-u-* reading was perhaps the poet's dialectal usage. Eigg has the *-u-* rhyme throughout the

stanza, whereas McL has it only in the final line. The 1741 Vocabulary has *An Tsheamair, Antsheamarag* (p. 62).

2029 *tiumrachd* Eigg *tiumarachd*, McL, C. Campbell *tiormachd* The Eigg form again indicates dialectal usage.

2031 *sìontaidh* McL *siontuidh*, C. Campbell *Siontaibh*, Eigg *siontadh*, later edd. *siantan*. The early versions imply the poorly-attested plural in *-aidh*.

2032 *deisear* McL *deasair*, Eigg *deisir*, later edd. *deàrrsadh*. The more muted sense of *deisear* 'having a southerly exposure' is more appropriate than that of *deàrrsadh*, which implies more intense shining and heat, and would sit uneasily with the reference to hoar-frost.

2033 *Feadh* Eigg *Feoth*

2034 *Cranna-shneachda* McL, C. Campbell *Crann-shneachda*, later edd. *Crann-s(h)neachd' a'*. This may imply the image of a snow-plough or snowploughs plucking snow from the skies.

2035 *Froiseadh* Eigg *Froishidh*

2037 *solta* Eigg *sollta* The syntax of this line seems a little strained, and perhaps the form *lomach* rather than *lom* is evoked by the rhyme scheme. I take the sense to be '(the land) that became bare of all mild/tender things'.

2038 *bronnach* 'well-fed, having a large belly'

2039 *croma* McL, Eigg *cromadh*

2040 *Fhaoillich* McL *aolaich*
Gart 'threatening aspect'. The sense of the line is 'the threatening aspect of January/February weather marks it at all seasons'.

2041 'all the time throbbing as with fever'

2043 *fadadh-cruaidh* McL *fada cruaidh*. The *fadadh-cruaidh* is the 'dog-tooth' rainbow.

2047 *doirbhe sileadh* Eigg *doirbh a shileadh*

2048–55 In C. Campbell, the order of these two stanzas is reversed.

2049 *a smig ga spagadh* The High. Soc. Dict. gives '*spagadh* an obliquity of the mouth', attributing this to Common Speech. The sense of the line is 'with his distorted chin' or possibly 'whose chin distorts him'.

2050 *glaistig* usually refers to a female; here presumably it is the quality of screeching that is emphasised.
sgreadaidh Eigg *sgreididh*, 1839 *sgreidich*

2051 *iumraich* The Eigg form is retained. Other edd. *imrich*
thogbhail Both McL and Eigg use this older form.

2052–5 This stanza is placed before 11. 2048-51 in McL, but the Eigg order is clearly preferable.

2053 *Bail' ion-mholta* All sources have *Baile*, and Eigg has *inn-mholta*. The hyphen is retained, as the original probably intended to stress *-mholta*, to rhyme with *solta*.

2054 *solach* 'sunny' (?) This word is not well attested, but *sol* was used of the sun.

2055 *sò-ghradh'ch* Eigg *so-ghradh*. The metre suggests a dissyllable but the adjectival form is required. In 1. 2063 the form with *ò* is indicated by the rhyme.
forach The later sources have *feurach*, but *forach* fits better metrically. It is difficult to pin down the sense precisely: perhaps 'productive' is close to it.

2056 *bhòcan* Eigg, C. Campbell *bhòchdan*

2057 *caisrigte – – – 's gach* Later sources *coisrigte – – – is*

2059 *cluaran* The commoner meaning is 'thistle', but the sense of 'corn-marigold' seems more appropriate here, going with the lilies and roses/primroses.

2060 *de* McL, Eigg *do*, later edd. *le*

2061 *de* As in 1. 2060

2062 *fòid* McL *fod*

2063 *barrach* A possible reading also is *bàrrach* 'rich in cream'.

sò-ghradh'ch 1924 *sòbhrach*. The weight of evidence is against the 1924 reading. As in 1. 2055 above, *sò-ghradh'ch* needs to be taken as a dissyllable.
2066 *anam fàis* Later sources *anma-fàis*. The sense of the line is 'putting the soul/spirit of growth, with warmth, in their pores' (i.e. into strath and mountain). The poet glosses the expression in 1751 as 'a vegetative soul'.
2067 *bòidhcheid* McL, Eigg *boichid*, later edd. *bhòichead*.
2070 *an* McL *air*, but with *ann* suprascript.
2071 *geum* Other sources have *seirm*, which is better for sense though less accurate for purposes of rhyme.
2073 *òran* C. Campbell *nan Oran*, 1924 *òrain*. The genitive plural is more appropriate than the genitive singular.
2074 *ainglidh* McL *aingle*
2075 *grèidhte* 'well-prepared, well-rehearsed'
2076 *gun* Omitted in Eigg.
2077 *dris* McL *dreis*
2079 McL, C. Campbell *Dh' fhionnagh m' fheoil dhi(o)m mar dhroch Reasar* Eigg *Dh fheannadh m' fheoil ma'r toirc dhroch rèasur* Later edd. – – – *mar chuirc* – – –

Eigg *toirc* is perhaps a dative form of *torc* in the sense of 'notch, indentation' (cf. Dwelly, quoting Alexander Carmichael). *torc* is normally a masculine noun.
2083 *O* – – – – *glasaibh* Later edd. *Bho 'n* – – – – *glasan*
2084 *piocaid* Eigg *piochdaid piocaid* is used of pick-axe and of pincers. Perhaps the latter is the sense here.
2085 'the man who was unquestionably surly'
2088 *ascart* Eigg *ascairt* The usual senses are 'tow, coarse broken flax'. Here perhaps used more loosely of inflammable rubbish (?).
2093 *braclainn* Eigg *brachdloinn* The sense is not clear. There is possibly a connection with the older forms *bracht* glossed in the R.I.A. Dict. as (1) juice, grease, fat; pith, and (2) breaking, cutting. Either of these senses may possibly go with the reference to the otter.
2094 *chàineadh* McL *chaine*, Eigg *chàine*, later edd. *chàin*. A two-syllable word is needed.
2095 *rium* McL *orm*, with *rium* in margin.
2096 *fraoch-sgriachain* 'crackling heath' (Dwelly, with reference to MacEachen, who quotes Arisaig forms). McL gives an alternative reading *bad an diorsain*, and Dwelly quotes *fraoch an diorrasain* in the sense of 'a kind of heather that sparkles when burning'. This suits the rhyme-scheme less well.
2097 *Loisgeadh* Apart from McL the other sources have *A loisg*.
2098 *'Cur* McL, Eigg *Cuir*, 1924 *Chur*
2099 *gun deireas* Literally 'without scarcity' i.e. all over the place.
chraiceann 1839, 1874 *chnaimhean*
2101 *eanghlas* McL, C. Campbell, Eigg, 1839 *earraghlas*. The reading of the later edd., accepted here, makes better sense. *eanghlas* was used of a weak drink, and is listed here with other undesirables, of which, surprisingly for the time, tobacco is one.
2102 *dam* Later edd. *'gam*
2103 *criothlagan* Later edd. *creathlagan*
2106 *trioblaid* Eigg *treobloid*

CUACHAG AN FHASAICH

Sources and Editions:

Eigg	115-17
McL 2	14-16
McL 148	7
McL 187	7-8
Campbell Collection A	3-6
Gillies	206-9
1806	112-14
1839	102-5
1841	127-8
1874, 1892	93-5
1924	234-6

Our text is based primarily on Eigg, as the earliest datable and extended version. The title there is 'Duanag *le* Alastair Mac Dhonuill, *air fonn* Banarach *dhonn a chruigh*', and this may suggest that the first line, or the whole chorus, was taken from an already existing song.

In McL 2, at the foot of p. 16, the title is given as 'Cuachag (uibhisteach) an Fhasaich', and both in this version and in McL 187 (but not in identical stanzas) there is reference to a girl named Màiri. It may well be that the song has a Uist location, or was partly inspired by the sight of a pretty Uist milkmaid.

Eigg has sixteen quatrains, Campbell and Gillies have eighteen, McL 187 has fifteen, McL 2 has ten and a half, and McL 148 has three quatrains only. McL 148 has one quatrain (11. 2160-63 in our edition) which does not appear in some other sources, and McL 187, Gillies and 1839 have two quatrains (11. 2159-66) which do not appear elsewhere. There is strong evidence of Gillies' acquaintance with the McL MSS. Gillies follows the same stanza order for the fifteen stanzas of the McL 187 version, and this differs markedly from Eigg. Gillies's final three stanzas are very close to the three in McL 148. Campbell (i.e. MacNicol) is often close to McL 148 and Gillies, but uses a fairly rough orthography. Lines 2175-6 here occur only in McL 2, as a half-stanza. There are other variants as between all these versions, and the significant ones are noted. The three extra quatrains from McL 148 and 187 are slotted in at appropriate points in this edition, but we have no clear evidence of their original position. There are considerable differences in stanza order between the sources.

None of the McL versions has an ascription to an author. McL 187 has a note on its final page: 'Cuachag an Fhasaich na Moirthir', which may suggest a Morar location as opposed to a Uist one. Thus we have to rely mainly on the Eigg ascription. Since the poem does not appear in the 1751 edition, it may have been composed later, and may indeed have a Morar component. No doubt the poem is as much a pastoral stereotype as an autobiographically inspired lyric. It certainly has stereotypical elements, but also a sharp, vivid turn of thought and phrase which carry the poet's recognisable stamp. We can probably accept the additional quatrains of the non-Eigg versions as genuine, though there are also present some of the expected variants and ambiguities that arise from multiple traditional channels.

CUACHAG AN FHASAICH

An Luinneag: A bhanarach dhonn a' chruidh,
Chaoin a' chruidh, dhonn a' chruidh,
Cailin deas donn a' chruidh,
Cuachag an fhàsaich.

A bhanarach mhìogach,
'S e do ghaol thug fo chìs mi,
'S math thig làmhainnean sìoda
Air do mhìn-bhasan bàna.

'S mòr bu bhinne bhith 'd èisdeachd
'N àm bhith bleoghan na sprèidhe
Na 'n smeòrach sa' Chèitein
'M bàrr gèig ann am fàs-choill.

Nuair a sheinneadh tu coilleag
A' leigeil mairt ann an coillidh,
Thigeadh eunlaith gach doire
Dh' èisdeachd coireal do mhànrain.

Ceòl farasda, fìor-bhinn,
Fonnmhor, faramach, dìonach
A sheinn an cailin donn, fìnealt
Bheireadh bìogadh air m' àirnean.

Ged a b' fhonnmhor an fhidheall
'S a teudan an righeadh,
'S e bheireadh danns air gach cridhe
Ceòl nighean na h-àirigh.

Tha deirg' agus gile
A' gleac an gruaidhean na finne,
Beul mìn mar an t-sirist
D' am milis thig gàire.

Deud snasta na rìoghainn
Snaighte, cruinn mar na dìsnean,
Gur h-i an donna-gheal ghlan smìdeach
'S ro mhìog-shuileach fàite.

Chuireadh maill' air do lèirsinn
Ann am madainn driùchd Chèitein
Na gathanan grèine
Thig o 'teud-chùl cas fàinneach.

'S ciatach nuallan na gruagaich
Ri bleoghan cruidh ghuailfhinn,
A' toirt torman air cuachaig
'S bodhar-fhuaim aig a clàraibh.

'S taitneach siubhal a cuailein
Ga chrathadh mu 'cluasaibh,
A' toirt muidh' air seist-luachrach
An taigh-buaile 'n gleann fàsaich.

A muineal geal bòidheach
Mu 'n iathadh an t-òmar,
A dhath fèin air gach seòrsa
Chìt' a' dòrtadh tre 'bràighe.

Dà mhaoth bhois bu ghrinne
Fon dà ghaoirdean bu ghile
Nuair shìnt' iad gu h-innealt
Gu sinean cruidh fhàsgadh.

Dà chalpa na mainmnich
Mar phileirean mairbhill
Cho gile ri cainichein
Chinneas fanna-gheal sna blàraibh.

Gum bu mhòdhar mo bheadrach
Teachd doṅ bhuaile mu eadradh,
Sèimh, sult-chorpach, beitir,
'S buarach ghreasad an àil aic'.

Do chùl amlagach, teudach,
Buclach, feòirneineach, glèidhteach,
De chnothan na gèige,
Cheapadh glèidhtich' a làn diubh.

Bheireadh dùlan na grèine
Deàrrsadh moch air òr-sheudan,
'S gum b' ait leam ra lèirsinn
Boillsgeadh èibhinn cùil Màiri.

Glac gheal a b' àrd gleodhar
A' stealladh bainne 'n cuaich bhleoghain,
A' seinn nan luinneag bog seoghach,
A' togail cobḣair ri Blàraich.

Nuair a thogadh tu 'bhuarach,
Cuach is curasan na buaile,
B' ao-coltach do ghluasad
Ri guanaig na sràide.

– – – – – – – – – – – –
– – – – – – – – – – – – – –
Gur cùbhraidh leam t' anail
Na caineal a' mhargaidh.

Cha bhanarach glinn' thu,
Cha tig àireach gad shireadh,
Ach duin' uasal den fhineadh
Thèid don fhireach le 'phàirtidh.

NOTES

2108–11 The chorus is not included in Campbell. It is set out as a chorus in all other versions except McL 2, where it simply appears as the second stanza.
2108 *A bhanarach* McL 2 *Ban-aireach*
2109 *Chaoin* McL 2 *Chiuin*
2113 *ghaol* Eigg *ghaoil*
2112–3 McL 2 has *A Ninghin na Miog-shul*
'S e do ghaol tha gam lionadh,
with *Ach* added before the start of 1. 2112.
McL 187 and Campbell have *do'n Tir* instead of *fo chìs*.
2114–5 McL 2 *'S maith thig Lamhainin side*
Dha do Mhin bhassan Bana.
This stanza comes as No. 9 in McL 2.
bhasan Gillies *bhosabh*
2116–9 Not in McL 2
2116 *bhith* Eigg *a bhiodh*
2117 *'N àm bhith* McL 187, Campbell *'s tu*
2119 *am fàs-choill* Campbell *Gleann Fasaich*
2120–3 This stanza is in Eigg, McL 2, McL 187, Campbell and Gillies, with significant variants between these versions. Eigg's version is followed, but the reference to a *Màiri* in 1.4 of McL 2 and in McL 187 (in a different stanza) may be authentic, though Eigg's version fits the metrical pattern better here.
2120 *tu coilleag* Eigg *tu 'n coilleag,* McL 2 *i Luineag*, McL 187 *tu choilleag*, Gillies *chaoilleag*
2121 Eigg *– – – ann coillidh*, McL 2 *Bleoghan mairt ann an Coile*, McL 187 *leigeadh – – – coille*
2122 *Thigeadh eunlaith* McL 2 *Thigeadh Niallain*, with the second word glossed 'Birds'. *Thigeadh* seems preferable to Eigg's *Thàladh*. McL 187 reads *Dh' fhalbhagh*, which is equally possible. Gillies *Dhèleaigh*, 1839 *Dh' eulaidh*. I take the sense to be 'When you sang a ditty, milking a cow in a wood, the birds would come/go from every grove to listen to the music of your humming'.
2123 *coireall do mhànrain* McL 2 *Ceilire Mairi* (i.e. Mary's sweet singing).
2124–7 Not in McL 2.
2125 *Fonnmhor* Eigg *Fonnar*

dìonach This adjective is more usually applied to piping, where the air control gives precision of sound.

2126 *an cailin* Eigg *a Cailin*. This word is masculine, though referring to a girl. Dwelly wrongly gives it as a feminine noun. The Inverness (1806) version has *a chailin donn fhinealt'*.
finealt McL 187, 1839 *miogach*, Campbell *migich*, Gillies *mìagach*

2127 Gillies *A bheireadh bìog air an Arainn*
m' àirnean McL 187 *m' airne*
The line means literally 'that would make my kidneys throb'. This picturesque expression refers to the effect of the music (*ceòl*) on the poet.

2128–31 This stanza is the first one in the McL 2 version, taking the form:

gur Buaghach air Fidhill
'S na Teudan ga Ruitheadh
Thogagh Fonn air gach Croidhe
Port Inghin na h Airidh.

The syntax of the Eigg version is more coherent, though the overall sense is similar in both versions.

2128 *Ged a* Gillies *'S ga*

2131 *nighean* McL 187 *Inghin*, Gillies *nighinn*

2132–5 Not in McL 2 nor in McL 187. This stanza is the second-last in Gillies and in 1839.

2133 *Gleac* Eigg etc. *gleachd*
finne Glossed 'The Fair one' in Eigg. Later sources *fine/fine*

2135 *D'am* Eigg *Da*, later sources *Do am*, but 1839 *O'm*
gàire Gillies, 1839 *fàilte*

2136–9 Not in McL 187

2136 *Snasta* Eigg *snasna* (the second *n* presumably a misprint).
rìoghainn Eigg *rìoghuinn*, 1874 *rìmhinn'*, 1924 *rìghinn'*

2136–7 The McL 148, Campbell and Gillies readings for these lines are (with minor spelling differences):

Mar Phairc thaitneach do'n Ibhri
Tha Deudach na Ribhin

and 1839 is almost identical.

2138 *donna-gheal ghlan* McL 148, Campbell *Donnaghealach smìdeach* This is probably a variant of *smèideach*, which can mean 'nodding, beckoning'. *smèid* is given the sense of 'wink' among other senses, in Armstrong's Dict., and this may chime in with the reference to smiles in 1. 2139.

2139 *fàite* 'smile'. The word occurs more usually with a short *a*, but the long variety is required for the rhyme-scheme here. Eigg glosses the word 'Smile'. 1839 has *fàilte*.

2140–43 Not in McL 2

2140 *maill'* McL 187 *maille*, later sources *moill'*

2141 *madainn driùchd* Later sources *madainn-dhriùchd*. The sense is probably 'in a morning of dew in May'. The syntax of the stanza is a little contorted: the subject of *Chuireadh* in 1. 2140 is *Na gathanan grèine* in 1. 2142.

2142 Campbell seems to offer an alternative line *Bheiridh Dealan na grèine* as an additional option.

2143 *'teud-chùl* McL 187, Gillies *d' theud chul*, Campbell *fod theud-chul*, 1839 *o t-theud-chùl*

2144–7 McL 2 has a related text which runs:

'S glan Ruidhe do ghruadhach
Dol timchioll chruidh ghuail-fhion
Toirt Cobhar air Cuaich
'S mor fhuaim aig a Claraidh.

2146 *torman* So Eigg, but the later edd. 'correct' to *tormain*, perhaps justifiably.

Campbell, Gillies, 1839 read *A' steolladh/stealladh bainn ann an cuachaig*

2147 *bodhar-fhuaim* Eigg *bothar fhuaim*. The meaning may be 'a dull noise' i.e. a dull sound of milk thudding against the wooden staves of the pail.

2148–51 Not in McL 2

2150 *seist* McL 187, Campbell *sop*
The sense of this line is not exactly clear. It seems to mean 'churning on a bed of rushes', and perhaps means 'sitting churning on a bed of rushes'. Armstrong (*Dict.*) quotes the line as coming from an 'old song'. The Gillies and later versions give *seid* rather than *seist* (Gillies *seit*, 1806 *Seid*, 1839 *seid luachraich*). The use of *toirt* with *muidhe* seems a little strange, but Dwelly quotes a Wester Ross usage: *Thoir a' mhuidhe* 'churn'. The general picture, however, is clear: the girl, with her tossing locks, is busy churning in a cattle-fold hut or sheiling in a deserted glen/glen of wild vegetation.

2152–5 Not in McL 2

2152 *A muineal* Gillies *Do mhuineal*

2153 'Round which the amber (complexion) would spread' or 'encircled by amber beads'(?)

2154–5 The sense seems to be that her throat is so white and clear that 'one could see its individual colour on any (liquid) pouring through her throat/upper breast'.

2155 *tre 'bràighe* McL 187 *throimh Bragad*, Campbell *ro' Braighid*, Gillies *tre d' bhràgad*, 1806 *tre braghad*, 1839 *tro d' bhràghad*.

2156–9 This gives another sensitive picture of the milking-girl, elegantly stretching her tender palms and white arms to squeeze the cow's udders. McL 2 gives the same picture in slightly different words:
Na Meorin is grinne
Fo'n ghairdin is gile
gan shineadh gu scileil
gu shinin Chruidh fhasgadh.

2158 *h-innealt* McL 187, Campbell, Gillies, 1839 *sgileil*

2159 *sinean cruidh* McL 187 *shininnin*, Campbell *sinninin*, Gillies *sininnean*

2160–63 This stanza is in McL 148, Campbell, Gillies and 1839

2160 *mainmnich* A variant of *meanmnaich* (?)

2160–61 Gillies *Do chalapanna menmneach – – – marabill*
1839 *Do chalpannan meamnach,/Mar phileirin marabuill*

2162 *cainichein* Gillies *canachein* This appears to be a variant of *cainchean*, itself a variant of *canach* 'cotton-grass'.

2164 Various meanings can be read into this line, depending on how we interpret *mòdhar*, e.g. 'my playful one would be mettlesome' or 'my lovely girl would be gentle/tender'.
bheadrach McL 187 *Bheadradh*

2164–7 McL 2's reading is rather different:
gur Binn' i na Feadan
Dol san Anmoch don Eadradh
Ninghin Donn 's i na Dreass
Buarach ghreasad an ail aic.
McL 2's last line seems to have been preferred by later editors, as against Eigg's *'S buarach greasadh an àlaich*. McL's *Dreass* is perhaps a dissyllabic borrowing of Eng. *dress*.

2165 *Teachd* McL 187 *Teidh'n*

2166 *Sèimh* McL 187 *sheang*, Campbell *seang-chorpach*, Gillies, 1839 *'Seaghach seang-chorpach*

2167 *ghreasad an àil* McL 187 *greasadh a h Ail*, Campbell *greassad a H'ail*, 1806 *greasadh an alaich*.

2168–75 These two stanzas appear in McL 187, Campbell, Gillies and 1839. There is some difficulty in fitting 11. 2170-71 into the sequence of thought, and whether this reflects the inadequacy of the redactor or of the editor is an open question at present. The reference to Màiri in 1. 2175 links this version to that of McL 2.

2169 *Buclach*, Gillies *Buchdlach*, 1839 *Buchlach*
glèidhteach McL 187 *gleatach*, Gillies *cèutach* The sense of *glèidhteach* may be 'well looked after'.

2170–71 The literal sense seems to be 'of the nuts on the branch a careful person would catch/keep his full share of them'. It may be over-fanciful to think that this is a metaphor for the thought 'she is well worth capturing'.
glèidhtich Gillies *gleatach* Glossed 'a careful person, provider' in High. Soc. Dict.

2172 *dùlan* challenge. The sun's rays challenge Màiri's hair to reveal their golden tints.

2173 *òr-sheudan* Gillies, 1839 *fhoir d' eùdainn/t-eudainn*

2175 *Boillsgeadh* McL 187 *Boisge*, Campbell *Boisgidh*, Gillies *Bòisgeadh*

2176–9 There are considerable differences between the sources here. Our text is based on Eigg, but several of the alternative readings are credible. On the whole, Eigg's rhyme-scheme, with strong dialectal preferences, is the most consistent.

2176 McL 2 *Glac ghrinn nam Mear Sheaghach*
gleodhar 1874, 1924 *gleadhar* The word refers to the sound made by the spurts of milk as they enter the milking-pail.

2177 McL 2 *Chuireagh Beinn an Cuaich Bhleoghain* (where *Beinn* represents a dialectal form of *bainne*).

2178 *seoghach* Eigg *sheothach* This represents a dialectal form of *seaghach*.
McL 2 *Le Luineag Beag Ladhach*

2179 *cobhair* Eigg *codhar* (Note the McL 2 reading, *cobhar*, in 1. 2146). McL 2 *'S i Bleoghann na Blaraich*, McL 187, Campbell, Gillies (with orthographical variants) *Na Suigh 'n gobhal na Blaraig*, 1839 *An gothal na blaraig*. The cow's name is either *Blàrach* or *Blàrag* (i.e. the cow with a white spot in its face). Eigg's reading translates 'raising foam (in the pail or bucket) which rises towards Blàrach'. The reading with *gobhal* has an authentic ring also ('sitting between the legs of Blàrach'). 1806 has a different (revised?) reading *ri clarabh*.

2180–81 McL 2 *Nar a ghlacagh i Bhuarach*
Agus Car'san na Buaile. McL 187 and Gillies also read *i*.
curasan McL 187 *Currsan*. Armstrong (*Dict.*) has the word *curasan*, giving the sense 'milk-pail' and quoting *cuach is curasan* from 'Macdon.'.

2182 McL 2 *bu Choslach a gluasad*, with *neo(?)* added above *Choslach*.
McL 187 *B'ea-coltas a gluasad*, 1839 *Bu coltach*

2183 *guanag na sràide* presumably refers to a street-girl, perhaps a prostitute.

2184–5 These two lines occur as the fragment of a stanza only in McL 2. McL 187 does not have a corresponding quatrain.

2186–7 This stanza occurs only in McL 2.

2187 *àireach* is used of cattleman, dairyman and shepherd. Here used to contrast with *duin' uasal*, 'nobleman, gentleman'.

2188 *den fhineadh* of the kindred/clan. The poet may well be referring specifically to the MacDonald clan here.

FAILTE NA MORTHIR

Sources and Editions:

McD	6-11
Eigg	118-21
McL 126	4-8
1839	91-5
1874, 1892	86-91
1924	36-42

This text raises some editorial problems. There is a version in Eigg, normally regarded as an authoritative source of Mac Mhaighstir Alasdair's poems, but in this case it is the shortest surviving version, running to 62 lines. The 1839 edition has 68 lines, and is generally close to the Eigg version. MacDiarmid's version runs to 100 lines, McLagan's to 104, Macpherson's (1874) to 114, and the MacDonalds' (1924) to 116. The present edition, which is a composite one, has 120 lines.

MacDiarmid's version comes near the beginning of his MS, suggesting a date for the copy close to 1770. MacDiarmid ascribes the poem as follows: 'le Mr Alastair Mac-Dhomhnuil', and this use of 'M.^{r}' may suggest that the poet was still alive at the time of writing down this version (this is MacDiarmid's general, though not his exclusive, practice). McLagan 126 may also be fairly early, and Macpherson (1874) says that his text is copied from the McNicol MSS, and so may be close in date to the McLagan version. The MacDonald editors (1924) seem to follow Macpherson in the main. There is much common ground between the MacDiarmid, McLagan and Macpherson/MacNicol versions, but considerable differences in stanza order, and a good many small variations.

The shortness of the Eigg version is particularly puzzling. The explanation may be that it comes from an early draft, subsequently extended by the poet, but surviving in his son's papers in its original form. The 1839 text is probably based largely on Eigg, though it has an extra eight lines. Mackenzie in 1839 evidently did not know or use the early MS texts.

This edition is based primarily on MacDiarmid, since it is both early and full. McLagan readings are given the next priority, and there is some commentary on the Macpherson and MacDonald texts. The stanza order of MacDiarmid is followed, with couplets added from the other sources (with appropriate references to origin). It is possible to detect some editorial input in all of these versions, most particularly in those of 1874 and 1924.

Our text is therefore a composite one, and presented frankly in that sense. The peculiar circumstances would seem to justify this approach, as the MS texts may all date to Mac Mhaighstir Alasdair's lifetime or not long afterwards, and they appear to be in a close relationship to the original poem, which was no doubt expanded by the poet himself, and may have undergone other small changes in transmission.

Such changes are especially noticeable in stanza order. It would be possible to impose an editorial order (relying on the editor's sense of logical development), but it would be impossible to assume that this coincided with the poet's. It would seem to be characteristic of Mac Mhaighstir Alasdair to disperse somewhat similar types or areas of description throughout a poem, so that the cows and heroes and curds and birds are not necessarily grouped strictly together. It also seems to be a deliberate device to punctuate the poem with couplets or runs of *-ach* epithets.

The precise sense of 'Mòrthir' is a little difficult to pinpoint. It is usually taken to refer to Morar, and the *Ailleairt* reference (1. 2211) fits comfortably there, as perhaps may the reference in 1. 2221 to the close loyalty to the Church (probably here the Catholic Church). But the reference to Shiel (1. 2213) goes more naturally with Moidart. The use of the feminine definite article in the title, and feminine lenition in 1. 2214, support *Mòrthir* rather than *Mòrar*. He perhaps sways between the Morar meaning and the wider usage of *Mòrthir* for the Clanranald mainland territories. Also, if what we have is an earlier text later expanded, it may first have been composed from the more southerly viewpoint, and added to once the poet moved to Arisaig and Morar later in his life.

The tone of much of the poem is contented, generous and outgoing, free of the rancour that colours the Eigneig poem, and more lyrical than the early descriptive poems. It may well reflect both the sensuous appreciation of Nature that often goes with youth and a philosophical appreciation that came after a robust and troubled career.

FAILTE NA MORTHIR

Fàilt' ort fèin, a Mhòrthir bhòidheach,
Anns an Og-mhìos Bhealltainn.

> Heitirinn à-rinn ù-rinn o ho ro
> Heitirinn à-rinn ò rò.

Grian-thìr òrbhuidh 's uaine còta,
Froidhneas ròs re h-alltaibh.

Tìr 'm bi pailteas coirc' is eòrna,
Beòir bho hòb, is dràm innt'.

Le biadh 's le dibh a' cur thairis
Cha tèid earrach teann orr'.

'S cannach, lurach slios a tulaich,
'S duilleach mullach chrann innt'.

Le h-uisgeachan èiteag-chlach geala
Ruith throimh bhaile geamhraidh.

'S loinneil a fir anns a' bhannal,
'S sgiamhach, barr-fhionn clann innt'.

Mnathan toinnte, mòdhar, coibhneil,
Làn de loinn 's de bhaindeachd.

Am meòir chaola 's grinn air anart
'S iad cho glan ri bain-tighearn'.

'S bainneach, bailceach, braonach, glacach
Bruachan tachdrach Ailleairt.

'S lìonach, slatach, cuibhleach, breacach
Seile ghlas nan sàmhnan.

Mòrthir ghlan nam bradan tàrr-gheal,
'S airgeadach cur lann orra.

Tìr làn sonais, saor o dhonas,
Gun dad conais dranndain.

Seirceach, caidreach, gun dad sladachd,
Saor o bhraid 's o anntlachd.

Pailt de chreideamh is de dh' eagnachd,
'S iad ri 'n Eaglais staingte.

'S àlainn a beinnean 's a srathan,
Is èibhinn dath a gleanntan.

Damh le rùtas dol sa' bhùireadh,
'S e ri bùirein cleamhnais.

Greighean dhearg' a' tàmh mu 'fireach,
Eilid bhiorach 's mang aice.

Boc air daradh timcheall daraig,
'N dèidh a leannain cheann-deirg.

Coilich-choille 's iad ri coilleig
Anns an doire chranntail.

Cnothach, caorach, dearcach, braonach,
Glasrach, raonach, aibhneach.

'S deiltreach, laomach, meiltreach, caoineach
A fuinn mhaoineach, leamhnach.

'S cùbhraidh suibhean, 's badach luibhean
Ris a' bhruithinn ain-teas.

'S feurach, craobhach, luideach, gaolach
An tìr fhaoilidh sheannsail.

Dìthein cheigeach 's neòinein eagach,
'S bòidheach leagail stàmp orr'.

Grian ag èirigh, 'g òradh slèibhe,
'S beachan gheug ri sranntaich.

'Choill gu h-uile fo làn duillich
'S i 'na culaidh bainnse.

Bàrr gach tolmain fo bhrat ghorm-dhearc
Air gach borrachain alltain.

Gu bheil a talamh 's a h-aeir
Làn de dh' aighear annsail.

Bric le sulas leum ri buinne,
Ruith nan cuileag greannmhor.

'Chearc ri tùchan 's i ri giùgail
Is fìor chùirteil cleamhnas.

Eòin gu foirmeil seinn an orgain
Is fìor òirdheirc canntachd.

Chìte Robin seinn is sog air
Agus frog air dreallan.

'S ceòlar èibhinn bàrr gach gèige
'S an eòin fèin a' danns' orr'.

Eòin na beinne an taobh eile
'S iad ri ceilear ranntail.

Cuthag chùl-ghorm cur nan smùid dith
Ann an dùiseal cranntail.

Crodh air dàir am bàrr an fhàsaich,
An fheòir nach fàs gu crainntidh.

Crodh air theas a' ruith le 'm buaraich
'S tè le cuaich gan teann-ruith.

Geum laoigh bheaga 's crodh gam freagradh
Anns an eadradh shamhraidh.

Na minn bheaga dol an creagaibh
'S iad ri ceigeis ghreannmhor.

Luisein chùbhraidh mach a' brùchdadh
'S pàirt diubh cùl-ghorm bainndearg.

Searrach suigeartach ri ruideis
'S e ri buigeirt dannsa.

Seillein ruadha diogladh chluaran,
Mil ga buannachd 's srann ac'.

Sòbhrach, mealach, creamhach, samhach,
Cluain is camhain cham-ghlac.

'S mithich dhòmhsa triall don Mhòr-thir
Anns an òg-mhìos shamhraidh.

A bhuain snodhaich, 's gach meas nodha,
Mar ri cnothan calltainn.

A bhuain fhaillein, 's a dh' òl bainne,
Rìgh! gur fallain m' annlan.

'S miosrach, cuachach, leabach, luachrach
Dol gu buail' as t-samhradh.

'S is òmhnach, uachdrach, blàthach, cnuacach
Lòn nam buachaill annta.

'S imeacach, gruthach, meugach, sruthach
'N imrich shubhach, ghreannmhor.

Cailin bhuidhe crathadh muidhe
'S i 'na suidh' air plancaid.

'S ùrail, àlainn, geal, dearg, blàthor
A daoin' àrsaidh 's clann innt'.

A fir buadhmhor, màrsail, sluaghmhor,
Meardha, cruaidh sa' chàmpa.

Fo 'n làn èide, le 'n toil èilidh,
Foirmeil, gleusda, sanntach.

Lom-làn de dhìlseachd do Shèasar:
Mo ghràdh fèin bhith cainnt riu.

Deoch gun tomhas dol mu 'm chomhair
Gun aon ghlomhar ganntair.

Tha mo chliabh 's mo ghoil' air lobhadh
Le uisg' odhar seanntaidh.

'S gheibh mi cobhair, bainne ghobhar,
'S e fo chobhar ceann-gheal.

'S bùrn briosg criostail, 's e ri briotal,
Ruith roimh chrioslaich bheanntan.

NOTES

2190 *bhòidheach* McD *bhoidhich*

2192–3 The chorus in McL 126 is written *Heideagan airin urin o uro/Heideagan airin o ro*, and in McD *Heitirin arin urin o ho ro/Heitirin arin oro*. The adjustments made here take account of the sung version of the chorus.

2195 *froidhneas* McD *Fronas*, Eigg *froinneadh*, McL 126 *'S Freine*, 1839 *froinidh*, 1874 *'S froidhneadh*

2196–7 Not in Eigg or 1839 or 1874

2197 *bho hòb* McD *fuidh hòb*, McL 126 *fo shop*, 1924 *fo shop*.
1924 does not confront the issue, translating the second line 'a dram for all providing'. Clearly the rhyme scheme requires a long *o*. I take the reference to mean 'beer from hops', and have amended *fuidh/fo* to *bho*. Another possibility may be 'hob' i.e. fireside hob, in which case *fuidh/fo* could be retained. In either case the long *o* seems to be a dialectal aberration on the poet's part.
innt' presumably refers to *tìr*

2198 *dibh a' cur* McD *dibhe a cuir*, McL 126 *dibh cuir*

2199 *orr'* Eigg, McD *orra*

2200 *cannach* Eigg *inach*, McD *ianach*, McL 126 *Canach*, 1839 *ianach*, 1874 *fàinneach*, 1924 *canach* translated 'with mountain down'. The emended reading, with the sense of 'mild, pretty' seems more appropriate; *canach* is normally a noun, not an adjective.

2202 *èiteag-chlach geala* McD *eiteig chloch-geala*, McL 126 *Eiteag Chlach geala*. It is difficult to be sure which grammatical construction the poet had in mind. Here it is taken to be a genitive plural of the compound *èiteag-chlach* 'quartz stone'. 1839 side-steps the problem, reading *Uisge fallain nan clach geala*. So too 1874 and 1924.

2203 *throimh* McD *roimh*, 1874 *romh*

2204 McD *'S boidheach a fir is a Bannail*, McL 126 *'S loinneil a Fir anns a Bhannal* (with the final word glossed 'Company'), 1874 *'S loinneil a fir a's a bannal*. The McL 126 reading is preferred here, with the sense 'Handsome are her (i.e. Morar's/Mainland's) men in the company'. 1839 does not have 11. 2204-5.

2205 *sgiamhach* McD *giomhach*, McL 126 *giomach*, 1874, 1924 *ciabhach*. The *g-* forms presumably come from a mis-hearing/misinterpretation of spoken *Is sg-*. *gìomhach* 'defective' is clearly inappropriate.

2206–7 These lines are not in McD nor in 1839; in McL 126 they come with two intervening lines (11. 2294-5 below) after 11. 2208-9. 1874 has *aoibhinn* instead of *toinnte*.

2208–9 These lines are not in McD nor in 1839, but occur in much the same form in 1874 and 1924.

2206–9 The order of these two couplets is reversed here, since the slender fingers of 1. 2208 refer back to the ladies of 1. 2206.

2210 *glacach* McD *glachdach*

2211 *tachdrach* McL 126 *tarbhach*, 1874 *tacrach*. Dwelly quotes the form *tachdrach* as a variant of *tàcarach* 'fertile' etc., and this seems the appropriate sense here.
Ailleairt McD *ail ort* (perhaps suggesting *àill ort*), Eigg *allieort*, McL 126 *allt innt*, 1874, 1924 *Ailleart*. The reading *Ailleairt* rhymes particularly well with *bain-tighearn* and *bhaindeachd* in preceding couplets.

2212 *cuibhleach* So too 1874, 1924. McD *coilleach*, McL 126 *Cuibh'leach*. The sense is 'wheeled, with wheels', continuing the reference to fishing gear: nets, rods, winding reels. The technique is typical of this poet: 'Grey Shiel of the large river-trout is a river of nets, rods, reels and trout'.

2215 *cur* McD and McL 126 *cuir*. The sense of the line is 'the arrangement of scales on them (i.e. the salmon) gives a silvery sheen'.
2216 *saor o dhonas* McL 126 *gun dad Conuichd*, 1924 *'s i gun chonas*
2217 McL 126 *saor o choin is Dranndan*, 1874 *Gun dad conais-dranndain*, 1924 *Saor bho choin an dranndain*. The double genitive of McD and Eigg has been retained.
2218 McL 126 *suirgheach, Caidreach gun dad slaid ac*. Both 1874 and 1924 have virtually the same reading as McD, but the couplet comes earlier in their versions.
2220–21 Not in Eigg or 1839
2220 *eagnachd* McL 126 *Eigneach*
2221 *staingte* McD *stannda*, McL 126 *stainnte*, 1874, 1924 *stannte*. The sense is 'and they are entrenched in (the beliefs of) their Church'.
2222 *beinnean* McL 126 *Beannan*, 1924 *beanntan*
2224–5 These two lines are not in McD, Eigg or 1839.
bùirein cleamhnais 1874 *bùirein-cleamhna*
2226 *Greighein dhearg* McD *Groidhinn dhearg* This is taken to be the plural of a form *greighean* 'a small herd'. McL 126 reads *Bith greidh dhearg am Braighe t Fhirich* which is equally credible; 1924 has a similar reading. 1874 has *Greighean dearga tàmh mu firich'*. Angus Matheson (1951), 268 interpreted Eigg's *Graighin deargoa' tàmh*, as containing an old epithet *deargóach* 'red-eared'. This seems unlikely.
2227 *bhiorach* McL 126, 1924 *Bhinneach*
2228–9 These two lines are not in McL 126.
daradh 1874, 1924 *dàradh*. The *a* of the stem of this word is usually long, but one does not expect Mac Mhaighstir Alasdair to rhyme a long *a* with two short ones.
cheann-deirg This form preserves the end-rhyme, whereas 1874, 1924 *chìnn-deirg* does not.
2230 *Coilich-choille* McL 126, 1924 *Coileach Coille – – – 's e*
coilleig McD *coillig* The sense is 'singing'.
2231 *chranntail* McL 126, 1924 *Challtuinn*
2232–7 These six lines are not in McL 126.
2234 *caoineach* 1839 *caointeach*
2235 *mhaoineach* McD *mhaonach*
leamhnach where elm-trees grow(?), where tormentil grows (*leamhnach* is usually a noun meaning 'tormentil', but its use as an adjective is possible).
2236 *suibhean* McD, Eigg *suthan*
2237 *bhruithinn ain-teas* 1874 *bhruthainn annteas*, 1924 *bhruthainn ainteas*. The forms *suibhean* and *bhruithinn* are preferred *metri causa*.
2239 *sheannsail* McL 126 *sheannsar*
2240–41 Not in Eigg or 1839.
2240 *cheigeach* 1874 *chreagan*, 1924 *ceigeach*
2241 'lovely is the imprinting (*leagail*) of (Nature's) stamp on them.
2242 *'g òradh slèibhe* McL 126 *air a sleibhtibh*, 1924 *air na sléibhtean*
2243 *beachan* McL 126 *beachain*
sranntaich McD *srantaich*, McL 126, Eigg *sranntraich*, 1874, 1924 *srannraich*
2244–5 These two lines not in 1874.
'na culaidh bainnse McD *na culaidh bhainnse*, McL 126, 1924 *fo culaidh bainnse*
2247 *borrachain* McL 126 *garbh thaobh*
The word *borrachain* is meagrely attested. It is related to such forms as *borradh* 'swelling' and *borr-fhuaim* 'low murmuring noise' (both in Dwelly), and here seems to have the sense of 'a swelling murmuring one', a playful description of a brook.

2248–53 These four lines are not in McD. 11. 2248-9 not in 1839.
2248 *h-aeir* 1874, 1924 *h-athar*
2249 *annsail* McL 126 *eabhsail*, 1874 *cheannsail*, 1924 *cabhsail*. McL 126's form represents a dialectal pronunciation not very likely to have been Mac Mhaighstir Alasdair's, in view of the long run of end-rhymes in this poem. *annsail* 'dear, well-loved'.
2250 *Bric – – – – ri buinne* Eigg, 1839, 1874, 1924 *breac – – – – a buinne*
2252–7 Not in Eigg or 1839.
2252 *ri tùchan – – – giùgail* 1874, 1924 *le tùchan – – – – giùigeil* The movement of the hen's head seems to be compared to a courtly bow.
2254 *Eòin* 1874, 1924 *Na h-eòin*
orgain McD *orragain* This spelling simulates the pronunciation, and such a pronunciation presumably rhymes with the long *o* in the next line. 1874, 1924 *organ*
2255 *canntachd* All the sources are in agreement on this unusual form meaning 'singing'.
2256 *Chìte Robin* McD *Chi thu 'm Bru-dhearg*, 1874, 1924 *Chìteadh – – – –* McD clearly has a faulty reading here, missing the internal rhyme with *sog* and *frog*.
2257 *frog air dreallan* McD *frog – –* McL 126 *Froig air Dreulan*, 1874, 1924 *– – – dreòllan*. The form *dreallan* may represent a dialectal form, since *dreòllan* does not fit the end-rhyme.
2259 *an eòin* McL 126 *a h Eoin*
orr' McL 126 *oirre*
2260–3 Not in Eigg or 1839.
2261 *ranntail* McL 126, 1874, 1924 *ranntachd*. Either McD's adjectival form, though more unusual, or the others' nominal form fits well, to give the sense of versified or structured singing by the birds.
2263 *dùiseal cranntail* McL 126 *Dusul – – – –*, 1924 *dùsal*, 1874 *dùslainn challtainn*. McD's reading makes good sense: 'in the gloom/shade of trees'.
2265 McL 126 *Feoirneach, fasaidh, Cranntaidh*; 1874, 1924 *Fiar/Feur nach fàs gu crainntidh*. McD's reading implies a change of direction in the poet's syntax, but is possible. It may be that the other versions are imposing a 'correction' on that syntax.
266–7 Here we depart from the verse sequence of McD, who does not write this verse until after the next four couplets. The other versions keep the two verses about cows together. Perhaps it is being too dogmatic to follow them in this – the question probably has to be left open.
2267 *teann-ruith* 1874, 1924 *deann-ruith*
2268–71 Not in Eigg.
2268–9 Not in McD, nor in 1839.
2268 *laoigh bheaga* 1874, 1924 *laogh beaga*
2270 *an creagaibh* McL 126 *'s na Creagaibh*, 1874, 1924 *'s na creagan*
2271 *ceigeis* McD *geigeis* The sense is not altogether clear: perhaps 'darting about'. For 11. 2271-2, 1839 reads *Na meinn bheaga 's iad ri beadradh,/Anns na creugan teann air*.
2272–3 Not in McL 126.
2273 *pàirt* Eigg, 1874, 1924 *cuid*
bainndearg Other edd. *baindearg/bàindearg*. McD's reading suggests the double-*n* rhyme better.
2274–5 Not in Eigg.
1839 reads *searrach bhuicin anns an ruicil,/'s e sir chruiteil dhannsaidh*
2274 *Searrach suigeartach* The other versions make this plural: *searraich shuigeartach*, with *iad* instead of *e* in 1. 2275.
2275 *buigeirt dannsa* McL 126 *Buiggeis Dhamhsaidh*, 1874, 1924 *buiceis-dhannsa*.

The word *buiceis*, in the sense of 'sporting, frisking', is better attested than *buigeirt*, but McD's form gives a sharper internal rhyme.

2276–7 Not in McL 126.
diogladh 1874 *deogladh*

2277 *ga buannachd 's srann ac'* McD *d'a ---*, Eigg, 1839, 1874, 1924 *'g a buain(n) le dranndan*

2278–9 Not in McL 126 nor in 1839.

2278 *Sòbhrach* McD *Somhrach sòbhrach* is a variant of *sòbhragach*, 'abounding in primroses'.
samhach 'abounding in sorrel'

2279 *camhain* The senses usually given for this word ('plain, cove') do not seem to fit easily here, though the High. Soc. Dict. gives the sense of 'hollow'. The association of *cam-ghlac* with *camhain* suggests smaller areas of ground pitted with hollows etc.

2280–85 Not in 1839.

2280 *triall don* McL 126 *do do* (for *dol do* as in 1874, 1924)

2281 *òg* McL 126 *òig*; 1874, 1924 *--- mhìos Bhealltuinn*

2282 1924 does not have this line, using the first line of the following stanza instead (presumably a printer's error in origin, for both lines begin with *A bhuain*).
snodhach was used not only of sap but also of foliage and bark. The use of *buain* with the word suggests a solid rather than a liquid.
meas nodha McL 126 *-- Nuadha*, 1874 *mì* (leg. *nì*) *nobha*

2285 *annlan* McD *aunlun*

2286–7 Not in McL 126.

2287 *buail'* 1874, 1924 *buailidh*. Both *buaile* and *buailidh* were used of the milking-place.

2288 *òmhnach* McD *oth'nach*, McL 126 *onach*. The adjective based on *omhan* 'whey'.
cnuacach McD *cruachdach*, 1924 *cruachach*. The basic sense is 'lumpy', here referring to clots of cream, pieces of butter in the butter-milk. The couplet may be translated 'The food of the shepherds in them (i.e. the milking-places or sheilings) is whey-ey, creamy, buttermilky, lumpy', but the Gaelic version has more finesse!

2289 *annta* McL 126 *samhraidh*, 1924 *shamhraidh*

2290–91 Not in 1924.

2290 McL 126 has a different word-order here: *'S meagach gruthach imich sruthach*
imeacach McD *iomachdach*, 1839 *ìmeach*

2291 *ghreannmhor* 1839 *shlambach*

2292–3 Not in Eigg or 1839.

2292 *bhuidhe* McD *buidh*, 1874 *buidhe*
crathadh 1874, 1924 *toirt*

2294–9 These six lines come near the beginning in the other versions (after 1. 2209 above).

2296 *buaghmhor* McD *buagh'or*, McL 126 *Buaghar*, 1874, 1924 *b(h)uadhach*; 1874 *'m màrsal uasal*, 1924 *'m màrsail ---*

2297 *meardha* McD *Mearradha*, other sources *Meara*

2298 *Fo 'n làn èide* McD *Fuidh 'n làn èitidh*, McL 126 *Fo Lan Eididh*, 1874, 1924 *Fo làn-éideadh*. *èide* and *èideadh* are both used of garments, but also of uniform and armour, as probably here.
le 'n toil èilidh 'with their choice of kilt'. 1874 adapts to *le 'n toigh fèileadh* 'people who like a kilt', and McL 126 (*leantail Eachdan*) and 1924 (*leantuinn euchdan*) 'in pursuit of heroic deeds' take a different tack.

2299 *gleusda* McL 126 *Eileach*. 1874 and 1924 have a quite different line: *Mo ghràdh fhéin bhi cainnt riu.*

2300–01 This couplet survives in full only in McL 126, though its second line was used by two sources, see 1. 2299 above.

The *Sèasar* here is presumably Prince Charlie, and the reference has an authentic Mac Mhaighstir Alasdair ring about it.

2302–3 These two lines not in McD. In most other versions they come after 1. 2293 above, and that is probably their natural location. In McL 126 they are followed by the equivalent of 11. 2288-91 above. In Eigg and 1839 they are placed at the very end of the poem.

2302 *mu 'm chomhair* Eigg *mar comhair*, 1839 *far comhair*, 1874, 1924 *mu 'r comhair*

2303 *ghlomhar* McL 126 *ghlothar*, with the alternative reading *sruithlein* written *supra*. The original reading is clearly the right one, on metrical grounds. It is a characteristically colourful reference, for *glomhar* was used of 'a piece of leather or wood, or sometimes a pine cone, – – – – which used to be placed on the snouts of lambs to keep them from sucking the mother' (Dwelly). 11. 2302-3 translate 'Drink without measure set before us, with no scarcity gag'.

2304–9 Not in Eigg or 1839.

2304 *Tha* Other sources *Bha*
ghoil' McL 126 *ghail'*, 1874 *ghial*

2305 *seanntaidh* McD *seannda*

2306 *'S gheibh mi cobhair* Other sources *Ach 's ma(i)th mo chobhair*
McL 126 has the *a* forms for *Chabhair, ghabhar, Chabhar*. The reading *Ach 's math* – – – has an authentic ring to it.

2308–9 McD's reading seems the most authentic; the other three are in agreement. McD's couplet translates 'And quickly-moving crystal water, spurting audibly, running through the girdlings of the hills'. McL 126 (the model, perhaps, for the other readings) has
'S uisge brisg-gheal 's e re Brittil
Ruith throimh Christil Bheanntan
i.e. 'with white quickly-moving water, spurting audibly, running through the crystals of hills'.

BIBLIOGRAPHY

A Dictionary of the Gaelic Language (Highland Society of Scotland), Vols. I and II (1828) (Edinburgh)

Almqvist, Bo et al. (1987), *The Heroic Process* (Dún Laoghaire)

Armstrong, R. A. (1825), *A Gaelic Dictionary* (London)

Bawcutt, Priscilla (1976), *Gavin Douglas, A Critical Study* (Edinburgh)

Black, Ronald (1986), *Mac Mhaighstir Alasdair. The Ardnamurchan Years* (Isle of Coll)

Calder, George (1923, 1980), *A Gaelic Grammar* (Glasgow)

Cameron, Alexander (1892-94), *Reliquiae Celticae*, Vols. I and II, ed. A. MacBain and J. Kennedy (Inverness)

Campbell, J. F. (1860), *Popular Tales of the West Highlands* (Edinburgh)

Campbell, J. F. (1872), *Leabhar na Fèinne* (London)

Campbell, J. L. (1933, 1984), *Highland Songs of the Forty-five* (Edinburgh)

Campbell, J. L. (1958), 'Notes on Alexander MacDonald's 'Oran a' Gheamhraidh', in *Éigse*, Vol IX, 57-60

Campbell, J. L. (1934), 'Some Notes on the Poems of Alexander MacDonald', in *Scottish Gaelic Studies*, Vol. IV, Pt. 1, 18-23

Campbell, J. L. (1971), 'The Expurgating of Mac Mhaighstir Alasdair', in SGS Vol. XII, Pt. 1, 59-76

Campbell, J. L. (1961), 'The R.I.A. text of the *Birlinn*', in SGS, Vol. IX, Pt. 1, 46-64

Carmichael, Alexander (1900), *Carmina Gadelica*, Vols. I, II; (1940), Vol III

Carney, J. and Greene, D. (1968), *Celtic Studies* (London)

Co-chruinneachadh Nuadh do dh'Orannibh Gaidhealach (1806) (Inverness)

Donullach, Alastair (1874), *Eiseirigh na Seann Chanain Albannaich* (Edinburgh)

Donullach, Alastair (1892), Reprint of above 1874 ed.

Dwelly, Edward, (1911 – 1994), *Illustrated Gaelic to English Dictionary* (Glasgow)

Eigg Collection (*Comh-chruinneachidh Orannaigh Gaidhealach*) (1776), ed. Ranald MacDonald (Edinburgh)

Eigg, rev. Turner (1809), *Comh-chruinneachadh Orain Ghaidhealach* (Glasgow)

Ellice, Edward C. (1898), *Place-Names in Glengarry and Glenquoich* (London)

Forbes, Robert (1895, 1975), *The Lyon in Mourning*, ed. Henry Paton (Edinburgh)

Gillies Collection i.e. *Sean Dàin* etc. (1786) (Perth)

Henderson, George (1910), *The Norse Influence on Celtic Scotland* (Glasgow)

Kennedy, Rev. John (1888), 'Alexander MacDonald, the poet', in *The Celtic Magazine*, XIII, 265-71, 302-10, 337-43 (Inverness)

Lhuyd, Edward (1707), *Archaeologia Britannica* (Oxford)

Lockhart Papers (1817)

Mac-Dhonuill, Alastair (1751), *Ais-eiridh na Sean Chanoin Albannaich; no, An nuadh Oranaiche Gaidhealach* (Edinburgh)

Mac-Dhonuill, Alastair (1802), *Orain Ghaelich* – – – (Glasgow)

MacDiarmid Anthology, See Thomson, D. S. (1992)

MacDonald, Alexander (1741), *Leabhar a Theagasc Ainiminnin* (Edinburgh)

MacDonald, Rev. A. and Rev. A., (1896-1904) *Clan Donald* (Inverness)

MacDonald, Rev. A. and Rev. A., (1924), *The Poems of Alexander Macdonald (Mac Mhaighstir Alasdair)* (Inverness)

MacDonald, Charles (1889, 1989), *Moidart or among the Clanranalds* (Edinburgh)

Macdonald, Keith Norman (1900, 1929), *MacDonald Bards from Mediaeval Times* (Glasgow)

MacFarlane, P. (1815), *A New and Copious English and Gaelic Vocabulary* (Edinburgh)

MacFarland, Peter (1813), *Collection of Poems* (Edinburgh). See MacPhàrlain, P.

Macinnes, John (1979), 'The Panegyric Code in Gaelic Poetry and its Historical Background', in TGSI, Vol. L, 435-98

Mackenzie, John (1834), Ed. of *Aiseiridh na sean chànain Albannaich; no, 'N nuadh òranaiche Gàelach* (Glasgow)

Mackenzie, John (1839), *The poetical works of Alexander Macdonald* – – (Glasgow)

Mackenzie, John (1841). *Sàr-Obair nam Bard Gaelach* (Glasgow etc.)

Mackenzie, John (1844), *Eachdraidh a' Phrionnsa* (Edinburgh)

MacLeod, Angus (1933), *Sàr Orain* (Glasgow)

MacLeod, Kenneth (1988), *The Gaelic Prose of Kenneth MacLeod*, ed. T. M. Murchison (Edinburgh)

MacPhàrlain, P. (1813), *Co-chruinneachadh de dh' òrain agus de luinneagaibh thaghta Ghae'lach* (Edinburgh)

Macpherson, Donald C. (Ed.) (1874, 1892), *Eiseirigh na Sean Chànain Albannaich; no, An Nuadh Oranaiche Gaidhealach* (Edinburgh)

MacQueen, John (1982), *Progress and Poetry*, Chap. 4 (Edinburgh)

Malcolm, David (c. 1732), *Focloir Gaoidheilge-Shagsonach* (prospectus and specimen of proposed vocabulary)

Malcolm, David (1738), *An Essay on the Antiquities of Great Britian and Ireland* (Edinburgh)

Matheson, Angus (1951), 'Some Textual Notes on the Poems of Alexander MacDonald', in *Éigse*, Vol VI, 265-9 (Dublin)

Mays, Walter J. (1955), 'Note concerning the date of Composition of Mac-mhaighstir Alasdair's Òran a Gheamhraidh', in SGS, Vol. VIII, Pt. 1, 53-5

Murchison, T. M. (1952), 'Alasdair Mac Mhaighstir Alasdair', in *An Gaidheal*, Vol. XLVII, 79-80

Ó Baoill, Colm (1979), *Bàrdachd Chloinn Ghill-Eathain* (Edinburgh)

Ó Baoill, Colm (1983), 'Gaelic manuscripts in the Colin Campbell collection', in SGS, Vol. XIV, 83-99 (Aberdeen)

Orain Ghaelich. An nuadh Oranaiche Gaidhealach (1802). Le Alastair Mac-Dhonuill, Bàilli Chana (Edinburgh)

Purser, John (1992), *Scotland's Music* (Edinburgh)

R.I.A. Dictionary: *Contributions to a Dictionary of the Irish Language*, various editors (Royal Irish Academy. Dublin)

Ramsay, Allan (1725), *Tea-Table Miscellany* (Edinburgh)

Reid, John (1832), *Bibliotheca Scoto-Celtica* (Glasgow)

Ruddiman, Thomas (Ed.) (1710), *Virgil's Aeneis Translated into Scottish Verse* (Edinburgh)

Scott, Hew (1923), *Fasti Ecclesiae Scoticanae* (Edinburgh)

Scottish Gaelic Vernacular Verse to 1730: A Checklist (1988), ed. C. Ó Baoill and D. MacAulay (Aberdeen)

Small, John (Ed.) (1874), *The Poetical Works of Gavin Douglas, Bishop of Dunkeld* (Edinburgh)

The Celtic Review (1908-09) (Edinburgh)

The Lyon in Mourning, ed. Henry Paton (1895, 1975) (Edinburgh)

Thomson, D. S. (1961), 'Alasdair Mac Mhaighstir Alasdair', in *An Gaidheal*, Vol. LVI, 65-7, 79-82 (Glasgow)

Thomson, D. S. (1991), 'Alasdair Mac Mhaighstir Alasdair: his political poetry', in TGSI, Vol. 56, 185-213

Thomson, D. S. (1974, 1990) *An Introduction to Gaelic Poetry* (London, Edinburgh)

Thomson, D. S. (1990), *Gaelic and Scots in Harmony* (Glasgow)

Thomson, D. S. (1993), *Gaelic Poetry in the Eighteenth Century* (Aberdeen)

Thomson, D. S. (1990), 'Mac Mhaighstir Alasdair's Nature Poetry and its Sources', in *Gaelic and Scots in Harmony*, 95-115 (Glasgow)

Thomson, D. S. (1968), 'The Harlaw Brosnachadh: An early fifteenth-century literary curio', in *Celtic Studies*, ed. Carney and Greene (London)

Thomson, D. S. (1992), *The MacDiarmid MS Anthology* (Edinburgh)

Thomson, R. L. (1970), *Foirm na n-Urrnuidheadh* (Edinburgh)

Thomson, William (1725, 1733), *Orpheus Caledonius* (Edinburgh)

Wade, W. M. (1822), *A Tour of Modern and Peeps into Ancient Glasgow*

Watson, W. J. (1918, 1959), *Bàrdachd Ghàidhlig* (Stirling)

Watson, W. J. (1915, 1929), *Rosg Gàidhlig* (Stirling)

GLOSSARY

A

a-nìos 58n down (from above); 1918n upwards
a-rèir 1689 in accordance with
àbhaist 168 habit, custom
abhsadh 1748, 1826, 1882 down-haul/slackening of sail
acain 55 complaining, bemoaning
acfhainn 1686, 1953 tackle, rigging (of a ship)
achlais 1591 armpit; angle between two crossing waves
achlaisean 1976 angle-piece (tying thwart to frame of boat)
achuinge 76 petition, entreaty
adharcach 1924 horned
aèir 1997 air
Aeolus 1309n
àgh 107, 628, 990 joy, success
àibheis 1568, 1928 sea, ocean
aibhneach 2233 with many streams
àibhseach 1950 spectral
aidmheach 1973n testimony
aigeal 1899n, 1916 sea-bed
aigeann 883 sea-floor
àigh 71, 706 happy, auspicious, glorious
àigh 2069 gen. of **àgh** joy, luck
aighear 2249 joyousness
aignidh 71n spirit, mind; 181 disposition; 274 nature
àile 950n air, wind
àilleagan 158, 241 pretty/lovely girl
ailm 1669 tiller
aimhgheur 133 blunt
ain-teas 2237 great heat
ainbhfhiach 626n great debt/obligation
aineamh 435 flaw, blemish
ainglidh 190, 2074 angelic
ainnir 147, 366 virgin, maid
ainnis 428 awkwardness
airc 32n distress, hardship
airceas 2018 scarcity
àireach 2187n cattleman, dairyman, shepherd
àirigh 2131 shieling
àirnean 2127n pl. of **àra** kidney
airteal 345n weariness
airtneal 1306n depression; 1575, 1828 weariness
aiseirigh 973 resurrection
aisig 547 ferry, deliver; 1007 ferry over, cross
aisne 1976n rib
aithridh 1351n repentance
àl 776, 1446 progeny, brood
àlach 1003 brood
àlach 1572, 1585 bank of oars
allail 722, 1880 excellent, glorious
amaladh 86 entwining, intertwining
amharc 1650 looking (closely)
amladh 193 intertwining
amlagach 2169 ringletted
anagrach 6n very quarrelsome
anam-fàis 972n, 2066n spirit of growth
anart 45, 2208 linen
anfadh Introd. to **Birlinn** 15 var. of **onfhadh** tempest; 1904 raging
annlan 2285 condiment, dairy produce
annsail 2249n dear, well-loved
anntlachd 2219 discontent
aognaich 858 grow death-like, grow pale as in death
aonrais 1716 tempest
aotram cèille 1935 frenzy
àr 1058, 1126, battle, war, slaughter
àraich 1195 battle-field
araichdinn 151n gift, deserving object, prize
aranach 942n bready
àrd-labhara 1772 loud-voiced
àrdan 208, 426, 1501 excessive pride, hauteur
arrail 1063 proud
arral 360n pride, insolence
àrsaidh 2295 old, ancient
àsainn 307 instrument
ascart 2088n tow, lint
ascaoin 1671, 2105 rough, harsh
ascaoin-eaglais 2086 excommunication
ascaoineachd 1387 harshness, brutality
asgall 1669 bosom, armpit

asnachadh 63n beseeching
at 1662 swell
atach 60n requesting, beseeching
atharrach 1356n another
athchuinge 96 entreaty, request
athlamh 370n, 1064 ready

B

babaid 795 cluster
bac 1532n, 1589 oar-rest
bac-bhrèid 1627 belaying pin
bacach 1270 lame, halting
bacan 1210 stake
bachallach 413 curled, ringletted
badach 2237 tufted, bushy
badan 1205, 1224 thicket
badanach 787, 905 in clumps, bunching, tufty
baganta 740, 788 plump, neat, tidy; 1192 warlike (The 1751 Glossary gives 'tight, compact; also vigorous, lively')
bagr' 1297 ‹**bagradh** threatening
baideal 759 pillar, tower; 993 standard, flag
baidealach 1842 sheeted, bannered
bàigh 1420 kindness
bailc 30 flood, spate
bailceach 2210 soft-showery (?)
baileach 1203n feeling at home (?)
bailleagach 477 pliable, lively
bain-iasg 138n hen fish
bain-tighearna 2209 lady
baindeachd 2207 womanly qualities
baindidh 169 womanly, ladylike
bainndearg 2273 var. of **bàn-dearg** pale red
bàirich 784, 1889 lowing, bellowing, roaring
bàirlinn 1555, 1773 surging billow(s)
bàirlinn 2048 summons of removal
baisgeanta 862 warbling
balcant 739 stout, boastful
balg 1048 belly
balgan 1486 quiver (for arrows)
ball 1855 rope; piece of equipment
ball-mhaiseach 961 with beautiful spots/markings
ballach 1857, 2005 spotted, speckled, striped
ballag 339n neat/plump little woman
ballart 368 noise, boasting
bàn-chraicneach 196 fair-skinned
ban-diùc 170 duchess
banail 425 womanly
banarach 2109 ff milkmaid
bannail 1859n vigorous, fierce
bannal 829, 2205n company, band
bàr 645 bar of lawcourt
barail 2046 opinion
bàrcadh 14 pouring
bàrr 1715 excess
bàrr-chas 1012 steep-topped
barr-fhionn 2205 fair-headed
barrach 693 top growth of birch/trees
barrach 2063 lush, productive
barrachd 364 surpassing
barradh 1986 clinching
bas 1590, 2116 palm
bas-bhàn 141 white-palmed
bas-leathann 1533n broad-bladed
basdalach 327 showy, outgoing
basgant 2008 melodious, making a melodious noise
basraich 1199 wringing hands
beach 2103, 2244 bee
beachach 717 full of wasps
beachainn 877, 1004 bees
beachd 1474, 1501 notice, care; confidence
beachd 834 in phr. **gu beachd** precisely
beachdaich 486 observe
beadarach 471, 728 sportive, playful, frolicksome
beadrach 2164n lovely/playful girl
beadradh 755 sport, play; 1214 flirting, caressing
beag-nàir 299 shamelessness
beairt 1969 article of boat's tackle
beairtean 1464 shrouds (of a ship)
Bealltainn 2191 May
beàrr 1882 crop, shorten
bearra 35 var. of **bearradh** cleft, ridge, precipice
bearraideach 531 giddy, delirious
beathair 1027n bear
bèic 894 roar
beiceil 735 curtseying
beilleach 732n lipped
bèin 1405n gen. of **bian** hide, skin, pelt
Beinn Shiant 1440n
beinnidh 523n unusual gen. of **beinn**
beirte 569 in phr. **nam beirte balbh e** 'if he were born dumb'
bèisteil 1551n beastly
beithe 689n birch; 1485 of birch wood
beitir 758 tidy
beò-chluig-chiùil 2070 living musical bells
beòlan 360 censoriousness, ridicule (1751 Glossary)

beucach 1549 roaring
beucail 1877 roaring
beud 1470 harm
beul-mòr 1972 gunwale
beulanach 1877 front wave, nearer wave
beum 1691, 1707n (noun) knock; furling (of sail)
beum 2004, 2095 (verb) furl
beura 2078 prickly, pointed
beus 476n, 1211 singing bass
beus 7 behaviour, character
beusach 152, 198 virtuous
beusadh 743n singing bass to
bhalet 907n valet
bheirte 1374 would be born
bhermilion 161, 399 vermilion
biadh-eunain 800 wood-sorrel
biadhchar 1326 fruitful, productive
biastag 2102 little beast/creature
bidean 1160 pointed object (?)
bil 133n lip, mouth
bil 912 blade, leaf
bile 747n (large/old) tree; 1132n tree, cluster of trees
bileach 1172 billed (with moving bill, as of a bird singing)
bileag 401 petal
binn 594 judgement
binn-fhoclach 672 having melodious vocabulary
biodag 1487 dagger
bìogadh 2127n throbbing
bionn-ghobach 724n, 732 with pointed beaks
bionnfhoclach 724n with pointed (well-projected) words/notes
bior 2022n thorn, prickle
biorach 403, 932, 2091 sharp; 2228 sharp-featured
bioradh 402 pricking, piercing
bith 930 being, type
bìth 1562n tar, caulking
bìth-dhearg 995n, 1847n red-resined, resin-red
biùthaidh 1149 champion, champions
blàr 2163 moor
Blàrach/Blàrag 2179n white-spotted one (cow)
blàth 702 blossom
blàth-mhaiseach 194 of lovely blooms
blàthach 2289 with much buttermilk
blàthor 747 blossoming, foliage-laden; 2295 with a healthy bloom
bleoghan 2117 milking
blìon 222 (var. **blian**) basking (in sun)
boc 318, 856 buck
bòc 1866 swell
bòc-thonn 1525, 1549 swelling wave
bocach 776 with many roe-bucks
bòcan 1071, 1275, 1928, 2056 spectre, hobgoblin, object of terror
bocsaich 1942 thumping
bodhar-fhuaim 2147n dull noise/thudding
bog 2178 soft
bog-bhailceach 769 with soft showers
bogadh 1213 softening, moistening
bogaich 1116 soften, make cowardly
bogan 807 marshy spot, moist patch
bogha 916n, 1483n bow
boglach 2025n marsh, marshy ground
bogladhrach 783 soft-hooved
boil 1096 frenzy, in phr. **air bhoil** eager
boile 2089 frenzy
boilich 291 var. of **boile** frenzy
bòilich 1295 blustering
boillsg 909 shine
boillsgeadh 2175 shining
boillsgeil 720 sparkling
bois 1518, 1593n dat. of **bas** palm
bolgain fhal' 1557 drops of blood
bòrcadh 2060 sprouting, growing in profusion
borrachain 2247n swelling murmuring one
bos-luath 1518 with palms of hands moving swiftly
braclainn 2093n greasy fat (?), cutting (?)
bràghad 1588 gen. of **bràighe** upper/forward part
braid 2219 theft
bràighe 2155 throat
braise 1506 compar. of **bras** bold, hardy
bramannan 2098 pl. of **braidhm/braim** fart
braoim-bhruic 1354n badger's fart
braon 75 drop
braonach 705, 2211, 2233 dewy
bras 1249 quick(ly)
bras-chaoin 484 quick and gentle
bras-chnapadh 1594n rapidly pittering
bras-ghaoir 1555 sudden throbbing cry
brat 892, 1860 covering, cloak
bratach 720n flag, banner, clothing
bratag 2039 caterpillar
breabadaich 474 jumping (from note to note)
breac 139 sea-trout

breac-iteach 861 speckled-winged
breac-laoghach 695 of dappled calves
breac-uigheach 705 of speckled eggs
breacach 2213n with many trout
breacan 1836 plaid
brèidgheal 1022n of white cloth
breisleach 1660, 1779 confusion
breug 221 beguile
brìodal 518 love-talk
brìodalach 275 fondling
briogadh 2022 pricking, stabbing
Brìos 1344n Bryce/Brice
briosg 2308n quickly-moving
briosg-ghlòrach 652n with quickly moving utterance, prattling
briot 1778 tattling
briotal 2308n spurting audibly
brisg 498, 762 brisk, active, lively
brìsneach 940 breeched, requiring breeches to be worn
broc 1486 badger
brochan 1920 brose
brodadh 2023 poking
brògach 941 requiring shoes/boots to be worn
bròn-bhinn 688n sadly sweet
bronnach 1608, 1612, 2038n big-bellied, gluttonous
brotagach 945 soupy
brothach 1446 scabby, mangy
bruach 1006 slope
brucach 800 spotted, speckled
brùchdadh 693, 2273 pushing out, exuding, bursting open
bruid 898 captivity, affliction
brùid 566 brute, animal
bruidhneach 1240 producing talk
bruithinn 2238n var. of **bruthainn** sultry heat
bruthaiste 943 bread or meal soaked in the fat of broth (1751 Glossary)
buadh 75, 971 virtue, accomplishment, endowment
buadhach 165 virtuous; gifted; 496 efficacious; 696 propitious
buadhaich 920 win, be victorious
buadhmhor 2296 successful
buagharra 932 boisterous, oppressive
buaidh 656, 666 etc. virtue
buailteach 695 of (cattle) folds
buaireach 166 enticing
buaireadh 286n temptation; 1181n turmoil; 1946 worry
buarach 395, 2168, 2181 tether, fetter, cow-fetter
buchallach 861, 1211 melodious
buclach 2169 budding, tied in knots (?)
buideal 1799 cask, anker
buig 902 gen. of **bog** marsh
buige 302 softness
buigeirt 2275n frisking
buil 609 consequence
buille-bheairte 1694n pl. of **ball-beairte** tackle rope
buin 1088 touch
buinne 1679, 1863, 2251 cataract, rapid current in stream, spout
buinnig 1337, 1340 winning
bùirdeasach 865 burgess, citizen
bùireadh 2224 roaring, bellowing
bùirean 1645 roaring, bellowing
bùirein 2225 var. of **bùirean**
bunailt 266 var. of **bunait** steadiness, constancy
bunnsaidh 1640 solid
bùrn-ionnlaid 259 washing water
burraras 827 a warbling purling noise (1751 Glossary)
buscadh 908n dressing

C

cabaisteach 947 cabbagey
càbhlach 896, 991, 1007 fleet
cagar 40 whisper
caidreach 2218 friendly
caigeann 1439 coupling, binding together
càil 1130 disposition, quality; 1936 pleasure
càileachd 152 temper, nature; pl. attributes; 936, 962, 988 temper, natural constitution
cailin 2126n girl
cailis 984 chalice, drinking bowl
càin 2094 revile
càineadh 631 reviling, slandering
caineal 422, 2186 cinnamon
cainichein 2163n var. of **cainchean** cotton grass
cainnt 564n talk, converse
cainnt-shnasda 129n dressed language
càird 64n, 1086, 1122 delay, respite
cairt/cart 1448 clean out
cairteal 887 quarter(s)
cairtibh 2007 imper. pl. of **cairt** clean out
càiseach 942n cheesy
caisean/caisein 2085n surliness
caisg 1317 satiate
caismeachdach 482 rousing, giving warning; 1049 with loud war-cries

caisrigte 2057 var. of **coisrigte** consecrated
caitean 800n catkins
caiteanach 1852 rough, shaggy
caitheamh 337 decay
caitheamh 1453 driving on (propelling a boat through the sea)
caithream 529 triumph, joyousness
caithreamach 1075 triumphant
caithreim 2041n throbbing
càl 943 kail
cala 1458 harbour
calg 1030 sting
calg-rasg 142 thickly-lashed eye
calltainn 2284 hazel
calma 1517 strong
calpa 1989n rivet, bolt
calpa na tàirne 1732 lower section of the halyard
càm-ghlac 2279n unevenly shaped hollow
camhan 2279n hollow (?)
canach 412 cotton-grass
cannach 516, 2201n mild, pretty
canntachd 2256n singing
canntaireachd 1203 warbling
caoch-chnuasach 119n empty fruit
caochlaideach 251 changeable
caogad 1934 fifty
caoidhearan 903 wailing, mournful sound
caoin 1424 gentle; 2105 smooth, kindly
caoin-dheàrrsadh 692 kindly shining
caoineach 2235 green-grassed (?)
caoir-gheal 1518 white with foam
caol 994n tightly-woven
caol-bhàirc 1461n slim bark/ship
caol-chòrcach 1821 narrow hemp
caomh 5, 1421 kindly, tender
caomhag 183 kindly/affectionate girl
caonnag 1871 strife, fight
caor 250 berry
caorach 2232 abounding in red berries
car 115 in phr. **am char** my way, in my possession
cara 1470n vicinity
carachadh 534 movement
càraid 1494, 1800 pair
carraid 359 strife
Carraig Fhearghais 2015 Carrick Fergus
carran 2058 scurvy grass
cas 889 (verb) frizzle, become wrinkled
cas 2143 (adj.) curly
cas 962 (adj.) steep
càs 1096n difficulty; case, cause; 1895 dilemma
cas-chruinn 141 with neat/elegant feet
casadach 937 inducing coughing
casagach 939 cassocked, long-coated
casaid2087 complaint
casarlach 414, 798 curled
casg 1426, 2107 check, stop, hinder
cath-chrith 1038 trembling eagerness for battle
cathach 931 with drifting snow
ceàird 144n craft, skill
cealgaire 1406 treacherous person
ceanal 427 kindness, gentility
ceannfhionn 781 white-headed
ceap 722n cap, top (of hill)
ceap 2171n (verb) catch, keep
ceapadh 768 catching
cearclach 417 circular
ceart 1360 right(s)
ceathrannan 464n quarters, thighs
cèidse 114n gage, pledge
cèidse 525 cage, (bodily) frame
ceigeach 1866, 2240 shaggy, lumpy, bunching
ceigeis 2271n darting about
ceil 453, 462 hide
cèile-còmhraig 1503n fellow-combatant
ceilear 2261 singing
ceilear-gràidh 2071 loving litany
ceilearadh 455 warbling, music
ceileir 967 var. of **ceilear** singing
ceileireadh 866, 1938 var. of **ceilearadh**
cèillidh 1772 steady, sensible
ceist 389 beloved, darling
Cèitean 691 May
Cèitein 2042 var. of **Cèitean**
ceòlar 2258 musical
Ceòlraidh 57n Muses
ceud-fath'ch 2075 contracted form of **ceud-fathach** well-judged (?)
ceum 1585n speedy movement (?)
ceum-tuislidh 353 a stumbling step
ceumadh 725n stepping, pacing
ceutach 694, 827 pleasant, lovely, pleasing
chaisgeamaid 501 we would allay/satisfy
cho-ainneamh 423 equally rare
chomh-còrr 336 as pre-eminent
chomh-snasmhor 336 equally gracious
chomh-tlachdmhor 333 equally pleasant
chuaidh 1452 var. of **chaidh** went
ciabh 513 lock of hair
ciabh-òrbhuidh 420 with golden locks
cianthar 759n singing plaintively (?)

ciaraich 899 turn brown/tawny
ciasanach 1888n a broad-bottomed wave
ciatach 139, 447, 655, 1327 comely, pleasant, pleasing, graceful
cinn 485, 787, 890 grow, increase; 1796, 2037n become
cinneadail 1187 clannish, showing clan loyalty
cinneadh 1185 kindred
cinneadh 304n would grow
cinntinn 1504, 1506 growing
cìocras 1141 ravenous hunger
ciorram 404 hurting, wounding
cion 1431 loved one
cìos 60n wages
cìosnaich 1149 conquer, overpower
cìs 2114 tribute; **fo chìs** captured, entranced
cith 932 snow-drift
ciùcharan 918 complaining
ciùthrach 718 showery
clabhsail 1827n loud (?), methodical (?)
clach-shnaighte 128 dressed stone
cladh 1878 ditch; rampart
clag 2095 bell
clàideag 190 lock, ringlet
claidheach 1124 reduced form of **claidheamhach** carrying swords
claidhean 1475n pl. of **claidheamh** sword
claiseach 1262 fluted (of sword-blades)
claisneachd 1936 hearing
clann 514 ringlet
clannach 1242 clannish, supportive of their clan
claoidh 4 harass, fatigue
claon 72, 378 awry, uneven, not straight
claonadh 439 straying, making to stray
clàr 1799, 2147n plank, wooden stave
clàranach 1636 'one of squat figure' (1933 ed.)
cleachdagach 415 curly, ringletted
cleamhnas 2225, 2253, intercourse, copulation; friendship
cleasachd 541 play
cleath 1513n, 1524 post, pole; oar
clèir 602 clergy
clì 321, 386 strength
cliabh 951n, 2023, 2304 chest
cliabhan 1202 little creel, wicker basket
cliar 1166 poets, poet-band
cliath 1543 (gen. **clèithe**) bank of oars
cliath-lùth 484, 756 musical fingering (The 1751 Glossary gives 'that division of a pipe-spring, so called, because the nine fingers are at once in the quickest motion playing it.')
cliathnach 1700n of wide span (?), having wide sides
cloch-iùil 146 loadstone, magnet
clogad 1190 helmet
closach 1138 corpse
cluain 768 guile
Cluanag 534 The deceitful Woman
cluaran 2059n, 2276 corn-marigold (1751 Glossary: 'a sort of gowan')
cluas 1650 tack (foremost lower corner of a sail)
cluasach 787n ear-shaped
cluigean 1294n little bell
clùmhor 869 sheltered, snug
cnag 1496, 1554, 1751, peg, pin, plug, thole-pin; 1798 plank (?)
cnàmh 1151 decaying, consuming
cnap 1563n lump etc. Here 'mass of water' (?)
cnaparra 1708 bulky, sturdy
cnatanach 937 inducing colds
cnead 1982 moan
cnocaireachd 1140 going the round of small hills
cnotadh 1942n unhusking, skinning (?)
cnothach 2232 abounding in nuts
cnothan 2170n pl. of **cnò** nut
cnuacach 1538 bulging (with muscles); 2288n cream-clotted
cnuasach 914n fruit, produce
co-ghrad 822 equally quickly
co-lorg 1632 (Introd.) conjunction
co-rèidh 1017n equally well-disposed
co-sean 1343 equally old
co-throm 835n equally heavily, giving equal weight to
cobhair 31, 2306 help
cobhar 2179n, 2307 foam, froth
cogach 1192 warlike
cogall 1589n friction, rubbing, saw-dust
coi-fhreasgradh 730n co-serving, contributing
coibhrich 1360 help, comfort
coileach-coille 2230 woodcock
coilleag 826 song, note, singing
coilleig 2230 var. of **coilleag** singing, cheerful song
coillidh 2122 dat. of **coille** wood
coilpein 1844n rope, tow, stay
coimh-bhiogail 460 equally lively/frisky
Coimh-dhia 1455n Lord, master
coimh-eireachdail 459 equally handsome

coimh-iomlan 459 equally perfect
coimh-teiridneach 460n equally healing
coimhliont 369 perfect
coineallach 112n flexible, pliable, accommodating
coinneal 290n candle; roundness (?)
coinnealta 1091n supple, flexible
coinnspeach 2103 wasp
coireal 727n choir, chorale (?); 2124n music
coirein 959n var. of **coirean** little corrie
coisinn 1508 win (the victory over)
còisir 965 choir
còisridh 2072 choir
coitcheann 973 in common
col 1175 sin
colainn 1528 sharp blow/stroke
colainn 288n var. of **colann** body
colann 441 body
colg 1243 sword-blade; 1847n point
colg 1508 fierceness
colgarra 930 fierce, angry
colgrasgach 781 with wild eyes, lively-eyed, with shaggy lashes
collaideach 497 clamorous, turbulent
collainn 1607n striking, thumping
colum 5 dove
com 84n body, breast
com-chochlach 940n breast-hooded
comas 123, 125 ability, power, capability
comh-luath 1601n equally fast
comhair 2302 presence
comharra-tìre 1728 landmark
còmhnard 359n smooth, level-headed; 1514 straight
compar 1214n body
comradh 103 help, assistance
conas 2217n quarrelling, wrangling
conasg 2021 furze, gorse, whin
confadh 1904, 1914 rage, howling (1751 Glossary: 'rage, madness, eagerness')
conn 182n, 313n sense, prudence, regulator
connan 287n lust (?)
cop 886 foam
cop-gheal 1560n white-foamed
copadh 1613 foaming
còpadh 1829n pursuing, catching
còrnach 414 curled (like a drinking-horn)
corp-rùsgadh 1137 stripping corpses/bodies
còrr (adj.) 427 abounding; 618n, 947, 1325 outstanding, excelling, surpassing
còrr (noun) 95 excess
còrr-ghleus 1068 excellent preparation
corraibh 968 dat. pl. of **còrr** tip, point
còs 806, 869 hollow
còsag 214 small crevice
cosgair 643 slaughter
cosgarrach (adj.) 1117 conquering, warlike
cosgarrach (noun) 1141 conqueror
cosnadh 1502 accomplishment, winning
cothachadh 1499 struggle, achievement
cothrom 1412n equally heavy
cothromach 1604n just, firm, with equal weight
cràbhach 198, 868 pious
cràcach 1869 horned, spreading
cràdh-ghèadh 1621 sheldrake
cràg 1711 lumpy fist
cràgradh 1929n pawing
cràin 1401n sow
crainntidh 2024, 2265 withered, withering, shrivelled
crambo 99n rhyme; name of a game
crann 496n bar, bolt; pipe chanter; 760, 2057 tree; 1465, 1964 mast
crann-tarrann 1984n wooden peg/nail
cranna-shneachda 2034n pl. of **crann-sneachda** a snow-plough
crannag 962n pulpit (1751 Glossary also gives 'the round top of a mast')
crannghail 1974 mast-rigging
crannghridh 995n mast-rigging (?)
cranntail 2231, 2263n (full) of trees
craobh-sheanchais 1361n pedigree, genealogical tree
craobhach 817 of the woods
craos 443 gluttony; 1868, 1927 wide mouth, gluttonous mouth
crap-lùth 500 a 'curl' in pipe music
crathadh 2149, 2292 shaking
crè 628 body
creach 1406 plunder; 1436 plundering raid
creachann 853 upper reaches of mountain
crèadhaich 243 clay
creamhach 706, 2278 (with lots) of garlic
creathnaich/criothnaich 1561 shake, make to tremble
creuchdach 1024 inflicting wounds
creuchdadh 1028, 1981 wounding, destroying

criomadh 43 nibbling, chewing
crioman 2090 morsel, small piece
crìon 544 trifling
crios Chù-Chulainn 794n meadow-sweet (1751 Glossary gives 'the herb my lady's belt')
crios-guaille 1482 shoulder-belt
crioslach 2309n girdling
criothlag 2103n var. of **creathlag** horse-fly
criothnachadh 1666 shaking, moving
criothnaich 1672 shake, tremble
crith-chiùil 1213 quivering of music
cròcach 1701 spreading, spread out
cròdh 878 fold (noun and verb)
cròdha 1103 valiant
croich 1426, 1435 gallows
croinn 215 pl. of **crann** lot. **Tilg croinn**, cast lots
crois 1993n cross
croiteag 295n pudenta
crom 1550n, 2039 bent, curled
crom-bhileach 1016 with curving crests
crom-ghobach 767 with curved gob/mouth
crom-ruaig 107n lit. 'bent-chasing'
crom-shoc 1447 bent snout
crom-shrònach 2049 hook-nosed person
cromadh 495 bending; 1194, 1526 descending, descent
cromag 1850 hook, clip
cruadhach 1685, 1806 hardship; 1704n difficulty, danger
cruadhach 1182, 1479 gen. of **cruaidh** steel
cruaidh 540, 1266 steel
cruaidh-bhall 1820 hard rope
cruaidh-phaisgte 342 firmly folded/encased
cruaidhteach 924 var. of **cruadhlach** rocky/stony ground
cruinn 2137 well-rounded, neat
cruinn-shnaighte 332 chiselled and gathered i.e. with even, well-shaped teeth
cruinne 410n, 583 world, universe
cruinneag 409 maiden, young girl
cruinnlùth 483 the most detailed late movement in **ceòl mòr**
cruit 1209 lute
crumpa 1788 bowl-shaped baling vessel
cruthaich 1459 create
cuach 703, 804 cuckoo; 1158 hollow of bird's nest
cuach 2178, 2181 milk-pail, bucket
cuachach 772, 2286 abounding in milking-pails
cuachach 536 curled
cuachag 2146 milking-pail
cuachag 2112 curly-haired girl
cuaich 1488 pleat
cuailean 2148 head of hair
cuairt 1384 a turn
cuan-choire 1015 sea-corry
cuanda 1709 trim, tidy
cuanna 1052 handsome
cuartag 1573 eddy (of waves)
cubhaidh 1288 fitting
cùbhraidh 2185 fragrant
cudthromach 1640 weighty, grave
cuglach 1387 (also **cugallach**) uncertain, uneasy
cuibhleach 2212n wheeled, with wheels
cuibhtich 2084 ff. quit
cuilidh 98 treasure-house
cuing 1445 yoke
cuinnsearach 1124 armed with swords/daggers
cuir fo 1619n pass (of a boat's movement)
cuireadh 280 inviting
cuireideach 275 coquettish
cùirnean 719 small heap, dew-drop
cùirnein 912 var. of **cùirnean**
cùirteach 209, 727 courtly
cùirteil 169, 622 courtly
cùis 596 case, legal case
cuisle 354 vein
cuislinn 701n, 746 little vein/artery; little pipe, flute
cùl 160, 2175 head of hair
cùl-aodach 1803 rear sails (?)
cùl-dearg 1617n red-backed
cùl-ghlas 1014 grey-backed; 1573 grey/foam-backed
culach 263n sonsy; well-dressed
culaidh 279n dress, instrument; means, qualities; 2245 dress
culaidh-chiùil 224n musical instrument
cùlanach 1878 back wave, farther wave
cullach 1401n boar
cum 2001n shape, put in shape
cumachd 271 shape, figure
cupladh 1970n coupling
cur 2215n arrangement
cur thairis 2198 overflowing
curaidh 1073n hero
curasan 2181n milk-pail
curraiceach 939 (‹**currac**) mutched, requiring mutches to be worn

cùrsadh 964 directing, taking a course

D

daga 1487 pistol
dagach 1125, 1191 armed with pistols
dàicheil 577 graceful, dignified; 648n haughty (?); 1566n, 1579 severe, hard
daillte 1948 blinded
dàimh 1403n relationship, kindness, love
daingeann 733, 1440 firm, strong, steady, steadfast
daingneach 36 stronghold
dàir 696, 2264 mating, calving
dàireadh 315n in a sexual frenzy
dall-cheò 1948 blinding fog
dall-churach 931 with blinding snow
daltachan 873 foster-sons
daltan 59 dimin. of **dalta** fosterling
dàm 507 draughts
damh 2224 stag
danarra 1583 steady, resolute
dàradh 2228n rutting, copulating
darag 2228 oak-tree
dasg 966n desk
dastram See 325n
deagh-bholtrach 689 fine-scented
dealanach 1077 lightning
dealbhach 1511, 1515 shapely
dealtach 718 dewy
deann 1664 in phr. **'na dheannaibh** in great haste, at great speed
deanntag 2058 nettle
dearcach 717, 2232 abounding in berries
dearg-bhallach 764 red-spotted
Dearg-chòt 1232 Redcoat
dearmad 1581, 2013 neglect, failure
deas 263 trim, accomplished, skilful
dèasgadh 1983 cracking
deathach 1954 smoke
dèe 1009n gods
dèideag 157 fair one; darling
deigheach 933 icy
deil 520 ardour
deilbh 568 fashion, shape; **deilbhim** 72 let me fashion
deileas 1034n eagerness, vehemence
deilich 519 var. of **dealaich** part
deiltreach 2234 golden, gilt
dèirc 80 alms, charity
dèirceach 197 good at giving alms
dèireach 1119n loud report
deireas 2099 scarcity
deireasach 461, 521 damaged, damaging, defective
deirge 2132 redness
deirgead 305 redness, rosiness
dèis See 681n
dèis 1158 in phr. **an dèis** after: **an dèis leum** having jumped (‹Old Gaelic **éis** track etc.)
deisear 2032n having a southerly exposure
deoch-thunta 856n decanted drink (1751 Glossary)
deud 2136 teeth
dh'fhuir'eas 1496 short for **dh'fhuiricheas** will stay
dìan 319, 323 fervent
dibh 2198 drink
dìblidh 1500 abject, weak
dìle 27 flood
dìlseach 931 flooding
dìlseachd 2300 loyalty
dinneadh 303 pressing
dìobhail 464 distressing
diog 1438n breath, life, being
diogladh 2276 tickling
dìol 68, 1277, 1281 pay, render, hand out
dìombas 520 lasciviousness (1751 Glossary)
dìon 752n airtightness
dìonach 994n, 1843 water-resistant, water/wind-tight, secure, closely-woven; 2125n well-tuned
dìosgan 1982 creaking
dìsne 2137 die (sing. of dice)
dìth 556, 610 lack, loss, what is lacking
dìthean 2240 flower
dìtheanach 716 abounding in flowers
dìthich 1162 destroy
dleasdannach 1369, 1432 rightful
dligheadh 544 duty, what is due
dlùth-dhuilleach 962 close-leafed
dlùths 1119n closeness, quick succession
dòbhran 8, 2093 otter
dochainn 1898 injure, damage
docharach 526 grievous, causing hurt
dòich 1505n more likely
dòid 1742 hand, grasp
dòideach 1537 muscular
dòigheil 1853 systematical, leisurely
doilleir 684 dusky, shady
doineannach 1302n stormy
doirbh 2047 difficult, hard
doire 697, 2123 wood
dòite 890, 1832 scorched, dark-coloured, singed, burnt

domblas 2101 gall
donas 2216 badness, unhappiness
donna-gheal 2138 fair tanned one
dòrainn 1313 torment, anguish
dos 862 tuft; 2070 plume, top foliage (?)
dosach 1271 tufted
dosrach 690 branchy, plumed, luxuriant
dragh 1911 pull, haul
dranndan 2217n snarling, complaining
draoidheachd 539 druidry, magic
dreach 140, 970 appearance (i.e. usual appearance)
dreach-lùbach 416 curling gracefully
dreach-mhìn 797 graceful
dreachmhor 418 elegant
dreag 1079 meteor
dreallan 2259n var. of **dreòllan** wren
dream 1102 people, company
dril 910 drop (of dew), sparkle
driom-robach 1012n ragged-backed, rough-ridged
dris 2077 briar, thorn
droigheann 2022 thorn
droineap 1465 tackle (of a ship), rigging
dronnag 1011 ridge, hump
druid 904 starling
drùidh 48 soak, penetrate
druimfhionn 780 white-backed
duaichneachd 708n gloom, ugliness
dualach 1480 stranded, layered (?)
dubh 1324 ink
dubhlosgadh 1150 burning until blackened, earth-scorching
dùbhlan 143n challenge
Dùghall 17n Dougal (used here of the raven)
dùil 50n, 143 element, being
duilleach 2201 leafage
dùiseal 2263n gloom, shade
dùl 1441, 1510 gen. pl. of **dùil** element
dùlan 2172n challenge
dùldachd 895 var. of **dùdlachd** depth of winter, December
dùldaidh 1832n 1878 dark, gloomy
dunach 395 gen. of **dunaidh** misfortune, disaster
dùrachd 144n desire
durrgha 1566n grim
durrghail 39 cooing

E

eadradh 756, 2166, 2270 milking (time)
eag 876 gap
eagach 2240 notched
eagarra 475 exact, precise (1751 Glossary)
eagnachd 2220 wisdom
èagsamhail 200 manifold, matchless
ealain 131 art, poetic art
ealamh 1087 quick, ready
eallach 917 herd (of cattle)
eanchainn 1906 brain
eanghlas 2101n weak drink
earalas 'Birlinn' 15, Introd. precaution
eàrr-ghobhlach 885 with forked tail
eàrr-loisgeach 188 with a sting in the tail
earra-gheal 831 white-tailed
earrach 764, 1264 tailed, long-tailed
earradh 432, 765 dress, garment
eàrrlainn 1615, 1795 bottom/bilge of boat
èibhinn 966 strange, odd
èibhlean 1522 pl. of **èibheal** ember
èibhlibh 1120n dat. pl. of **èibheal**
èide 2298n uniform, armour
èidichte 1033 clothed, dressed
èididh 47n clothing
èifeachdach 1322n effectual
èighre 926, 1312n ice, frost
èile 1488n kilt
eileabor 519n hellebore, snuff
eilid 2227 hind
eilideach 466 of the hinds
èilidh 2298n kilt
èille 1037 gen. of **iall** leash
eiridneach 460n, 467 healing
eirmseach 1642 quick, expert
eirthir 1245 coast
èis 592 lack, defect
èisg 630 satirist, lampooner, satirical poet (1751 Glossary: 'a satyrist, a censorious nipping poet')
èisl' 1967n contracted form of **èislean** (?)
èislean/èislein 1586, 1828 sorrow, melancholy
èiteag-chlach 2202n quartz-stone
eitean 120n kernel
eochair 79 key
euchd 1032 valiant deed
euchdag 149 lovely girl
eucoir 648 guilty one; 1373 injustice
eucoireach 1350 a guilty person
eud 150 jealousy, source of jealousy
eugcoir 124 (later **eucoir**) wrong, injustice
eun-dealbhach 1480n bird-decorated
eunlaith 903 birds
eur 1255 refuse

F

fa-dheòidh 1509 eventually
fabhar 1420n favour
fad-luirgneach 796 long-stemmed
fadadh 1215, 2027 setting alight, taking fire
fadadh-cruaidh 1838, 2043n dog-tooth rainbow
faicleach 1638 careful
faigse 1396n closer
failbheag 1851 bolt ring
fàileanach 164 sweet-perfumed
fàilidh 780 gentle
faillean 2284 twig
failleanach 714 with many shoots
fàillinn 579, 1006 failing, dropping down
fàillinneach 860 failing
fàillnich 1694 fail
fàinneach 2143 ringletted
fàinneagach 415 having ringlets
faireachadh 533 awakening, consciousness
faireagan 293 bravo (1751 Glossary: 'a word of admiration')
fairtlich (air) 1960 fail
fàite 166n, 206, 2139n smile
faite-gàire 1962 smile
fàl-rùisgte 860 turf-stripped
falbh 1016 motion
falbhach 825 quick-moving
fallas-mhail'ean 1620 short for **-mhailghean**, pl. of **mala** (sweat from the brows)
falluing 818 mantle, robe
falmadair 1980 tiller
faloisg 1083 heath-fire
fann 513 light, dreamy (?)
fann-gheum 778 soft lowing
fanna-gheal 786, 2163 pale white
fannaich 1782 weaken
faobhar 107 keenness; 88, 1478 (cutting) edge
faobharach 1031, 1188, edged, sharp-edged, ready to show sword's edge
faodail 154 treasure (-trove)
faoilidh 2055, 2080, 2239 hospitable, generous
faoineag 183 giddy girl
faoisgneadh 1830 unhusking, emerging
faothaich 1686 relieve, loosen
faramach 2125 merry
farasd 371 gentle, mild
fàrdal 1002, 1603 delay, dilatoriness
farmad 1298 envy
fàs 118 empty
fàs-bheò 846n living growth
fàs-choill 2119 growing woodland
fàsach 898 wilderness
fàsach 1005n laying waste
fasdadh 1037 stopping, checking
fàsgadh 2159 squeezing
fàs(mh)or 551, 783 thriving, swift-growing, burgeoning
fathrom 372n noise
feachdraidh 1110n armed infantry
fead-choill 1224n wood-whistle (?)
feada-coille 806 flower of wood-sorrel (1751 Glossary)
feadag 1223 whistle, flute
feadan 470, 477, 487, 685 chanter
feadan 853 streamlet
feadh 1907 extent (of time or space); throughout
feall 1179 deceit
feann 1405n, 1708 (Introd.), 2079 flay
fear-cluaise 1708 (Introd.) a man to attend to the tack (of the sail)
fear-sgòid See **sgòid-fhear**
fearas-bheairte 1690 working of the tackle (of a boat)
fearas-ùrlair (**Birlinn** 15, Introd.) deck management
feardha 1117 manly, brave
fearthainn 923n rain, showers
fearthainneach 1301 rainy (See 923n)
feasgarain 868 vespers
fèath-ghrùnnd 882n calm bed
fèith 1584 sinew
fèitheach 1537 sinewy
feòirnean 2069 blade of grass
feòirneineach 892 grassy; 2169 piled (like grass or straw?)
feòrag 1822 squirrel
fiabhras 2041 fever
fiadh-ghleann 1608 wild glen
fiamh 147, 960 aspect; 2064 appearance, smile
fiamhach 1757 fearful, timid
fiasag 2097 beard
fideag 456n whistle
fidheall 2128 fiddle
fidreachdainn 17 (‹**fidir/fidrich**) discovering, ascertaining
fil 114n var. of **filidh** poet
fileanta 90 fluent
fineadh 2188n kindred, clan
finealt 205, 516, 541, 2126 fine, elegant, gentle, sophisticated
finid 1269 end

finn-mhèagach 771 with white whey
finne 160 superlative of **fionn** fair
finne 2133n gen. of **fionn** (used here as noun) a fair woman
fionnachd 467 cooling
fìor-shaor 207 truly liberal
fioruisg 761 freshwater
fireach 890 moor, high ground; 2189 deer-forest
fise faise 1971 onomatopoetic expression to suggest breakage
fitheach 1139, 1403n raven
fiùran 1065 warrior, hero
flaith 591 pl. of **flath** noble
flichneach 935 sleety
flùthar 229n var. of **flùr** flower
fògair 709, 1313, 1385 banish, expel, exile
foghainn 92, 95 suffice
foghar 1940n noise, sound
fòid 2057 turf
foidhneul 802n gleam
foil 1347n act in a hurry
foill 1367 deceit
foindeal 155n wandering
foinealach 1483 shining (?)
foinn 1365n twist (?)
foinneachadh 1092n tempering (1751 Glossary)
foinnidh 367 comely, elegant; 1095, 1735 active, lively
fòir 93 help, relieve
foireann 1075n company, troop
foirmeil 491, 740, 1071, 1097, 2300 brisk, lively, noteworthy; 735, 1281, 2254 formal, ceremonious
fòirne 1063, 1565 troop, band, crew. The usual sing. form is **foireann**
fonn 893 land
fonnmhor 181, 209, 1586, 2126, 2128 cheerful, melodious
forach 2055 productive
fosghaoir 1942n loud shouting/noise
fòtas 428 blemish; 2058 refuse
fraoch 1039 anger
fraoch-sgriachain 2096n crackling heath(er)
frasach 1281 pouring
freasdail 67 attend
freasdal 1582n, 1670, 1854 waiting on, watching, taking precautions against, attending to
freumhach 679 root, origin
freumhaich 847 roots
frìd 524n insect; pigmy
frìth 1569n anger, rage
frìth 216, 318 moor ('deer-forest' becomes the commoner sense later)
fritheilteach 1082 attentive
frithir 1745n ticklish, hard to handle
frog 2257 quick movement
fròg 870 nook, cleft
froidhneas 801n, 2196 fringe
froiseadh 2035 showering
fuar-licneach 928n cold-stoney
fuarachd 878 cold
fuaradh 1711 windward, weather side
fuaradh, air 1651, 1656 on a windward tack
fuaradh cluaise 1672 luffing (causing the sail to flap)
fuaradh frois(e) 1761, 1841 breeze before a shower
fuasgail 596 unravel
fuasgailt 1633, 1781 active, nimble
fuasgailteach 1734 nimble
fuasgladh 33, 1687, relief; 1977 coming apart
fuath 1433 hatred
fuathas 1106 dread; 1497, 1630 horror, apparition
fùidreadh 1145 mixing, sprinkling
fuinn 2235 pl. of **fonn** land
fuirbidh 1535, 1558, 1666 strong/ powerful man
furachail 1638 observant
furachair 1760 alert, watchful
furanach 269 welcoming
furas 393 patience

G

gàbhadh 1576 danger
gabhail 1648 course, tack (of a ship); 1674n taking the wind
gad 111 withy
gaganach 905 bunched, clustered
gailbhinn 1582n, 1914 storm, tempest
gaill-fheadan 745n Lowland chanter
gailleacha 1523 pl. of **gailleach** stormy
gailleann 926 storm; 362n snow-storm, white ground
gairbhe 203n fullness
gairbhneach 1801 rugged
gaire 1890 nearness
gaiseadh 1969 defect
gaisge 1492 heroism, warrior-like deeds
gaisgeach 1461 hero
gaisridh 1023, 1121 warlike troops, warriors
galla-bhodaiche 590n **bodaich Ghallda**, Lowland carles

gallan 367n straight young tree; 1533 branch, stalk, young tree (here 'oar'); 1170 handsome young man, hero
ganntar 2303 scarcity
gaoirdean 2157 var. of **gàirdean** arm
gaoisid 1695 horse-hair
gaoisneach 1538, 1698 hairy
gaol-thàirneach 146 attracting love
gaorr 1145, 1922 gore
garbh-mhothar 161 rough clustering
garbhlach 1230 the Rough Bounds, Highlands; 1430, 1530n rough/rugged country; 1457 roughness (here 'sea billows')
gàrradh 1004 garden
gart 894, 1498, 2040n threatening/surly appearance/aspect
gasda 138 neat, beautiful
gasraidh 1462 people, crew
gath 871 ray; 340, 1031n sting, dart; 1541n spoke, oar
gathan 192, 1327n 2142 small ray; 1617 dimin. of **gath** 'oar' (?)
geal-bhuidh 785 primrose (colour)
geal-sgiortach 829n white-skirted
geal-thuraid 391 white-turreted
geal-ùiseil 210 fair courteous/dignified one
gealtair 1759 coward
geanail 1238 cheerful
geanmnaidh 200, 269 chaste
geàrr 188 lit. 'cut'; form, utter
geàrr-chollainn 499 a short sharp stroke
geàrr-fhiadh 1818 hare
geàrr-fhionnach 780 short-haired
geàrr-ghobach 802 short-billed
gearradh 753 cutting, definition
gèill 1353 submit, yield
geòcail 946 voracious
geoic 1217 twist
geug 194n branch (used metaphorically here)
geum 2071n utterance (lit. 'lowing'); 2268 lowing
geumnaich 1879 lowing
geur-ghruaim 710 bitter/harsh gloom
geur-leanmhainn 1429 hotly pursuing
geur-tholltach 950n sharp hole-making
geurag 1426n little sharp-pointed one
ghlacas 137n
giall 1926 gill (of a fish)
gidheadh 51n yet, nevertheless
gin 1175 beget
giobach 1644, 1897 rough, fringed
giobagach 797 fringed, having protruding growth
giollachd 908 attending to
gìomh 983, 1179 defect, fear
gionach 946, 1239 greedy
giorag 1070 fear, terror
gioragach 1276 timid, frightened
giùgail 2252 lowering the head
giùlan 169 deportment; 555 conduct
giùthsach 1533n, 1567n pine forest; oar made of pine
glac 890 hollow, small valley
glac 2176 palm of hand, grasp
glac-gheal 180, 1534n white-palmed
glac-mhor 1684 having a good grip
glacach 2210 full of hollows
glacag 749 hollow
glacaireachd 1436 seizing, capturing
glagan 117, 1207 rattling noise
glaic 968 small glen
glainne 927n glass
glaistig 2050n, 2056 she-devil, hag
glaodhan 848n wood-pith
glas-ghoib 863n gag
glas-leug 928n gray jewel
glasrach 2233 with green meadows
gleac 1941, 2133 wrestling, contending
gleann-chladhach 1013 with glen-like troughs
gleanna-gharbh 1671 with rough/huge valleys
glèidhteach 197n frugal; 2170n well looked after
glèidhtich 2171n a careful person, provider
gleodhar 2176n noise, noisy blow
gleus 106n action, working parts, invention; 634n means, potential
gleus 91 sharpen
gleusda 1588, 1601, 1739 well-tuned, expert; 2299 ready for action
glìb-shleamhainn 933 made slippery by sleet
glob 888 globe, world
glocan 1212 clucking
gloic 1206n dat. of **gloc** throat
gloic 1681n embrace, charge
gloine-thrìdeach 201 transparent as glass
glòir 586 glory
glomhar 2303n gag
glòr 504n, 583, 611 speech, language, talking; sound
gluasad 2182 movement
gnàth 1442 in phr. **a ghnàth** always

gnè 235, 944n sort, species, kind
gnùis 909 face
gò 587, 1103 deceit, blemish
gob 832 bill
gobhal 2179n crotch
gogan 1217 nodding; cackling
goile 2304 throat; stomach
goireas 1974 apparatus
gòireileas 316 foolishness
gòisnichean 440 pl. of **gòisinn** snare, trap
gorm-dhearc 219, 2246 blue berry
gòrsaid 1479 gorget (a piece of armour to protect the throat)
gort 920 famine, scarcity
grad-fhad 952n swiftly kindle
grad-phongail 1883 quick and accurate
gradag 2051 hurry
graid-bheairteach 1052 quick to don arms etc.
graid-leumnach 1029n leaping swiftly
graimpidh 1683n unyielding, resolute
grama 1632 (Introd.) gen. of **grèim** grip
gramail 1718n, 1800 (Introd.) 1838 with a strong grip, secure
gràsmhor 482 graceful
greann 728n noise; 953n surly appearance
greannach 1858 surly
greannaich 889 become rough/surly
greannmhor 2231, 2271, 2291 lively
greasad 2167 preparing; hastening
grèidhte 2075n well-prepared
greighean 2226n a small herd
grian-dheàrrsgnaidh 832n sun-burnished
grian-lasda 420 shining like the sun
grian-stad 838 solstice
grian-thìr 2194 sunny land
grianan 760 sun-bower
grinnead 305 handsomeness, elegance
griobhag 1642, 1736, 1778n hurry, confusion
grìomach 2026 grim, barren
grìosach 1134 burning embers
grodan 1178 rot, putridity
gruag 908 head of hair
gruagach 2144 maiden (with long hair)
gruaidh 2133 cheek
gruamach 920, 1486 surly
grùnndail 185 sensible
gruth 942n crowdie
gruthach 773, 2291 abounding in crowdie
guaillionn 2145 fair/white-shouldered
guaineiseach 782 sportive
guamach 165 smiling; 1737n careful, exact
guamag 486 neat (smiling) girl
guanach 500 giddy, wavering
guanag 2183n coquettish girl
gucag 809 bud, sprout
gucagach 715 abounding in buds; 875 bunched (1751 Glossary: 'covered, or abounding, with bells etc.')
guibean 1206 little beak
guileag 975n warbling, chirping
guin 411 wounding
guineach 583, 1353 sharp, keen; 935, 1023 penetrating, wounding; 1075 venomous, eager
gunnach 1197 armed with guns
gur 1173 brood
gusgal 1778 idle talk

H

hòb 2197n hops (?), hob (?)
hùgan 1553n

I

ial 2030n time, season
iar-àird 1935 west, western point of compass
iargain 571 regret, sorrow
iargalt 1835, 1859 fierce
iarmailt 1837 sky, firmament
iasad 653 loan, borrowing
iath 2154n surround, enclose
ìbhri 163 ivory
imeacach 942n, 2291 buttery, with much butter (1751 Glossary: 'butterish, or abounding with butter')
imeachd 254 movement
imrich 1712, 2291 removal (here to the shieling/milk pastures)
inbheach 1237 prestigious, eminent
innealt 2158 neat, elegant
innealta 1069 well-ordered (1751 Glossary: 'neat, tight, conformed to art')
innleachdach 542 clever, well-organized
innsginn 468 mind (?)
innsginneach 370 sprightly, lively, vigorous
ìobair 343 sacrifice
ìobairt 66, 122 sacrificing, offering as sacrifice
ìobradh 558 sacrifice
ìochdaran 1362, 1910 underling
ìochdrach 1956 lower/infernal

ìocshlaint 987 salve, remedy
iolach 488, 1171 cry (often of exultation), call
iomad 1071 var. of **iomadh** many
iomain 1551 drive
iomarcaidh 1618 abundance, superfluity
iomchar 1482 carrying, carriage
iomluas 1386 fickleness
ion 619 fitting, proper
ion-eug 846n practically die
ion-faileis 530, 1345n a near shadow, virtual shadow
ion-mholta 2053n praiseworthy
ion-slugaidh 1884n possibility of being swallowed
iongnach 1924 with nails/claws
ionmhainn 1228 well-loved
ionnsaigh 1045 attack
ioraltach 487, 672n ingenious, inventive, intertwined, well-contrived
iorghail 1129 battle, contest
iorghaileach 1543n loudly shouting
iorram 1545 rowing song
ìot 501, 1317 thirst
ìota 1259 thirst
ìslich 1501 lower, weaken
iteach 764 finned
iteach 820n feathers
iteagach 11 with fluttering wings
iteagaich 23 fluttering of wings, flying
iubhair 1483 of yew wood
iùbhrach 1551 vessel
Iuchar 909, 2042 dog-days, July
iùl 1466 guidance; 1472 course
iumallach 1400n at the edge
iumlan 2030 var. of **iomlan** perfect, perfectly developed
iumluath 2031 var. of **iomluath** changeable
iumraich 2051n of **iomraich/imrich** removal
iùnnrais 1456n stormy sea, tempest

L

Là Fhèill Brìghde 'Birlinn' 16. Introd. St Bridget's Day, Candlemas (1st February)
labhradh 577 discourse
lachdann 939 tawny, swarthy
ladarn(a) 1812 bold, daring
lag-ìobairt 967 softly uttered offering
lagach 2024n with hollows
lagadh 1706, 1975 weakening
lagaich 537, 954 weaken
laghach 339 pleasant
làghanach 947 sowany, abounding in sowans
laigead 737 weakness
laigh---air 1740-41 put full weight on
lainnir 357, 958 sparkle, sheen
lainnireach 766 glittering
làmh-ghnìomhach 210 dexterous, good at working with (her) hands
làmhach 1815 good with (their) hands
làmhainn 2115 glove
làmhann 1479 gauntlet, glove
lann 1340, 1476 blade; 1563n, 1658, 1986 metal rove, washer; 1428 enclosure; 2216n (fish) scale
lannach 763 scaly; 1244 involving blades
laoghdaich 338 lessen, reduce
laoidh 635 lay, hymn
laoigh 65n, 557n calves/lays
laom 1020n crowd, over-growth
laomach 2234 gleaming
laomadh 1786 falling
laomsgar 1026 fierce, fiery
lapaich 1784 weaken, benumb
lasadh 1521, 2027 lighting up, flaming
lasair-chlach 330 shining stone, gem
lasgarra 1121 brave, fiery
leabach 2286 abounding in beds
leac-ruiteach 328 ruddy-cheeked
leadan 704, 2074 litany; 1210 lay
leadanach 469 melodious
leadarra 473, 686 harmonious; melodious, elegant
leagail 2241n imprinting
leagh 451 melt(ed)
leamhnach 2235n where elm-trees grow, where tormentil grows
leanaba 918 pl. of **leanabh** child
lear 20 ocean
leasachan 805n pl. of **leas** garden
leasraidh 1267 loins
leathoireach 1398 remote, marginal
lèig 1308n, 1359 league
leigeadh 757 milking
leigeil 2122 milking
leigeil See 1216n
leighis 1008 heal
leirg 1062 dat. sg. of **learg** battle-field
lèirsinn 2140 sight, faculty of seeing
leòb 1593 shred, fragment
leòis 1590 pl. of **leus** blister
leth-eaglach 1756 half-frightened, cautious
leth-phàirteach 463 partial, biassed
leug 155, 165, 759 jewel

liagh-leabhar 1541 long-bladed
liagh-lom 1514 with bare/polished oar-blades
lianach 770n with fields/meadows
liath-reothadh 2032 hoar-frost
liath-reothtach 933 hoar-frosty
lìnigeadh 951n lining
lìobhair 345n var. of **liubhair** deliver
lìomhtha 595, 612 polished
lìonach 2212n with nets commonly in use
liteach 947 porridgey
litir 18n letter
litleimneach 762n
lobhadh 2304 rotting
locair 87 plane
lòchran 956 lantern
lògh(mh)or 623, 804 precious, distinguished, excellent
loidhne 1370n line
loinideach 772n with whisks
loinn 156n, elegance; 218, 2208 lustre
loinneach 796n downy, spongy
loinneil 807, 825 bright, shining; beautiful; 500, 2204n elegant, handsome
lom 937 bare (subject to winds blowing)
lom 1718n bare, reduce
lom-dharag 748 bare oak
lomach 2037n bare
lomarra 493 bare, closely judged
lompair 902n bare surface/plain
lòn 302n, 875, 2025 meadow; brook
lòn 2289 food
lònach 770n with grassy meadows; full of pools
long 1451 ship
longphort 886, 1473, 2014 harbour, haven
lonnach 1611 surging
lorcach 1922, 1925 lame, splay-footed, crawling
los 1750 with the effect of
lot 1526 wound(ing)
lotach 1047 inflicting wounds
luachach 1173 precious, valuable
luachrach 716, 2286 with many rushes, rushy
luaidh 1, 580 mention(ing)
luaidhe 540n lead
luaineach 1739 restless
luas 992 speed, **ri luas** speedily
luasgan 1649 uneasy movement
luathrnadh 1178n covering with ash
lùb 980 twist
lùb-ruithe 1747 a running knot
lùbhghort 803 garden
lùdag 499 small finger
luibh 845, 2236 plant
luideach 2238 with long hair (vegetation?)
luig 900 gen. of **lag** hollow
luigh 1536n var. of **laigh(e)** lying
lùireach 1190, 1477 breastplate, coat of mail
luisean 2272 little plant
lùnn 408 roller, bar, pole
lurach 716, 1202, 2200 lovely
lusanach 713, 892 abounding in plants/herbs, plant-covered
Lùth 1377n Luther
lùth-chleas 1146 athletic exploit
lùth-chleasach 733 nimble, merry, sportive
lùth-chleasan 1264 athletic feats
luthadh 61n, 1484 bending
luthaibh 1595 (2 pl. imperat.) bend, flex
lùthmhor 482, 495 supple, agile; 1641, 1792 nimble, muscular
lùths 1534, 1570 strength, power

M

mac-samhailt 409 like, equal
macnas 323 wantonness, lasciviousness
madadh 7 dog, cur
magh 893, 2060 plain
màgradh 1931 pawing, handling clumsily
maide 1556 stick, plank
maidean 681n morning
maidinn 220 var. of **madainn** morning
maidnean 867n matins
maill 511 delay, impediment
maille 2140 hindrance, obstruction
màilleach 1477n made of mail
mainmneach 2160n var. of **meanmnach** spirited one (?)
màirnealach 1720n mariner
mairbhill 2161 marble
mairt-fheòil 943 beef
mairtear/mairteoir 1386n martyr
maistreadh 1900 churning
maith 599 noble
màl 879 tax
mall 652 placid, deliberate
màm 1873n large round hill
mang 2227 fawn
mànran 2123n humming, melody
mànranach 162 melodious, amorous
mantal 1862 mantle

maoineach 183, 658, 2236 rich, richly endowed, full of wealth; 775, 2054 productive, rich in produce
maoiseach 318, 856 doe
maoiseach 776 with many roe-deer/does
maor 2048 bailiff, steward
maorach 1916 shellfish
maoth 2156n tender
map 1364n map
marcaich 1085 horseman, rider
margadh 1329 sale, sale-price; 2185 market
màrsail 2296 good at marching
màrsal 481 march, march-time
mart 2121 milk-cow
màsach 1637 big-buttocked
masgadh 1599 mash, mixing
math-shluagh 430 congregation
meacain 855 sobbing
meachair(e) 371 tender
meadar 897n pasture, meadow
meadh-bhlàths 1326 lukewarmness
meadrach 72 metre, verse
meal 532 enjoy
mealach 713, 2063, 2279 abounding in honey
meall 959 mountain
meallach 165 alluring
mealladh 2046 deceiving
meallanach 923 of hail stones
meanbh 4 small, delicate
meang 579, 736, 1103 blemish, fault, defect
meang 1147 lop, cut off
meannanach 775 with many goat-kids
mear 1044, 1182n active, lively
mear-bhuillean 725 lively strokes/notes
mear-stoirmeil 490 brisk/quick-moving and stormy
meardha 886, 2298, vigorous, brisk, lively
meatagach 941 var. of **miotagach** gloved
meataich 1498, 1784 weaken, frighten
meiltreach 2234 smooth, level
meirbh 12, 888, 1058 feeble, slight, lacking spirit
meirghe 1057 standard, flag
meirgich 1059 rust
mèirleach thief; in l. 986 'rascal'
meomhair 91 memory
meugach 2290 with much whey
meur 1399 line (in pedigree)
mì-dhiongmhalta 1372 ineffective, unworthy
mì-rùn 588 ill-will
mial-mhòr 1902 whale
miann 943 desire
mìlidh 1081, 1934 warrior, soldier
mìlteach 666n numerous
mìn-bheumanach 1638 'of delicate touch' (1933 ed.)
mìn-fheur 2025 smooth grass
mìn-lunnach 1515, 1617 smooth-handled
mìne 203 smoothness
mìneachadh 1000 smoothing
mìnead 306 smoothness
minn 2270 pl. of **meann** kid, young roe
mìnneach 204n affable, affectionate
mìnneil 152n affable, tender
mìodachadh 702n increase, swelling out
miodrach 774 with many milk-pails/churns
mìog-shùil 171 smiling eye
mìog-shuileach 2139 smiling, inviting
mìogach 206, 2113 smiling, sparkling
mìogchuiseach 512n genial, flirtatious
mion-bhallach 779 with small spots/patches of colour
mion-bhreac 766 with small speckles
mion-dhìonach 480n carefully controlled
mion-iasg 1912 small/tiny fish
mionach 1241 stomach
mionaideach 490 detailed
mìorunach 1380 showing ill-will
mios 2061 var. of **meas** fruit
miosgadh 819 mingling
miosganach 774 with many kits/wooden butter-vessels
miosrach 773, 2286 var. of **measrach** abounding in churns, with much churning
miotagach 11n frightened; mincing
miotaich 974 make fearful
mire 1182n sport, merriment, movement (?)
miread 492n sportiveness, rousing
mireag 212 playing, sporting
mireineach 489 merry
mìslean 1260 sweetness
mith 599 commoner
mithich 2280 in phr. **is m.** it is time to
mochthrath 1143 early in the morning
modh-sìolaich 37 manner of breeding
mòdhar 167, 2206 modest, mild, gentle; 2164n mettlesome
mogach 783n shaggy, hairy
mogal 1831 husk, mesh
moit 208 surliness (?)

molach 1006, 1742 (Introd.), 1865 rough, shaggy
mòr-shliochd 675 descendants
mòralach 1044 great, majestic
mòrchuis 270, 368 (excessive) pride
mosgail 1305 waken up
mosgladh 1765 wakening, arousing
mothaich 1500 notice
mothar 1014 cluster
mothar 1939 snort
muidhe 2150n, 2292 churn
muime 97 foster-mother
muineal 201, 1786, 2152 throat, upper chest
muir-bhàite 1768 sea of drowning, drowning sea
muirichinn 31n children, family, brood
mùirneach 209, 982 loving, joyful; 2055 cheerful, hospitable
mùirneanach 425 affectionate
munar 173 trifle
munaran 284n trifling, playing about
murtachd 355 sultry heat
murtaidh 1304 close (of the atmosphere)
musga 901n musk (?)

N

nàistinn 1639n care, circumspection
Naoi 13n Noah
naoinear 69 nine persons
naomha 2082 pious, consecrated
nathair 1029 serpent
nathrachan 2020n place of adders
neamh-churaidh 273 not warrior-like
neamh-dhoitheamh 158 gentle, mild (lit. not un-gentle)
neamh-fhiamhach 1076 fearless
nèamha 1423n of heaven
neimhneach 2023 poisonous
neo-chearbach 1580, 1849 accurate, without fault
neo-chladharra 1579 uncowardly, not timid
neo-chlèireach 602 lay person
neo-fhad-bheairteach 1106 not slow to take action, quick to don arms
neo-lapach 1710 neat(ly), unfaltering(ly)
neo-liotach 650 not stammering
neo-sgaiteach 133 not keen/cutting
neo-thruaillidh 707 undefiled
neòinean 2240 daisy
neònachas 256 oddness
Neptiun 1309n
neulaich 897 cloud over
nidean 1158 small nest
nodha 2282 new, newly ripe
nogan 1234 (wooden) cup
nòin(e)in 2028n, 2060 daisy
nuallan 1553, 1769, 2144 roar, rumble, humming
nuallanaich 1908 howling
nuaranta 929 wild, tempestuous

O

obadh 1975 failing
ochanaich 1134 groaning
odhar 1835, 2305 dun-coloured, dirty
òdhraich 891 grow dun-coloured
ògalachd 324 youth
ògan 320, 726 seedling, young tree
oglachd 1833 gloom
oide 113 fosterer, foster-father
oideachd 1376 nurture
òigh 177, 236 virgin
oighre 1359 heir
oighreachdail 1366 hereditary
oir 999 modern **ear** east
òir-cheard 1344n goldsmith
òir-chrios 620n golden girdle
oirceanach 1446n like piglings
òirdheirc 820, 2061, 2256 glorious, brilliant, famous
oirfeid 475, 2072 music, melody, harmony
òirleach na h-òrdaig 1652n inch of the thumb
òirseid 232n orange
oiteag 1706 breeze
òmar 2153n amber
òmhnach 772, 2288n with much froth of milk or whey
òr-chrios 1189 golden belt
òr-dhìthein 874 yellow flower
òr-pheall 960n golden covering/veil
òr-sheudan 2173n golden jewels
òradh 2065 turning golden in colour
òrainsean 312n oranges
òranach 252 fond of songs/singing songs
òrbhuidh 2194 golden-yellow
òrdag 619 thumb
òrdha 954 golden, gilded
òrrachan 452n pl. of **òrtha** charm, enchantment (?)
osnaich 1200, 1615, 1717 sighing

P

paidir 49 **pater noster**, (Lord's) prayer
pailis 624 palace

pàirt 170 accomplishment; 182n ability, attribute
pàirtich 552 share
pàirtidh 2189 (hunting) party
pàiste 172 youthful person, youngster
pàrras 606 paradise
Pàrthas 2080 Paradise
pearsan 343 person, body
peileirean beithrich 1952n fire-balls
peiteagach 941 waist-coated, vested (i.e. wearing vests)
peucach 189n long-tailed
peur 915 pear
peurlach 189 rippling, curling
Phèbus 711 Phoebus
Phènix, phènix 150n, 423n Phoenix, phoenix
pilear 2161 pillar
pill 814 clump of heather
piocaid 2084n pincers
planaid-cùrs' 235n journey among the planets
plancaid 2293 blanket
pliutach 1925 clumsy-footed
plocach 1637 stout, sturdy
plùir-mhìn 195 fine as flour
plùndrainn 1194n plundering
plùr 233 flower
poimp 1151 pomp, glory
pòiteach 948n given to imbibing
pongail 490 exact
pòr 728 race, clan, crew; 2066 pore
preas 868, 2120 bush
priob-losgadh 1107 sudden blazing/ eagerness (1751 Glossary: 'a prickling burning, occasioned by being quickly touched with any hot thing; also a twinkling blaze or sparkle')
prionnsaidh' 591n princes
prìs 171 esteem
pronn 1410, 1573 mash, smash
pronnadh 494 beating out; 1196 smashing, mangling
pronnor 742n struck
prosnachadh 1587 inciting, encouraging
puinnseanaich 1390 become poisoned
puinnseanta 1123 poisonous
punntainneach 935 numbing (1751 Glossary: '**Phuntuinn**, exquisite, cold, benumming')

R

rac 1966 ring or traveller fitted round mast
racan 1467 dimin. of **rac**
rag 36, 109, 1300, 1844 stiff, stubborn, obstinate; 918n hard, tough
rag-eàrlaid 1783n stubborn confidence
rag-chur 538n stiff putting
ràmhachd 1574 oarsmanship
rang 1050 rank
ranntail 2261n verselike
raonach 2233 with many fields
rap-ghaoth 998 stormy wind
rapal 1186 nonsensical talk
rath 338 luck
ratreut 1284 retreat
reang 1658 rib, rung
rèasair 2079 razor
rèidh 480 steady
rèidh-shlios 966 smooth side
rèimeil 185 authoritative, even-tempered
rèir 1336n
rèitich 82 untangle
reub 1427 tear
reubadh 1027, 1966 tearing to pieces
reubal 1256 rebel
reul-iùil 81, 1731 guiding star
reula 357n var. of **reul** star
reulag 417 little star
Reumhair 149n Rhymer
riabhach 802 brindled
rian 1650n regulating
riasladh 1840 tearing, tossing
Richard 745n Richard the wren
rifeid 742 reed, musical note
righ 1584 stretch
righeadh 2129 stretching, tautness
righinn 1513, 1845 tough, durable
rinn 88n point; 1574n sharpness, precision
rinn-bheurra 1031 sharp-pointed
riochd 1163 guise
riochdail 960, handsome, lovely; 1759, 2085n positive
riofa 1954n sulphur
rìoghainn 263, 327, 2137 maid, young lady, beautiful young maiden
rionnag-iùil 237 guiding star
rò-bhog 622 exceedingly soft/pliable
rò-choill 1823 huge wood
ro-ghairbhid 1800 (Introd.) excessive roughness
ro-lurach 274 very lovable/attractive
ro-mheud 1002 over-great extent
ro-thlàth 105 very mild
robach 1865 rough, shaggy
rocadaich 1139 fierce bird-cries, cawing

ròd 2017 roadstead (used of harbour mooring place)
roghainn 1578 choice, the best selection
ròiceil 948 gluttonous
roimh 1850 through
roinn 754 dividing, proportion
roisg 979 pl. of **rosg** eye
ròmasach 948 shaggy, bearded
ròmhan 1932 groaning, raving
ronn 824 slaver
ronnaireachd 497 spittling (1751 Glossary: '(among pipers), when the notes seem to be played with wet fingers etc.')
ròpal 372 vain talk (1751 Glossary: 'rapsody, vain and idle talk, vapour, vaunting')
ròs 2195 rose, primrose (?)
rosg 641n war-ode
rosg 167 eye
roth 106n wheel
ruadh-mheirg 1184 red rust
ruadhaich 893 grow rusty
ruagadh 285 pursuing, persecuting
ruaimleach 1921 muddy, turbid
ruideis 2274 sporting, leaping (1751 Glossary: 'frisking')
ruidil 1797 riddle
ruighe 1698, 1805 forearm
ruisg 242 pl. of **rosg** eye
ruiteach 830 ruddy, rosy
ruith 1674n
ruithteach 649 flowing
rùmail 185n roomy; well-positioned (?)
rùnach 977 loved
rùsgadh 553 lay(ing) bare; 1590 peeling (of skin)
rùtas 2224 rutting instinct (?)

S

sad 924n dust; thud
saidh 1550n prow of a boat
saidhbhir 658 rich
saidhbhireas 174 riches (more usual **saidhbhreas**)
saighdibh 1123 dat. pl. of **saighead** arrow
sàil 1898 keel of boat
sàil-ghlas 1582n grey-seas (adj. here)
sàil(e) 1452n sea, salt sea water
saimir 804n trefoil clover, shamrock
sàl 140, 992 sea-water, sea, ocean
salmadair 961n psalmist
samhach 2278n abounding in sorrel
sàmhach 888 quiet
sàmhnan 2213 large river-trout
sanntach 2299 eager
saobhadh 1372n prevarication
saothair 1599 hard work
sàr-thuigseach 186 very sympathetic
sàth 1142 fill, sufficiency
sàth 1513 thrust
seabhag 1272 hawk
seac 849 wither
seach 836 in phr. **mu seach** in turn
seachainn 1627 avoid
seacharan 15, 21 straying
seaghail 651 full of meaning
seanchaidh 1321 historian, story-teller
seang-mhear 761 lithe and lively
seang-shlios 363 lithe side
seangan 2090 ant
seannsail 2239 prosperous
seanntaidh 2305 ancient
searbh-ghlòireach 1994 bitter-sounding
searbh-thùrsach 1909 bitter and mournful
searbhag 2100 bitter drink, acid
searg 1018n wither, fade away
searra-bhuain 1231n reaping and cutting
searrach 2274 foal
seas-ghrian 840 solstice
Sèasar 2300n Caesar
seasmhach 1268, 1722 steadfast, reliable
seile 1259 saliva
seillean 2276 bee
seilleanach 717 full of bees
seillein 512 bee
seinn 686 singing, playing
seirceach 2218 affectionate
seist-luachrach 2150n bed of rushes
sèitrich 1547 blowing, panting
seobhag 1115n hawk, falcon
seobhgain 1066n hawks
seoghach 2179 var. of **seaghach** gentle
seòl 963 fashion
seòlaid 1622n harbour, haven
seòlta 276 ingenious, methodical
seth 104n in phr. **gu seth** likewise
seudach 193 jewelled
sgailceadh 1054 giving a sharp blow to
sgàileadh 872n spreading
sgailleagach 478 making sharp, sudden notes
sgairt 1256 vigour, bustle
sgairt 1770 shout loudly
sgairteil 1283, 1502, 1734 vigorous
sgaiteach 1023n, 1243 cutting

sgalag 615 servant, inferior person etc.
sgallais 366 flattery
sgaoilt 373 unloosed, freed
sgaoilte 2083 free
sgapach 197n generous; 661 scattering
sgar 1748n sever, stop
sgaradh 1196 separating; 1966 wrenching, tearing
sgath 1626n drop
sgàth 1062 fear
sgàthachas 'Birlinn' 16. Introd. fear, dread
sgathadh 1267 lopping off
sgàthan-mais' 239 mirror reflecting beauty
sgeadas 707 decoration, gay dress
sgealpaireachd 1056 striking, skelping, slapping
sgeap 878 bees' skep
sgèimh 954 beauty
sgiamhach 2205n beautiful
sgiath 1480 shield
sgiathach 1124 wearing shields
sgibidh 821, 1114, 1646 neat, trim, tidy
sgiobalta 2107 smart, quick
sgioladh 2045 unhusking, taking off the skin
sgìomhach 796 lovely
sgiùrsadh 1893 scattering
sgobadh 1586 pulling, tugging
sgòd 1650 sheet (rope) of a sail
sgò(i)d-fhear 1691 sheet-man (man in charge of sail sheet)
sgoil 131 schooling
sgoinn 1368 firmness
sgol 113n (later **sgoil**) men of learning, bardic school, **literati**
sgoltadh 1048, 1549, 1602, 1980 splitting
sgorach 2078 notched, hacked
sgòrnan 2071 throat
sgrainngeil 2036 sullen, scowling
sgread 1080 crunch
sgreadach 1938 screeching
sgreadaidh 2050n screeching
sgreadail 1111 screeching
sgreadan 727, 1227 screech, screeching
sgreamh 1094 horror, nausea
sgreamhail 1932 horrific
sgreataidh 1863 horrible
sgreitich 895 terrorise
sgriachaidh 1932 shrieking
sgrios 852 decimate
sgròbadh 1703 clawing, clutching
sgrogach 2021 shrivelled
sguit-asgaill 1978n fixed seat in the angle (at bow and stern)
shuas 1544n
siab 1252 sweep, snatch
sian-ghaoth 1958 stormy wind
sicir 1757 prudent
sileadh 2047 pouring
simpleachd 1491n meekness
sìn 1531 stretch
sine 875, 2160 teat, dug, udder
sìneadh 1995 lying down i.e. abating
sinnsreadh 1450 ancestry
sìobhaltachd 543 civility, good manners
siola 1794 gill
siolladh 87 syllable (1751 Glossary: 'Siollad, a syllable')
sìolmhor 665 prolific
sìon 1313 (bad) weather
sionnach 1005 fox
sionnachain 1874 cf. **teine-sionnachain** phosphorescence
sìontaidh 2031n a pl. form of **sìon** weather
sìor-chonfach 1133n steadily furious
sioras 161n cherry
sìoth-shàimh 1992 peace
sir 116 search for, ask
siris 915 cherry
sirist 397, 2135 cherry
sìthe 489 fairylike
sìthein 891 little hill
siubhal 2149 movement
siumrag 2028n shamrock
siùrsach 1382 prostitute
slacraich 1918, 1940 thudding
slad 34 robbing, plundering
slad 386 snatch, plunder
sladachd 2218 thieving
slaiseadh 1266 slashing
slamag 413 small lock of hair
slamanach 773 abounding in curds/ curdled milk
slaoidmheoirich 497 lazy fingering (1751 Glossary: '**Slaodmhearaich**, (among pipers), an awkward and tardy motion of the fingers')
slat 1467, 1966 yard-arm
slat-bheòil 1978n wale
slatach 2212n with rods commonly in use
sliabh 2430 high ground, mountain
sliabhchnoc 801 moorland hill
sliasaid 1564n side, quarter
sligneach 1899 shelly
slinn-leumnach 762 leaping over flat stones

sliochdmhor 651 prolific
sliom 621, 885 smooth, sleek
slios 2200 side
sloc(hd) 884 hollow
slocach 1198 full of hollows/cavities
sloistreadh 1615 dashing
sluaghmhor 2296 used to joining the host/army
slugan 1233 gullet
sluistneadh 1900n mixing
smal 1178 stain, blemish
smàl 712 vapour, cloud
smeòrach 703, 904, 1156ff, 2119 thrush, mavis
smìdeach 2138n beckoning, smiling
smig 2049n chin
smodan 1177 spot, blemish
smuaintidh 551n
smùd 1177n dust, mote
smùid 2262 blast (of song)
smùid 911 fragrance
smùirnean 979 mote, speck of dust
smùis 1618, 1804 var. of **smuais** vigour, strength
smùis 1055 bone marrow
smùisridh 1148n smashing
smùr 237 dross, blemish
snaigheadh 1108 hewing, slashing
snaighte 2137 chiselled, well-shaped
snàithean 1366n thread
snaoim 82n, 379, 596 knot, difficulty
snaomanach 1734 robust fellow
snaompach 1848 knotted, knotty
snasda 87 neat
snasta 2136 well-shaped, elegant
snìomh 1591 twisting, twining
snìomhain 701 twisting, winding
snìomhanach 514 pleated, curled
snodhach 699, 847 sap, juice; 2282n foliage, bark
snuadh 199 complexion, beauty
snuadhor 786 comely
so-ghràdhach 2055, 2063n amiable, easy to love
so-laist' 1291n easily fired
so-lùibte 111 pliable
sòbhrach 2028 primrose
sòbhrach 2278n abounding in primroses
socair 1516 well-balanced
sodan 1179 fawning (1751 Glossary: 'Soddan, joy, blytheness')
sog 2256 good homour
sogan 1219, 1235 delight
sòghmhor 674 luxurious, sappy
sòigh 945 luxurious, sumptuous
soilleir 1585n a clear, smooth patch of sea
soillsean 765 gleam
soillsein 959n var. of **soillsean** shining
soineann 1311n fair weather
sòinneadh 145n excellent fashioning
soirbheas 1714, 1762 fair wind
soistinn 187n sense; 1733n tranquillity
soitheamh 157 gentle, mild
solach 2054n sunny (?)
solar 1159 gathering
sòlas 955 joy
solta 1641, 1735, 2037n, 2053 quiet, mild, tender, kindly
somaltachd 1093 laziness
sonn 186 admired one; 1881n hero (here of wave)
sonn-bhrochan 938n gruel (fit for heroes)
sòradh 1102 grudging, sparing
spadh(adh) 1740 strong quick pull, jerk
spàg 1066 claw
spagadh 2049n distorting
spaglainn 1295 ostentation, bombast
spaglan 1185n ostentation
spàinnichibh 1053 dat. pl. of **spàinneach** Spanish blade, Toledo blade
Spàinnteach 1476n Spanish
spalparra 483 strutting
spàrr 1183n intrusive wedge (?)
spàrr 1547, 1567 thrust
sparradh 1342n thrusting
sparraig 1744 rivet, nail
speachadh 2091 biting
spealg 1485 (verb) split
spealtadh 1055 cleaving, splitting
speilg 110 (usually **spealg**) splinter, fragment
spèirid 970, 1545 vigour, courage
speur 125n sphere, sky, firmament
spioladh 43 unhusking
spìonadh 2034n plucking
spionnadh 307, 1636 strength, power
spìsridh 164n spices
spòg 1930 paw
sporach 2078 flinty
spòrsail 484 sportive
sprachdalachd 485 strength, activity
sprèidh 2117 cattle
spreigeil 671 lively, vehement; 2048 peremptory, reproving
sproc 854 dejection, lament
spùill 34 despoil
spuing 2026 tinder
spuir 2092 claw

spuir 1119n pl. of **spor** gun-flint
sracadh 1437 tearing away
srad 1088, 1519, 2097 spark
sradadh 1906 scattering; 2026 sparking
sradanach 1874 sparking
srann 2277 hum, drone
sranntaich 2243 humming
sreath 102 series
srian-bhuidh 873 yellow-striped
srianach 1085 reined
sròl 45 satin
sruthach 2290 with much liquid (milk?)
stacan 1212 little stake/post
stagh 1469, 1968 stay
staid 121 state, condition
staideil 168n, 481 sedate, stately; 1682n steady
stailceadh 1208 stamping
staingte 2221n strongly bound, entrenched
stalcadh 538n stiffening
stannart 426 coyness (1751 Glossary: 'stint, want')
staplainn 1563n crashing
starbhanach 1812 strong fellow
stàtail 1099 stately
stealladh 2177 spurting
still 1678 pl. of **steall** spout, torrent
stoc 1719n gunwale
stocainneach 940 stockinged
stocan 1211 small trunk/stump of tree
stoipt 519 blocked
stoirm-shìonach 930 stormy and tempestuous
stòite 195, 298 projecting, swollen (1751 Glossary: 'prominent')
stopadh 1269 stopping
stràchta 2061 filled completely
stràic 986 fill to the brim
streap 880, 1820 climb
streup 1357 combat
strìochd 1502 submit
strìochdadh 1961 submitting
strìopachas 443 fornication, prostitution
strioplach 1921 foul, dirty
stròdhalachd 444 dissoluteness
strònag 228 var. of **srònag** hillock, small projecting rock
stròthail 946 prodigal
struidh 845 waste, go to waste
stuagh-thorrach 1015 pregnant with waves
stuagh-leimneadh 1968 a flaw caused by the waves (?)
stuibein 1208 var. of **stuibean** little stake, stick
stuirt 485 pride
stuirteil 479 steady, assured (1751 Glossary: 'stately, grave, calm')
stùr 1184 dust
stuth 944n stuff
suain-cheòl 489 twisting music
suairc 168 affable, gentle
subhach 2291 happy
subhailc 449 virtue
sùdh 1494n seam (here of boards)
sùgh 1647 billow
sùgh 848 suck
sùgh-bheath 848n life-giving juice
sùgh-dhlùth 1013 with billows close together
sùgh-talmhann 913 sap/moisture in soil
suibhean 2236 pl. of **subh** fruit berry
suibseic 132n subject
suigeart 738, 1235 joy, verve, cheerfulness
suigeartach 2274 lively, frisky
sùil-bheachd 1729 visual observation
suinn 1559 pl. of **sonn** hero
sulas 281, 2251 great joy
sult 948, 2038 fatness, fat
sultmhor 669 in good condition, fertile (used here of language)
sumaid 1634n, 1654 billow, surge of sea
sùrd 556 cheerfulness, alacrity; 1010, 1508 eagerness, exertion
sùrdag 1655 spring, bound
sùrdail 1571 spirited
susbaint 131 substance, efficacy

T

tabhann 1999 barking, clamour
tàbhachdach 646 effectual, effective
tachdrach 2211n fertile
tagach 1189 nailed, studded
tagha 271 choice
taghadh 1577, 2084 choosing, choice
tagradh 1293 pleading
tagraichean 1396 claims
taiceil 1636, 1708 solid, substantial, supportive
taigh-buaile 2151 cattle/milking fold
taigh-comhairl' 593 council house/ chamber
taigh-taisge 659 store-house
taip 179n portion
tàir 944n contempt
tairbheartach 1049n abundant, numerous

tàirneanach 1950 thunder
tàirneant 1802 strongly pulling
tàirnibh 1595 pull (2 pl. imperat. of **tarraing**)
tais 1504 soft
taisdeal 996 traversing
taise 1491, 1830 (Introd.) softness, weakness
taisich 1660 soften
taith-bheothaich 988n revivify
taitneachdainn 334 pleasuring
taca var. of **taice**, in phr. **an taca** together with, in collusion with
taghte 83 choice
taisbein 80 reveal
taisg (verb) 91 deposit, treasure
taitne 257 pleasing, giving pleasure to
talach 433 reproach
talcarra 740 sturdy (1751 Glossary: 'sturdy, corpulent')
taod-aoire 1673 bolt-rope, sheet
taom 377 impulse; 1780 water coming into a vessel (needing to be baled out) (1751 Glossary: 'a fit of any passion')
taosgadh 1870 pouring
tapaidh 652 healthy, strong; 1854n active, quick
tarbhach 1523 efficacious
tàrr 173, 1622n (more usually **tàir**) get, obtain, acquire, reach
tàrr-gheal 1913n, 2214 white-bellied
tàrr-gheal(ach) 763, 782, 885 white-bellied
tàrr-lachdann 1834 tawny-bellied
tarraing 1076 drawing (sword)
tarraing 1469, 1970n halyard
tartar 663 clamour
tartarach 1050, 1105 noisy, clamorous
teachdaire 15 messenger
teann 614 integrated; 1845 tight
teann-bheairtichte 1053 firmly adjusted
teàrn 881, 1884 descend
teàrnadh 202 descending
tein-adhair 925 lightning
tein-èibhinn 952n, 1215 bonfire
teine-dealain 1951 lightning
teine-sionnachain 1521 phosphorescence
teirce 31 scarcity, poverty
teirig 900 fail, come to an end
teis-meadhan 1809 absolute centre
teòma 1812 skilful, active
teud 864, 1391, 2130 string (of fiddle), musical string; 1468 rope
teud-bhinn 2074 sweet-stringed
teud-chùl 2143 stranded hair
teudach 1913, 2168 stranded, of strands
thadhlamaid 226 we would visit
thagras 625 fut. of **tagair** claim
theannamaid 225 we would set about
thogbhadh 1934 older form of **thogadh** (they) would lift/produce
thùbhradh 1991 was said
tìgear 1109 tiger
tinnead 306 firmness
tinnisneach 1067n urgent, violent
tiochd 1128 var. of **teachd** coming
tiom 65 timid, fearful
tiomachas 1068 hesitation, timidity
tiomaich 1413n soften; 1782 frighten, become frightened
tionndaidht' 1913 turned (upside down)
tionnsgain 337 begin
tionnsgnadh 1046 beginning, attack
tioram 671 dry, pert
tìth 508 square (on draught/chess board)
tiumrachd 2029n var. of **tiormachd** dryness
tiunnail 265, 384 match, likeness
tlachd 1310 joy, pleasure
tlachdmhor 2081 pleasant
tlàths 935 mildness, warmth
tlus 950n, 1414, 1424 kindness, compassion
tobhta 1972 thwart
tobhtainn 1696n var. (?) of **tobhta** thwart, oar-bench
togair 38 desire, challenge, be forward
togarrach 1115 eager, keen
togbhail 2051n
togbhar 1171n 'is lifted/sung'
tograch 2027 willing, keen
tòicte 196n swollen
toil 129 will
toinnte 1873, 2206 twisted, plaited, well-coordinated
toirleum 851 jump quickly, tumble (1751 Glossary: 'dismounting')
toirm 736 sound
toirteal-laoch 1680n a bulky hero
toirteil 1047, 1517, 1559 strong, vigorous
toite 296n tight
toiteanach 945 abounding in chops/collops
toll 2099 make a hole in
tolman 2246 knoll
tom 889 hillock

tomach 1530, 2036 hilly, full of knolls or tufts
tombaca 2101n tobacco
tomhas 2302 measuring
tonn-anfaich 1525n wave-overflowing
tonn-ghorm 1834 splashed with blue, with blue splashes
tonn-ghreannach 894 surly-waved
torc 2079n notch, cut
torchairt 527 happening
torman 2147 noise (here of milk falling into the milking-pail)
torrach 614n, 2054 productive
torraichim 528n numbness (1751 Glossary; 'sound sleep')
torrann 925 thunder
torrannach 634 thunderous, resounding
tosdach 1767 silent
tràigh 16 ebb
tràilleil 615 thrall-like
traisgeach 198 good at observing fasts
trealaich 1489 paraphernalia (the Gaelic word in singular)
trèas 980n treason, treachery
trèin 1454 pl. of **treun** a strong man
treubhach 1824 valorous
treud 1133, 1360, 1428 herd, band, flock, company
treun-fhear 1453 warrior
treun-ghlac 1583 with a strong clasping
treunant 1668n, 1802 valorous
triall 11, 835 motion, travelling, journey
trian 382n a third part
Triath 967 (the) Lord
trileanta 479 quickly moving; 751n trilling, warbling
trioblaid 2106 trouble
trochladh 1988n decaying, damaging
trod 1180 conflict
trogbhail 'Birlinn' 16 Introd. n setting out
trom-straichte 850 heavily filled/laden
tromdha 181n serious, dignified
truaill 670 deteriorate
truailleadh 1175, 1183 defiling
trusgan 698 covering
trustar 1346 miscreant, reprobate
tuagh 1435 axe
tuairgneadh 1979n smashing, battering
tuairmse 578 conjecture, venture; **gun t.** without doubt
tuar 3, 766, 990 hue, appearance
tuarapadh 1631n mishap, accident
tuasaid 492, 1484 tussle
tùchan 815, 2252 hoarseness, hoarse cry
tugh 949n thatch
tuil 1318n flood
Tuil-ruadh 584n Red/Mighty Flood
tuilich (verb) 584 flood
tùilinn 1643n descending (of seas)
tùillinn 2005n twilled linen
tuim 797 pl. of **tom** mound, clump
tùir 537n (verb) sense
tulach 889, 2200 hillock, knoll
tulgadh 1565 rocking, jolting
tulganach 2012 rocking
tulman 799n little mound
tunna 1316 barrel (Eng. tun)
tùr 245 sense
tùr 195, 1067 tower, pillar
turranaich 825 twittering, warbling
tururaich 1207 warbling, rattling (1751 Glossary: 'a warbling, purling noise')

U

uachdrach 1956 upper, heavenly; 771, 2288 creamy, with much cream
uaibhreach 494 proud, spirited
uaimhinneach 1908 in terror
uamh(a) 1198n care
uchd 952n breast
uchd-àrdach 831 high-breasted
ugan 1213 throat
uidhe 1597 way, journey
uilt 495, 1148 pl. of **alt** joint
uireas 63, 93n, 1339 want, necessity, need, lack
uireasach 610 defective; 1319 deprived, lacking
uireasaibh 136n, 264 lack
ùirneach 197 prayerful
uiseag 904 lark
ulaidh 94, 280n, 389 treasure(-house)
ullamh 1087 ready, prepared
ùmhlachd 978 humility, obeisance
ùmhlaich 1509 make humble, become humble
ùrail 690, 2295 fresh, flourishing
urchoid 1715 harm, calamity
ùrlar 473 ground (of pipe tune)
urracag 1713, 1744 thole-pin, belaying pin
urramach 276 honourable
usgar 418 jewel
usgraichean 886 pl. of **usgar** (1751 Glossary: 'jewels, equipage; also bells on liquor')

INDEX